A WORLD BANK COUNTRY STUDY

Slovakia

Restructuring for Recovery

The World Bank
Washington, D.C.

Copyright © 1994
The International Bank for Reconstruction
and Development/THE WORLD BANK
1818 H Street, N.W.
Washington, D.C. 20433, U.S.A.

World Bank Country Studies are among the many reports originally prepared for internal use as part of the continuing analysis by the Bank of the economic and related conditions of its developing member countries and of its dialogues with the governments. Some of the reports are published in this series with the least possible delay for the use of governments and the academic, business and financial, and development communities. The typescript of this paper therefore has not been prepared in accordance with the procedures appropriate to formal printed texts, and the World Bank accepts no responsibility for errors. Some sources cited in this paper may be informal documents that are not readily available.

The World Bank does not guarantee the accuracy of the data included in this publication and accepts no responsibility whatsoever for any consequence of their use. The boundaries, colors, denominations, and other information shown on any map in this volume do not imply on the part of the World Bank Group any judgment on the legal status of any territory or the endorsement or acceptance of such boundaries.

The material in this publication is copyrighted. Requests for permission to reproduce portions of it should be sent to the Office of the Publisher at the address shown in the copyright notice above. The World Bank encourages dissemination of its work and will normally give permission promptly and, when the reproduction is for noncommercial purposes, without asking a fee. Permission to copy portions for classroom use is granted through the Copyright Clearance Center, Inc., Suite 910, 222 Rosewood Drive, Danvers, Massachusetts 01923, U.S.A.

The complete backlist of publications from the World Bank is shown in the annual *Index of Publications*, which contains an alphabetical title list (with full ordering information) and indexes of subjects, authors, and countries and regions. The latest edition is available free of charge from the Distribution Unit, Office of the Publisher, The World Bank, 1818 H Street, N.W., Washington, D.C. 20433, U.S.A., or from Publications, The World Bank, 66, avenue d'Iéna, 75116 Paris, France.

ISSN: 0253-2123

Library of Congress Cataloging-in-Publication Data

Slovakia : restructuring for recovery.
        p.   cm. — (A World Bank country study, ISSN 0253-2123)
    The report is based on findings of an economic mission to Slovakia
in April 1993; it was prepared under the direction of Kemal Dervis
and others.
    Includes bibliographical references.
    ISBN 0-8213-3066-7
    1. Slovakia—Economic policy.   2. Slovakia—Economic conditions.
3. Post-communism—Economic aspects—Slovakia.   4. Structural
adjustment (Economic policy)—Slovakia.   5. Slovakia—Economic
conditions—Statistics.   I. Dervis, Kemal.   II. International Bank
for Reconstruction and Development.   III. Series.
HC270.3.S56   1994
. 338.94373—dc20
                                                    94-35172
                                                      CIP

Contents

Contents (Contd.)

Map

v

Figures

Tables

Boxes

ABSTRACT

This is the first report by the World Bank on Slovakia's economy. It is based on findings of an economic mission in April 1993 and has been discussed with the authorities in April 1994.

The report focuses on macroeconomic and structural reform issues related to the transition to a market economy, and presents recommendations for policies and institutional reforms. The recommendations fall into two broad categories: (i) facilitating resource reallocation through further privatization, increased job mobility through informational, training and housing market reforms, and the elimination of regulations that discourage employment and new business start ups; and (ii) redefining the economic role of the government by reducing the fiscal deficit which is crowding out private activity, by shifting expenditure away from subsidies to enterprises and non-targeted social benefits and toward public capital formation that crowds in private investment, and by providing more generous transfers to the truly needy.

The members of the economic mission that visited the Slovak Republic from April 19 to May 7, 1993 were Messrs./Mmes. Nemat Shafik (mission chief), Marie-Renee Bakker (enterprise finances), Rune Barneus (banking), Marinela Dado (macroeconomic framework and financial sector), Andrew Ewing (enterprise restructuring and privatization), Albert Martinez (financial sector), William McGreevey (social sectors), Michael Mertaugh (labor markets), Kent Osband (private sector development and privatization), Mansoora Rashid (social sectors), and Sweder van Wijnbergen (macroeconomics). Raquel Fernandez commented extensively and participated in revising the report prior to yellow cover. Substantial revisions were also made by Bob Anderson (privatization), Stanislas Balcerac (enterprise finances), Luis de la Calle (macroeconomics), Jean-Jacques Dethier (agriculture), Yves Duvivier (restructuring and privatization), Nena Manley (private sector development), Kaushik Rudra (statistical annex), Shamsher Singh (financial and enterprise sectors) and Alfredo Thorne (monetary policy) who participated in subsequent missions to the Slovak Republic. Zuzanna Murgasova provided research assistance. Sahra Harbi was the staff assistant during the mission. Anita Correa was responsible for report preparation. Laila Tushan was responsible for revisions after the green cover version. Meta de Coquereaumont edited the final version of the report. Alexander Kasjanov assisted with the translation of the report into Slovak. The report was prepared under the general direction of Kemal Derviş (Director), Michel Noël (Division Chief), and Christine Wallich (Lead Economist). Discussions on the green cover version of the report were held in Slovakia from April 18-22, 1994. The mission is grateful to the numerous individuals in Slovakia whose insights and knowledge contributed to the quality of this report.

CURRENCY AND EQUIVALENT UNITS

Currency Unit = Slovak Koruna (Sk)

	1992	1993	May 1994
US$1.00 =	28.3	33.0	32.4

WEIGHTS AND MEASURES
Metric System

ABBREVIATIONS AND ACRONYMS

CMEA	-	Council of Mutual Economic Assistance
CSOB	-	Československa Obchodni Banka
CSFR	-	Czech and Slovak Federal Republic
EBRD	-	European Bank for Reconstruction and Development
EIB	-	European Investment Bank
EU	-	European Union
GATT	-	General Agreement on Trade and Tariffs
GDP	-	gross domestic product
IB	-	Investični Banka
IBRD	-	International Bank for Reconstruction and Development
IMF	-	International Monetary Fund
IRB	-	Investična a Rozvojová Banka
KB	-	Komerčni Banka
KBB	-	Konsolidačna Banka Bratislava
Kcs	-	Old Czechoslovak koruny
KON	-	Konsolidačna Banka
NBS	-	National Bank of Slovakia
NPF	-	National Property Fund
OECD	-	Organization of Economic Cooperation and Development
SAL	-	Structural Adjustment Loan
SBCS	-	Statni Banka Československa
SDR	-	Special Drawing Rights
SEP	-	Slovak Power Company
SFMR	-	State Fund for Market Regulation
Sk	-	Slovak koruna
SPP	-	Slovak Gas Company
SSB	-	Slovak Savings Bank
SSP	-	Slovenska Statni Poistovna
STF	-	Systemic Transformation Facility
SSS	-	Slovak Savings Bank
SZB	-	Slovenska Zaručna Banka
VAT	-	value added tax
VUB	-	Všeobečna Úverová Banka

SLOVAK REPUBLIC-FISCAL YEAR

January 1 - December 31

EXECUTIVE SUMMARY

The Slovak Republic started down the road to economic transformation with a legacy of policies and resources both favorable and unfavorable. Slovakia inherited a tradition of macroeconomic prudence, low inflation, and modest debt. Its skilled and competitively priced labor force and strategic location in the center of Europe hold out the promise of economic prosperity at the end of the transition. But Slovakia also inherited an industrial structure at odds with its comparative advantage, weak banks, and a large and inefficient system of social transfers. Thus the inevitable adjustment required of the economy and its people is large and has already been costly in social terms. Real incomes have plunged by 24% since 1990 (Figure 1). The major challenge for Slovakia will be to continue and deepen the program of structural reforms while minimizing the social costs and the number of people excluded from its benefits.

The recommendations of this report fall into two broad categories: facilitating resource reallocation and redefining the economic role of government.

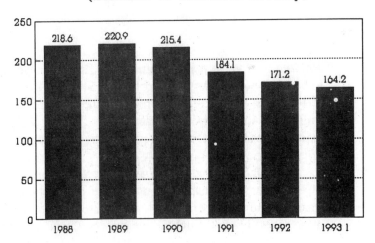

Figure 1: Fall in Real GDP
(billions of constant koruny)

1 Estimate.
Source: Slovak Statistical Office.

- *Facilitating reallocation.* Helping the private sector expand and flourish will require further rounds of privatization, increased job mobility through informational, training and housing market reforms, and the elimination of regulations that discourage employment and new business startups. Accompanying measures are needed to privatize state-owned enterprises and to eliminate incentives to produce for inventories and accumulate debt—activities that cloud distinctions between enterprises that would be viable in an efficient competitive system and those that would subtract value under all circumstances. In particular, debt workouts should be facilitated through development of an institutional arrangement for bankruptcy and introduction of out-of-court conciliation procedures. Mechanisms for facilitating the reallocation of resources—human, physical, financial—toward more productive uses in enterprises, banks, and labor markets are the themes of chapters 2-4.

- *Redefining the economic role of government.* The composition of government spending needs to facilitate rather than impede economic restructuring. That implies reducing a fiscal deficit that has been financed largely by domestic borrowing and so has crowded out private activity. It also means a shift in expenditures away from subsidies to enterprises and nontargeted social benefits and toward public capital formation that crowds in private investment, and more generous transfers to the truly needy. But despite the gains over the medium to long term, the restructuring of the economy is likely to imply a greater fiscal burden over the next few years because of greater demands on the social safety net, the need for recapitalizing selected banks, and the costs of closing down insolvent enterprises. Postponing these restructuring costs means postponing and endangering economic recovery. The need to change the economic role of the state is the central theme of chapters 1 and 5.

Macroeconomic Policy for Recovery

Despite some uncertainty immediately following independence in January 1993, the Slovak Republic has succeeded in preserving its tradition of macroeconomic prudence. Inflation was contained through a prudent monetary policy and an important fiscal adjustment in 1993 that cut expenditures by 8.4% as revenues fell 2.8%, thereby bringing down the underlying deficit from 13.1% of GDP in 1992 to about 7.5%. Cuts in public investments bore the brunt of adjustment on the expenditure side, a worrisome sign for the sustainability of adjustment. Large cuts in capital expenditure may be symptomatic of the difficulty of cutting current expenditures. A 10% devaluation in July 1993 restored equilibrium to the foreign exchange market and improved competitiveness. Preserving macroeconomic stability in the face of numerous external shocks was a major accomplishment.

The key role for macroeconomic policy is to create the conditions for growth. The main issues are:

- *Holding the line on fiscal adjustment*. The challenge for macroeconomic stabilization continues to be fiscal policy. Any compromise of Slovakia's macroeconomic stability would undermine the effectiveness of structural reforms designed to improve the performance of enterprises and banks. Following a large fiscal adjustment in 1993, a shrinking tax base and increased demand for expenditures associated with restructuring are putting new pressures on the budget.

- *Reducing crowding out of the private sector*. Nongovernment borrowers have been crowded out of the financial system, a consequence of the budget deficit and the lack of well-developed financial and treasury bill markets (Figure 2). Seeking to lower interest rates and to make credit more accessible to the productive sectors, the National Bank of Slovakia (NBS) suspended credit auctions in May 1993 and relied on the low interest rate rediscount facility as the main instrument for providing liquidity to banks. This move distorted the structure of interest rates and discouraged banks from mobilizing deposits—since NBS credit was a less expensive alternative. In addition, the government fixed yields on treasury bills at 12%, which discouraged private investors and banks from buying the bills and forced the NBS to finance an increasing proportion of the fiscal deficit. The NBS responded to these undesirable consequences by reintroducing credit auctions; the government abolished the ceiling on treasury bill yields in November 1993. Behind the credit squeeze on the enterprise sector lie the public sector's borrowing needs and the ongoing retrenchment in the financial system (discussed below). To ease this situation, there is no real alternative in the medium term to continuing deficit reduction, though financing from foreign banks and other external financial institutions should help to provide some financing to the private sector in the interim.

- *Changing the composition of government spending*. Total government spending needs to drop but, equally important, the composition of that spending needs to change as well. Despite substantial reductions in subsidies to enterprises (particularly to agriculture), which simply postpone needed restructuring, direct budgetary subsidies still constituted about 5% of GDP in 1993.

Figure 2

Provisioning against government guarantees of loans to enterprises, both direct and indirect, is a small portion of total spending but could rise rapidly as restructuring and bankruptcies increase. More worrisome in scale is the burden of social transfers—a hefty 40% of total spending and a major cause of distortion in microeconomic incentives in the economy. Meanwhile, other claims on the budget—such as social assistance to the poor, training for the unemployed, and government support to strengthening the banking system—require additional funding. Managing these fiscal tradeoffs will be the most difficult political challenge of the reform process.

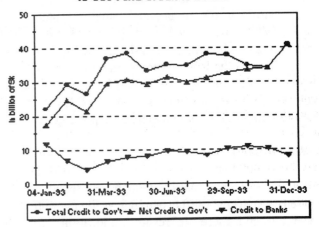

NBS Total Credit to Gov't, Net Credit to Gov't and Credit to Banks

Source: National Bank of Slovakia.

- *Maintaining competitiveness.* The collapse of aggregate demand for Slovak goods is the proximate cause of the large decline in economic activity. The breakdown of the CMEA, embargoes imposed upon a number of Slovakia's export markets and the decline in trade with the Czech Republic resulted in a loss of Slovakia's major markets. The government has successfully resisted protectionist pressures and maintained average tariffs (weighted by imports in 1992) at 4.6%. A 10% devaluation in July 1993 also helped to restore competitiveness. As a small, open economy, Slovakia has little choice but to use the exchange rate and monetary policy to stay competitive and to continue to lobby aggressively for access to foreign markets.

Stronger, More Competitive Financial System

While reform of the financial system has gone far, the legacy of past banking practices—weak competition and lending on a noncommercial basis—continues to reduce the efficiency of intermediation. Progress over the past three years includes market determination of interest rates, liberalization of entry, partial privatization of two of the three major banks, introduction of a legal and regulatory framework for banking, establishment of the Banking Supervision Department in NBS, and increased reliance on market-oriented instruments of monetary management. There has been some transformation of the financial system, mainly in the form of more financial institutions, more financing of private sector activities, banks exhibiting more caution in lending to state enterprises, and a slight improvement in intermediation margins.

Despite these advances, financial intermediation remains low with inadequate financial savings and with the government absorbing a large share of financial resources. The underlying problems of the financial sector are twofold: the burden of inherited bad loans and inadequate competition among the major banks and a lack of nonbank sources of financing.

Competition and Financial Market Development

A more liberal licensing policy has increased the number of banks from two in 1990 to seventeen banks and fifteen branches of foreign banks in 1993. But there is still a high degree of concentration in the commercial banking system, which is largely controlled by Vseobečna Úverovā Banka (VUB), the Slovak Savings Bank (SSB), and Investična Bank (IB). VUB's dominance in the commercial lending market has diminished substantially over the past two years, however, and increasing competition in the lending market makes it unnecessary to split VUB. SSB retains its dominance in the deposit market, however, and plans for its privatization should consider ways of reducing this monopoly. The development of nonbank sources of financing should also be encouraged through measures that facilitate the trading of commercial papers, government securities, and equities.

Inherited Bad Loans

Bad loans, although they reflect a loss of resources that has already occurred and not the current efficiency of the banking system, continue to be a problem to the extent that they distort incentives and, therefore, resource allocation. Overdue loans increased from 1.9% of outstanding loans in the banking system in 1991 to 21.8% in 1993. It is possible that the major banks, which have considerable market power, could increase interest spreads to pay for the cost of bad loans, thus effectively imposing a tax on both depositors and good borrowers. Problems of adverse selection and moral hazard also arise. The need to secure higher spreads leads to adverse selection, a problem exacerbated by poor information and the lack of risk-evaluation skills, while expectations of government bailouts create a moral hazard situation by encouraging banks to engage in excessively risky lending. Weak auditing and supervision enable banks to continue financing insolvent enterprises to prevent them from going bankrupt, an outcome that would make the true size of the bad loans evident. Debtors, for their part, are kept afloat through indirect subsidies, delaying the restructuring of enterprises and complicating the privatization process. While improving bank solvency through retained earnings is desirable, it should occur in a competitive environment where effective supervision insures that retained earnings strengthen the banks' capital base, rather than pay for dividends or other current expenditures.

The next round of reform should focus on strengthening existing institutions and creating an environment that encourages diversification of the financial system by types of banking and regulatory products, services, and financial institutions. Major recommendations:

- *Complete privatization of the banking system.* Privatization of banks is more likely to improve their performance and behavior when majority control is in private hands. Partial privatization of VUB still leaves control with the government. Similarly, the privatization proposal for SSB allocates majority shares to the government or to quasi-public institutions.

- *Deal with the bad debt problem.* There are two alternatives: a centralized program in which a workout agency consolidates the loans and implements a top-down solution and a decentralized program in which banks and enterprises negotiate a solution. Whichever approach is chosen, there are likely to be fiscal costs involved in the resolution of the bad debt problem since banks will probably not be able to cover the entire cost out of future earnings.

- *Upgrade supervision capacity.* With the fundamental regulatory framework in place, the focus of reform should be to accelerate the upgrading of supervision capacity, both off- and on-site. Supervision strategy should focus on each bank's weaknesses and risks. In monitoring the banks' lending practices and their behavior in credit auctions, supervisors should be on the lookout for anticompetitive behavior and imprudent risk taking. With privatizations increasing and the number of firms in the insurance industry growing, regulation and supervision of that industry also need strengthening.

- *Invest in information capital.* Lack of information prevents the effective allocation of financial resources. The new accounting and auditing law should provide a good starting point for the development of financial information systems. More detailed financial and operating information should be required of those issuing securities, and public companies should make their financial statements available to the public on a regular basis. In addition, the government can require and develop an efficient system of registration of mortgages.

- *Design measures to encourage financial market development.* NBS should continue to rely on credit auctions for managing liquidity, and not reintroduce rediscount facilities that allow banks to borrow at below-market rates. Laws relating to movables as collateral should be reviewed, and the judicial system's capacity to handle commercial and bankruptcy cases should be improved rapidly. The regulatory framework and supervision capacity for securities issues should be developed to encourage diversification of financial instruments and the emergence of nonbank financial institutions for which securities issues are the major source of funds.

A Stronger, Private Sector

The Slovak Republic is well-advanced in privatizing its economy. Virtually all small enterprises have been privatized, with over 9,300 small shops auctioned off or returned to their original owners over the last two years. Housing is the major remaining sector requiring privatization; enabling legislation has been approved by Parliament. The lack of private housing remains an impediment to labor mobility, to greater investment in housing quality, and to small business development, since mortgages on housing are the major source of collateral for loans.

About half of all medium- and large-scale enterprises, including banks, were privatized under the first wave, most of them through mass privatization or coupon scheme which ended in 1992. The largest single owner of these enterprises is the National Property Fund, the trustee set up by the government to handle the affairs of privatized enterprises prior to their privatization. By the end of 1992, the fund owned all or part of 533 companies with a total book value of Sk 153 billion. With a staff of only sixty-five people, most of them occupied with processing privatization projects, the fund has little choice but to manage its enterprises passively. The next largest owners of privatized firms are the 184 Investment Privatization Funds that participated in the coupon scheme; together they control 45% of the shares in Slovak firms sold through that scheme. These funds are in a good position to represent the interests of their shareholders but will be under pressure to distribute dividends.

Preparations for the second wave of privatization are ongoing. Between 1992 and 1993, the government relied more on standard methods of privatization, such as direct sales and public tenders, and tried to attract more foreign investment. This strategy was motivated by a desire to get better prices for the companies and to improve their governance, but the pitfalls became apparent as privatization slowed dramatically and enterprises remained in ownership limbo. The government has introduced a new multitrack approach that prepares enterprises for privatization through a variety of methods, including coupon privatization. The government intends to offer about half of the remaining state-owned assets in the second wave of voucher privatization scheduled to begin in September 1994.

Removing Constraints to a Growing Private Sector

Thanks in large part to rapid privatization, the private sector is growing quickly. From virtually no economic presence in 1989, the private sector now accounts for about 20% of output and 30% of employment. But because the base is small, this growth does not yet compensate for the decline in the state sector. Since the "Velvet Revolution", the government has dramatically improved its stance toward private business, but there are still problems. Many property and contractual rights remain unclarified or poorly enforced, and setting up businesses and effecting normal payments involve unnecessarily cumbersome procedures. Instead of focusing on these problems, past government efforts to promote the private sector have stressed tax holidays and directed credits.

Making it easier for businesses to do business should be the government's priority. Poor infrastructure and a cumbersome regulatory framework are major obstacles to private sector development. Registering a business is complex and time-consuming, involving separate paperwork and often fees for environmental impact assessments, health and safety inspections, social security payments, customs, and taxes. With the courts deluged by more than 250,000 commercial cases, debt collection is a major problem. Licensing rules should be simplified, so that approvals can be given more quickly. Startup fees should be reduced to make entry less costly. A fast-track procedure for small and medium-size claims and voluntary arbitration procedures would expedite debt collection, while the establishment of a central registry for debt claims could provide the information basis for a credit-rating industry. The government recognizes many of these obstacles and is taking measures to address them.

Restructuring Enterprises

Enterprises have adjusted slowly to the macroeconomic shocks experienced since 1989, and in some cases their responses—and those of the government—have increased the eventual adjustment costs. Forced bank financing of enterprise losses and further investment in some loss-making industries may have created significant overindebtedness. To preserve their liquidity in the face of collapsing sales, enterprises responded initially by continuing to produce for inventory and to run up overdues on their liabilities. The financial distress of a few large enterprises has reverberated throughout the economy, creating a chain of arrears. In an attempt to cushion the initial impact of the shock or to finance investments in military conversion, the government responded by providing support through the financial system and, for some enterprises, through direct budgetary subsidies—amounting to 5% of GDP in the 1993 budget. The government also used extrabudgetary means, such as guarantees by the National Property Fund against privatization revenues, to channel resources to troubled enterprises.

There are some signs that enterprises have started to adjust by laying off redundant workers and tapping new markets, particularly in the wake of privatization. But the process of enterprise restructuring and liquidation must be accelerated. Four components are key:

- *A hard budget constraint.* By rapidly phasing out subsidies and abolishing loans and guarantees from the National Property Fund, the government could signal to enterprises that they must renegotiate existing debt and attract commercial financing if they want to survive.

- *Market-based workouts.* There is a need for an efficient institutional arrangement for bankruptcy and liquidation including the introduction of an out-of-court conciliation scheme to accelerate progress of restructuring and break the inherited culture of creditor passivity and inertia. Such a scheme could include a rule stipulating that the concessions granted by the lead banks are also granted by the other creditors, thus reducing coordination problems and ensuring an even distribution of losses among creditors. In privatized enterprises, the government should encourage the use of a menu of options to restructure debt that respects the rank order of creditors and equity holders. In state-owned enterprises, creditors and incumbent managers are well-placed to develop restructuring plans; they know their enterprise best and might be expected to become stakeholders in the process of privatization.

- *Enterprises remaining in state hands.* For failed privatized enterprises with government guarantees and for state-owned enterprises with poor privatization prospects, the government needs a policy for reprivatization or liquidation. An efficient, out-of-court mechanism is needed that allows any remaining assets in these firms to be released quickly for alternative purposes.

- *Government as facilitator of restructuring.* The government needs to create a legal framework that makes market-based debt workouts possible. The framework might include a policy for treatment of government claims on enterprises, financial assistance for liquidation (such as for severance pay and environmental costs), and better debt collection and enforcement mechanisms.

Flexible Labor Markets

Slovakia has a highly skilled labor force that for the first time in recent history is experiencing high rates of unemployment (averaging 14%, with substantial regional variation; Figure 3). Its educational attainment compares favorably with that in the most economically advanced countries. The Slovak labor force is also highly competitive relative to workers in OECD countries (where wages are about ten times higher) and many of its neighbors. Major job losses have occurred in the public sector, particularly in trade, construction, and certain heavy industries. In many enterprises, managers are delaying staff layoffs by instituting involuntary part-time work or extended holidays. These delays have led to considerable labor redundancy, as evidenced by the greater decline in labor productivity in Slovakia than in other transition economies.

Unemployment benefits are provided for a six-month period at 60% of wages and are financed through an insurance scheme based on a 4% payroll tax. The benefits are administered by a network of 137 local employment offices, which also provide job placement services and requalification training. As enterprise restructuring proceeds, further unemployment is inevitable. If workers are to be matched with new jobs, it will be essential that actions be taken that make it easier for workers to switch jobs, including requalification training,

Figure 3: Number of Unemployed, 1990-93 (in thousands)

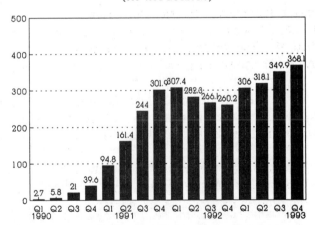

nationwide job placement services, and privatization of housing. Unemployment should also fall over the medium term as a result of policies to encourage small business development and, eventually, a reduction in payroll taxes that discriminate against hiring. Such policies will only be effective if the social safety net preserves incentives to work while protecting the truly needy.

Greater Efficiency of Social Spending

Slovakia's large and complicated social safety net, with more than forty categories of often overlapping entitlements, provides extensive coverage at fairly high benefit levels over a long period. The system is financed by a 50% payroll tax that raises the marginal cost of hiring labor and reduces incentives to create jobs. Given its current budgetary stringency, Slovakia can no longer afford to devote some 20% of GDP to its social safety net. At the same time, Slovakia's transition to a more efficient economy is likely to be painful, and vulnerable groups need to be protected from some of the harsher effects of the transition.

That can be done by improving efficiency and directing social services to the poor. Social protection needs to move toward a more rational and sustainable system, all the while keeping current fiscal pressures in mind. Targeting benefits more carefully—such as further means-testing of child benefits, raising the retirement age, making employees and firms bear more of the costs of sick leave, and introducing actions to control costs and collect contributions more effectively—are measures that can be taken right away. The effectiveness of the social safety net will need to be evaluated carefully, to ensure that social protection is provided to the neediest. Particular attention is needed in five areas:

- *Developing an effective program of social assistance.* Legislation similar to the Law on a Living Minimum, which (generously) defines minimum household incomes to reflect basic consumption requirements, could serve as the basis of a social assistance program for people whose income is below the defined minimum.

- *Reducing unnecessary social assistance programs.* As other means of support become available (including higher wages and new insurance programs), social benefit programs no longer necessary to keep households out of poverty should be phased out. Candidates for downsizing include many family allowances, sickness benefits, and parent benefits.

- *Developing a multi-tier retirement program.* The state pay-as-you-go social security system is currently the only source of retirement income for workers. As the economy becomes more market oriented, the private sector ought to take over some of the state's role in providing for income security in old age. Immediate measures to reduce benefit levels and tighten eligibility—and so to lower payroll taxes would improve both fiscal sustainability and incentives, and would be essential precursors to the future development of a private insurance market. Private markets would allow individuals to provide for income in their retirement in direct proportion to their own contributions. The government, through a second-tier, mandatory scheme, could require individuals to obtain such coverage.

- *Monitoring the costs of the social insurance program.* Under certain demographic and productivity assumptions, the social insurance program is projected to run a surplus. The program should be kept under review to consider the possibility of lowering the contribution rate, which would reduce the employment disincentives of the current payroll taxes.

- *Containing costs in the health care system.* A tight budget-capping mechanisms and an effective regulatory framework with well-designed incentives are necessary to contain the cost escalations inherent in a third-party health care payment system. Preventive health care and basic health services should take priority over expensive and sophisticated procedures that benefit only a few high-risk groups. The country needs to strengthen primary and community health care, public health services, and health care management training and to promote private sector health care.

The Outlook

Slovakia shares with about a dozen countries in Eastern Europe and the former Soviet Union favorable medium-term prospects based on a skilled and competitively priced labor force, a strong manufacturing tradition, and proximity to European markets. What, if anything, distinguishes Slovakia from these other countries? Most important, Slovakia inherits and maintains a tradition of macroeconomic prudence. Inflation has remained low (even after the breakup of the monetary union with the Czech Republic in February 1993), and the country adjusted successfully to the enormous loss of fiscal transfers from the former federation. Slovakia is also far more advanced in privatization than its neighbors (with the exception of the Czech Republic), with almost half its state-owned enterprises now in private hands. And Slovakia is much closer to wealthy markets in Europe—Vienna is only 60 kilometers from Bratislava, for example—than are most of the transition economies. The country's strategic position in the European pipeline network is also important as a source of substantial transit fees. Add to this Slovakia's modest foreign debt, and prudent financing of the transition appears to be a viable option.

But favorable characteristics and prudent macroeconomic management are not enough. Like all successful, small, open economies, Slovakia will have to find its niche in the world market. The private sector will have to move into the forefront as the government pulls out of directly productive activities and focuses on facilitating the reallocation of economic activities to increase efficiency. This reform program will have important fiscal implications, because the government will have to assume certain costs associated with strengthening the banking system and associated closure costs of liquidated enterprises. As insolvent enterprises are liquidated, their liabilities to the banking system will have to be written off and actions taken to improve banks' capital adequacy. This restructuring of enterprises and banks will inevitably lead to a greater demand for certain kinds of social transfers. These legitimate demands for social protection during the transition can be met only through a rationalized safety net targeted to the truly needy.

There are a number of risks associated with the reform strategy described in this report. Slovakia is a new country with limited institutional capacity in many areas. Its industries tend to cluster in sectors in which there is already substantial overcapacity in other countries (such as steel, chemicals, aluminum, and armaments) and where high levels of protection often impede access to export markets. Thus far, private sector investment, both domestic and foreign, has been limited. There is also the danger that the social consensus for reform will unravel unless economic recovery starts soon. The differences in economic recovery outcomes possible in the long run are large enough to justify taking the risks associated with a more aggressive reform effort now.

CHAPTER 1: THE CHALLENGE OF RECOVERY

Entering its first year as an independent country in 1993, the Slovak Republic enjoyed some of the most favorable initial conditions of any economy in transition. It had inherited a tradition of macroeconomic prudence, low inflation, and a modest debt. A skilled and competitively priced labor force and a strategic location in the center of Europe augur well for the economy's longer-term prospects. But other undesirable legacies—heavy industries ill-suited to Slovakia's comparative advantages, weak banks, and unsustainable transfer payments—mean that the adjustments ahead will be difficult. The transition has already been costly in social terms—real incomes plunged 24% between 1990 and 1993 (Figure 1.1). Economic reform has reached a critical juncture: macroeconomic stabilization has been broadly successful and there are promising signs of fiscal retrenchment and of private sector growth, and the restructuring of recently privatized state-owned enterprises. Decisions must be made now about structural changes that will determine the nature of future economic recovery. Economic projections for the next decade, developed later in this chapter, suggest that the gains from launching a rapid, comprehensive reform program now would be substantial (per capita income some 25% higher at the turn of the century) compared with the outcome if reform is delayed.

Slovakia's output decline since 1990 originated in two major shocks: the loss of markets associated with the collapse of the CMEA and the dissolution of the Czechoslovak Federation. With the collapse of the CMEA, the major markets for Slovak goods effectively disappeared and, because of extensive price and trade liberalization in 1991-92, firms faced a new set of relative prices that often revealed a lack of comparative advantage in their original activities. With dissolution of the Czechoslovak Federation at the end of 1992, fiscal transfers to Slovakia equivalent to 7% of GDP ceased abruptly. Interrepublic

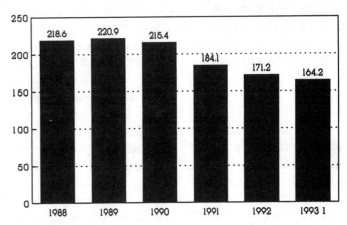

Figure 1.1: Fall in Real GDP
(billions of constant koruny)

1 Estimate.
Source: Slovak Statistical Office.

commerce, which accounted for half of Slovakia's trade, was also disrupted. Intensifying the impact of these shocks was the ongoing transition to a market economy and the need to establish a new institutional infrastructure—central bank, foreign ministry, and the other institutional structures of a new nation.

The decline in output, a natural consequence of resources deployed in the wrong activities, was exacerbated by widespread illiquidity. The government kept inflation in check, but the fiscal deficit mounted following the loss of transfers and the shrinking of the tax base. Financing of the deficit led to a crowding out of the private sector. An anticipated devaluation of the Slovak koruna led to heavy capital flight, further reducing liquidity. Enterprises reacted to the shocks by borrowing more than they were able to repay. Interenterprise arrears (estimated at 3% of GDP in 1993) and a large stock of bad debts in the banking system accumulated, leading to a decline in bank lending. The resulting gridlock impeded the necessary shift of resources to more competitive economic activities.

Three actions are needed on the macroeconomic front to restore growth:

- *Recovery of demand.* Export growth will have to be the major source of demand recovery as fiscal retrenchment begins to bite. The key will be to maintain competitiveness and to achieve or retain a foothold in markets that are often protectionist. As the health of the enterprise sector improves and wages and employment rise, more growth in private consumption can be expected.

- *Fiscal reform that facilitates restructuring.* Deficit reduction is a priority, but so are changes in the composition of revenues and expenditures. In the longer run, the economy needs to rely on lower tax rates and a wider, more consolidated tax base to generate revenue. Expenditures have to shift from subsidies and universal social benefits to investment and more generous transfers directed only to the truly needy.

- *Growth in credit to the private sector.* Reduced government borrowing from the banking system will help, but eventually it will be necessary to address the stock of bad debts that distort the effectiveness of financial intermediation.

This chapter explores the macroeconomic reasons for the collapse of output in Slovakia, beginning with Slovakia's economic legacy from the federation with the Czech Republic and the collapse of aggregate demand associated with the demise of the CMEA in 1991 and 1992. Ongoing fiscal and monetary policy—and the implications for prices, wages, and the exchange rate—are also considered. A medium-term scenario based on structural reforms in the financial, enterprise, and social sectors is outlined briefly and then presented in greater detail in subsequent chapters.

Slovakia Under the Federation

Slovakia's economic development was influenced heavily by the imposition of Soviet-style central planning on a primarily rural economy—one much poorer than the neighboring Czech lands with which it had been joined since the breakup of the Austro-Hungarian empire. This unified state became the Federation of Czech and Slovak Republics in 1968. The communist government that came to power in 1948 began a strong push for rapid industrialization in Slovakia, to achieve a convergence of incomes across the federation. Slovakia's measured per capita income rose from around 60% of that in the Czech lands in 1948 to almost 80% in 1968 and reached near parity in the 1970s.[1] This growth was fueled by large-scale industrialization financed in part through transfers from the federation. The outcome is a highly industrialized economy with a distorted emphasis on semifinished goods, engineering products, and armaments and highly dependent on markets in the former CMEA. The magnitude of the distortion in Slovakia's productive structure can be grasped by comparing its distribution of GDP across sectors with that in other countries—a 40%/54% split between services and industry compared with an average of 61%/33% for OECD countries (Table 1.1).

---

[1]   As is the case throughout the formerly communist economies, the real value at international prices of Slovak industries is not easy to determine. Only privatization followed by a period of integration with the world economy will reveal the true level of Slovakia's per capita income and wealth.

Table 1.1: GDP by Sector, Slovakia and OECD Countries, 1990 **(percent)**			
Country	Agriculture	Industry	Services
Australia	4	31	64
Austria	3	37	60
Belgium	2	31	67
Denmark	5	28	67
Finland	6	36	58
France	4	29	67
Germany	2	39	59
Greece	17	27	56
Italy	4	33	63
Japan	3	42	56
Netherlands	4	31	65
New Zealand	9	27	65
Sweden	3	35	62
Turkey	18	33	49
Average	6	33	61
Slovakia[a]	6.0	53.8	40.2
[a] 1992 Data			
Source: *World Development Report 1992* and Slovak Statistical Office.			

This industrial structure has imposed greater costs on Slovakia's transition to a market economy than might otherwise have been the case, given its favorable macroeconomic legacy. Slovakia shared in the macroeconomic stabilization success of the former Czechoslovak federation following the "Velvet Revolution" of 1989. Inflation remained low (10% in 1992), external debt was only 27% of GDP in 1992, and progress has been good in price decontrol, privatization, trade liberalization and reorientation of exports to the West, and the creation of a social safety net.

The output losses associated with the federal stabilization program were massive in both the Czech and Slovak Republics—a decline of 15% in 1991 and another 7% in 1992. Employment rates, however, have displayed a sharp divergence across republics since the beginning of the transformation program (Figure 1.2). Slovakia was hit much harder by the federal government's decision to stop arms exports, which were far more important for the Slovak than the Czech economy, and by the slow growth of its private sector and low rates of foreign investment.

Dissolution of the Federation

The breakup of the seventy-four year old federation on December 31, 1992 occurred after the victorious parties in the republic-level elections in June 1992 were unable to agree on the composition and policies of a federal government. A series of negotiated agreements accompanied the country's dissolution throughout the autumn of 1992. These covered a monetary and customs union, the division of publicly owned assets and liabilities, and the treatment of international and domestic obligations.

Monetary and Customs Union

The planned monetary union was to remain in force for up to six months starting January 1, 1993, though it collapsed within six weeks. The central banks in the two republics were to coordinate monetary policy through a joint committee. The agreement specified that the monetary union could be terminated if limits on the size of the budget deficits, foreign exchange reserves, and interrepublic capital flight were exceeded or if monetary policies were at odds.

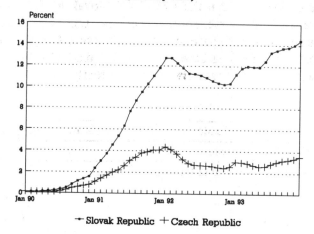

Figure 1.2: Unemployment Rates
(monthly data)

Source: Slovak and Czech Statistical Office.

A large loss in foreign exchange reserves in late 1992 and January 1993 in both republics precipitated the decision to dissolve the monetary union on February 8, 1993. Foreign exchange reserves were drained by capital outflows and by a sharp increase in import payments driven by uncertainty over the dissolution of the federation and preemptive buying prior to introduction of the value added tax on January 1, 1993. Net outflows of foreign assets were estimated at about US$200 million in 1992 because of widespread expectations of a devaluation.

The republics ratified a customs union agreement on October 29, 1992, in recognition of the extensive trade links between them and the need to ensure the free movement of goods and services and capital and labor. The agreement, which complies with the policies of the General Agreement on Tariffs and Trade (GATT) and the European Union (EU), prohibits the use of tariffs within the territory of the former federation and stipulates a common customs policy toward third countries. The agreement also prohibits trade discrimination through the use of fiscal instruments (except in agriculture), bans activities that thwart competition, and protects intellectual property.

When the monetary union was dissolved, a clearing arrangement was established for inter-republic trade flows. Transactions prior to February 8, 1993, were cleared under the common currency, but thereafter trade imbalances were cleared regularly and financed up to a ceiling of ECU 130 million. The agreement also allows for adjustments of exchange rates under the clearing arrangement within a 5% band against the clearing ECU.

The Velvet Divorce

The division of federal property was based on territoriality and population. Immovable federal property went to the republic in which it was located. Movable and divisible assets and liabilities were divided between the Czech and Slovak Republics in a ratio of 2 to 1, according to population. There were, of course, some exceptions. Embassies abroad were assigned to one of the republics, with some shared use of space until alternative accommodations could be found for the other republic. Quota allocations providing access to the EU market were divided on the basis of production and export capacity. Property was divided in an orderly manner, guided by the desire to ensure stability.

Table 1.2: External Debt of Hungary, Poland, and Slovakia 1990-93				
Debt measure	1990	1991	1992	1993
Debt per capita (current US$)				
Hungary	2,037.8	1,235.7	2,199.2	2,386.2
Poland	1,277.5	1,235.7	1,225.1	1,218.1
Slovakia	377.9	506.0	532.9	626.9
Debt as share of GDP (%)				
Hungary	65.4	74.1	70.6	67.4
Poland	78.3	60.7	56.1	55.7
Slovakia	14.0	26.7	26.5	32.7
Debt service as share of exports of goods and services (%)[a]				
Hungary	38.0	40.1	31.1	40.6
Poland	53.9	23.7	23.4	19.4
Slovakia	---	---	7.5	8.0

[a] Debt service figures for debt contracted as of end-1992 for Slovakia are estimates. Debt service ratios are based on total exports of goods and services.

Source: World Bank data.

Slovakia inherited a relatively small debt from the federation (Table 1.2): about US$2.8 billion in debt to the rest of the world (27% of annual GDP) and $900 million in debt to the Czech Republic (still under negotiation). Major creditors are commercial banks, bondholders, the International Monetary Fund (IMF), and other official creditors. The Slovak Republic is current on all its debt servicing, which in 1993 amounted to about 8% of exports of goods and services.

6

Box 1.1: The Slovak Republic in Context

Slovakia, which became independent on January 1, 1993, is a land-locked country at the center of Europe. Its population of 5.3 million people is stable, with fertility at about replacement rates. Enrollment in primary and secondary schools is virtually universal. About one-quarter of the population go on to colleges, specialized schools, and universities. Women's participation in the labor force is high at 82% of working-age women. Average life expectancy is also high at 72 years, but male life expectancy is only 67 years, mainly because of high rates of cardiovascular disease and cancer.

In per capita income, Slovakia is in the middle range of its Central and Eastern European neighbors (see figures below). Measured in terms of purchasing power parity exchange rates that adjust for prices of nontradables, however, Slovakia's per capita income exceeds that of Poland and is well above the regional average. Real wages have declined since the beginning of the transformation program. Declining output and growing unemployment have meant declining living standards for much of the population over the last three years.

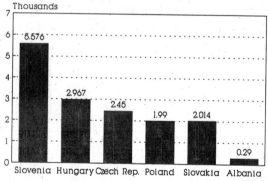

Box figure 1.1: Indices of Average Real Wage (1989 - 100)

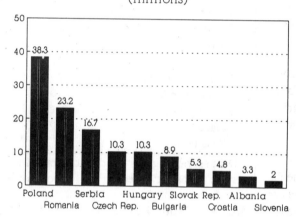

Box figure 1.2: Population in 1992 (millions)

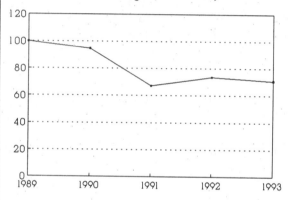

Box figure 1.3: Per Capita GDP in 1992 in Dollar Terms (Atlas)

Source: World Bank data.

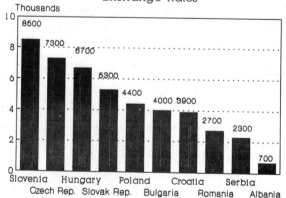

Box figure 1.4: Per Capita GDP in 1992 in Dollar Terms Based on PPP Exchange Rates

Coping with Shocks

Since independence, the Slovak Republic has preserved a good degree of macroeconomic stability, though macroeconomic imbalances persist, a consequence of the conflicting objectives of the government's fiscal, monetary, and exchange rate policies. The interrelated needs for fiscal adjustment to the loss of transfers from the federation, a prudent monetary policy to control inflation, and an exchange rate policy to protect the external position have contributed to the decline in economic activity in 1993. The fixed one-for-one parity with the Czech koruna through July 1993 meant that exports could not stimulate demand recovery, while the uncertainty led to capital flight that drained the economy of foreign exchange.

Loss of Markets: the Collapse of Foreign and Domestic Demand

The collapse of demand for Slovak goods is the root of the crisis in the economy. Aggregate demand fell by about 24% between 1990 and 1993 (Figure 1.1). Part of the demand shock reflected external factors—the collapse of the CMEA, embargoes on trade with a number of Slovakia's major trading partners, and the recent disruptions to trade with the Czech Republic. But domestic consumption and investment also contracted severely (35% between 1990 and 1993) as both government and households restrained spending during the transition. This loss was only partly offset by the gains in exports to Western markets as the direction of trade shifted away from the CMEA.

An open economy subject to massive trade shocks. The Slovak Republic is an open economy, with merchandise imports and exports equivalent to about 60% of GDP. Extensive trade liberalization after 1990 resulted in the abolition of most quantitative restrictions,[2] and import-weighted tariffs currently average 4.6%, unweighted tariffs 6.2% (Table 1.3).[3] By comparison, the average unweighted tariff is 13% in Hungary and Poland.

Collapse of trade. Czechoslovakia's trade collapsed in the wake of the dismantling of the CMEA trading arrangements in January 1991, depressing economic activity (Figure 1.3). The impact was particularly dramatic for Slovakia, which depended more on trade, especially CMEA trade, than did the Czech Republic. The impact was greater in volume than values because import and export prices both rose to world market levels following liberalization of prices, trade, and the exchange rate. The net impact was nonetheless a deterioration in Slovakia's terms of trade, because import prices (especially of energy products) rose faster than export prices. Consequences were especially severe for industries that depended heavily on imported inputs.

---

[2]   Exceptions are import licensing requirements on crude oil, natural gas, uranium, coal, copper, aluminum, lead and paper products, firearms and ammunition, certain clothing products, and narcotics. Export licenses are required for weapons and explosives and goods subject to voluntary export restraints based on quantitative limits or minimum prices (such as textiles, steel, meat and live animals exported to the EU).

[3]   The low tariffs were phased in. A 20% temporary import surcharge in effect in 1990 (Federal Ministry of Finance Decree 569/90) was reduced to 18% on May 1, 1991 (Decree number 108/1991), to 15% on June 1, 1991 (Decree 234/1991), to 10% on January 1, 1992, and abolished at the end of 1992. Article 22 of the customs union agreement with the Czech Republic allows for temporary measures under special circumstances if both parties agree. The Slovak authorities imposed a temporary import surcharge on consumer goods in March 1994. The Czech Republic followed the Slovak authorities' decision by devaluing the Czech koruna by 3 percent in the clearing system.

Table 1.3: Nominal Protection Rates, 1992					
Sector	Minimum tariff	Maximum tariff	Average tariff Unweighted	Weighted	Standard deviation
Economywide	0	80.0	6.2	4.6	5.6
Agriculture	0	80.0	4.0	6.9	7.7
Mining	0	5.8	0.2	0.0	1.0
Manufacturing	0	65.0	6.4	5.4	5.4
Consumer goods	0	65.0	8.4	9.7	.4
Intermediate goods	0	25.0	5.2	3.4	3.7
Capital goods	0	27.0	5.4	5.2	2.8
Manufacturing subsectors					
Food, beverages, tobacco	0	65.0	11.3	9.5	12.3
Textiles and leather	0	35.0	7.7	8.9	4.3
Wood and cork products	0	12.0	6.4	7.5	3.1
Paper and printing	0	25.0	8.1	6.6	5.5
Chemicals, petroleum, and coal	0	20.0	4.9	3.7	2.9
Nonmetallic minerals	0	20.0	7.9	7.6	4.5
Basic metal industries	0	10.0	3.9	2.0	2.7
Metal products, machinery	0	27.0	5.6	5.6	2.9
Other manufacturing	0	45.0	5.7	6.9	5.1

Note: Rates exclude the temporary import surcharge reimposed in March 1994.

Source: World Bank data and staff estimates.

Figure 1.3: Czechoslovakia Exports and Imports, 1989-92

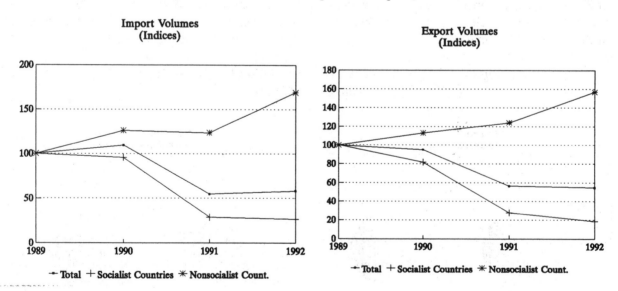

Import Volumes
(Indices)

Export Volumes
(Indices)

-◦- Total + Socialist Countries ✳ Nonsocialist Count.

-◦- Total + Socialist Countries ✳ Nonsocialist Count.

Source: World Bank Data

Before Slovakia was able to adjust to these shocks, it was hit by another external shock, the collapse of the monetary union with the Czech Republic in February 1993 and the resultant need to establish a border. Slovakia had an estimated trade deficit with the Czech Republic in 1992 of about US$640 million in merchandise and US$300 million in services. Until then, the imbalance was financed by transfers through the federal budget. The transfers, equivalent to about US$750 million, reflected the underlying current account adjustment that Slovakia needed to make in 1993. The border complications associated with the implementation of the VAT and the general uncertainty about procedures at the beginning of 1993 were corrected as procedures were streamlined. Nevertheless, trade with the Czech Republic declined sharply, with dollar exports dropping by 25% and imports by 39%. Although the trade balance with the Czech Republic did move into surplus (US$44 million) in 1993, some contraction in trade between the Czech and Slovak Republics seems to be an inevitable price of independence.

Despite the modest surplus in trade balance with the Czech Republic, Slovakia had an overall trade deficit of US$200 million in 1993 (10.2% of GDP). Slovakia's merchandise trade declined by 19% for exports and 12% for imports in nominal dollar terms. About half the merchandise trade deficit occurred in the last quarter of 1993, some US$200 million of it the result of imports of military airplanes from Russia and of equipment for nuclear power plants. The airplanes were delivered as repayment for loans from Slovakia to Russia, and thus there is a corresponding entry in the capital account. The services account showed a surplus of about US$370 million, due primarily to transit fees on the gas pipeline. The current account recorded a deficit of US$570 million (5.6% of GDP), but the capital account had a surplus large enough to allow for the accumulation of gross reserves of US$377 million (US$318 million of which represented an increase of short-term assets of commercial banks).

Shifting markets. The Slovak Republic has been increasingly more successful at shifting its trade to the OECD market (Figure 1.4). The importance of the Czech Republic as a trading partner diminished throughout 1993, reflecting both the shift to trade on a convertible currency basis and the continuation of a trend emerging in 1992, as Slovak exports to the Czech Republic fell by 17% and imports by 8% in nominal terms.[4] Trade with the Czech Republic fell from an estimated 50% of total trade in 1992 to 39% in 1993. The former Soviet Union has diminished in importance as a trading partner as well, its shares increasingly replaced by the EU, which now accounts for almost one-quarter of Slovak exports. Considering the severe economic dislocations in the former CMEA markets, this shift toward the OECD is clearly a positive outcome. But with recession and growing protectionism in many of the major OECD markets, Slovakia will continue to face difficulties in export markets (Box 1.2).

Figure 1.4: Direction of Trade (excluding the Czech Republic)
(percentage of value)

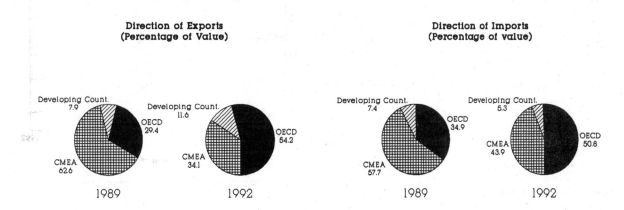

Note: The increase in the share of exports to OECD includes the reclassification of the former German Democratic Republic.

Source: Slovak Statistical Office.

4   PlanEcon, April 30, 1993, p.23.

Box 1.2: The EU and Slovakia—Trade not Aid?

The Europe Agreement (also known as the Association Agreement) between the EU and the former Czech and Slovak Federal Republic of December 1991 has not been ratified, but some provisions have been implemented through an interim agreement since March 1992. The objective is to establish a free trade area between the EU and the Czech and Slovak Republics over a transitional period of ten years. However, trade in agricultural products is not covered, and provisions for contingent protection—safeguard measures and antidumping - will remain indefinitely in industrial goods. Meanwhile, the Czech and Slovak Republics are obliged to adopt competition laws compatible with EU law within three years. The full agreement provides additionally for the liberalization of trade in services, political and economic cooperation, and technical assistance. The EU also provides Slovakia aid amounting to about US$40 million per year under the PHARE program and access to financing through the European Investment Bank (EIB).

Under the agreement, the EU will abolish all quotas and tariffs on industrial goods over five years, but the pace of that liberalization would vary. For "nonsensitive" products, liberalization is immediate. For "sensitive" industrial products, including footwear, motor vehicles, some chemicals, glass, and furniture, quotas will be raised by 20% a year (linearly) for five years, and then be abolished completely, while tariffs both within and above the quotas will be lowered. With the breakup of the Czech and Slovak Federation, access to the EU market was divided on a product-by-product basis between the two republics according to export performance and production capacity. The Czech and Slovak Republic's quota allocations to the EU will increase linearly by 20%, using 1991 exports as the base year. In general, the pattern of liberalization for Slovak imports is similar, but somewhat slower, with complete liberalization for industrial goods after nine years.

Quotas and tariffs on coal have been abolished except for imports to Germany and Spain, which are allowed to retain them for up to four years. Tariffs on textiles will be phased out over six years, with quotas phased out in ten years. For agricultural products, most quotas are increased by 10% per year, with levies on quantities within the quotas reduced by 50% to 60% over one to three years.

Steel, Slovakia's most important export, illustrates the EU's somewhat ambiguous attitude toward market access. Under the agreement, quotas were abolished immediately, while tariffs (already relatively low) were to be phased out over a period of five years. However, since the agreements came into force, the EU has imposed antidumping duties of over 30% on steel tubes and, under the safeguard provisions, has reimposed quotas on Slovak steel imports until 1995, based on their 1991 level.

Increased access to EU markets has brought clear benefits to Slovakia. Czechoslovak exports to the EU expanded by more than 40% a year in both 1991 and 1992. But the speed of future Slovak integration into the EU market depends most on factors over which Slovakia has little control—economic and political developments within the EU, and progress in multilateral trade negotiations. The Slovak economy is more open than that of the EU, and Slovakia is often competitive in precisely the "sensitive" sectors in which EU protection remains relatively high, such as steel, textiles, and potentially agriculture. The more Slovakia finds foreign markets for these traditional industries, the less painful restructuring will be and the less external assistance will be required.

Recognizing this, the European Council decided in June 1993 to advance unilaterally some of the measures described above, with the removal of duties on "sensitive" industrial products being brought forward by two years, the agricultural concession advanced by six months, and a number of other improvements. The European Council also committed the EU to eventual full membership for Slovakia, subject to various conditions, including "the capacity to cope with competitive pressures and market forces within the Union," although no target date is specified.

The composition of trade reflects Slovakia's legacy as an economy dominated by heavy industry. Slovak exports are composed largely of manufactures such as iron and steel, nonferrous metals, metal manufactures, cement, and wood and paper products (SITC category 6) and machinery and equipment (SITC category 7), which together account for 60% of exports (Figure 1.5). About one-third of imports from the Czech Republic consist of electric power, coal, metal products, and machinery and equipment; imports from the rest of the world consist largely of mineral fuels and machinery and equipment.

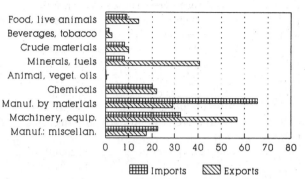

Figure 1.5: Composition of Trade in 1993 (excluding Czech Republic) (billions of current koruny)

Source: Slovak Statistical Office.

Contraction in domestic demand. The collapse of domestic aggregate demand has contributed to the recession and to the contraction of import demand. Both consumption and investment fell sharply in 1991 (by 25.1% and 15.5%) in real terms. Real personal consumption fell by about 28%, as household savings increased in precautionary response to rising unemployment and the declining real value of deposits after price increases associated with liberalization. Domestic demand contracted faster than output in 1991, resulting in a substantially improved foreign balance in constant prices (reflecting the large terms of trade deterioration), although only slightly improved in current prices. Domestic absorption fell by about 10% in 1992, while the negative external balance was reduced. The collapse in domestic demand continued in 1993 as consumption fell by 8%, much of it due to a sharp reduction in government consumption of about 18%.

Investment demand has also suffered. In 1991, gross investment fell by 16%, while fixed investment contracted by 25% as stocks equivalent to 6% of GDP accumulated. The collapse of investment reflected weak consumer demand, declining profitability, and the uncertainty created by price and trade liberalization and the impending privatizations. Fixed investment declined another 19% in 1992, and inventories accumulated the previous year were run down (equivalent to 4% of GDP). Continuing uncertainties about reform and the dissolution of the federation, as well as worsening enterprise profitability, lay behind the falling investment level. While firms' internal resources for investment were reduced, tight monetary policy raised the cost of external funds and limited their availability. Gross investment decreased slightly in 1993 as the rundown of inventories continued and fixed investment fell by 2%.

Adjusting to a Loss of Fiscal Transfers

With the breakup of the federation, the Slovak government had to adjust the budget for 1993 to an estimated loss of fiscal transfers equivalent to about 7% of GDP. At the same time, Slovakia had new expenditure obligations associated with the dissolution of the federation and the establishment of an independent country (such as establishing embassies, issuing a new currency, establishing a customs administration). Further complicating matters was the new tax system introduced on January 1, 1993, which greatly increased uncertainty about revenue projections (Box 1.3). Upheaval and adjustment in the enterprise sector also meant that the government's traditional tax base was shrinking. Meanwhile, the initial restructuring efforts were creating a greater need for social transfers.

Thus in the first year of independence, as transfers from the federation were eliminated and the government sought to maintain macroeconomic stability, the fiscal adjustment required was considerable. The budget deficit was cut back from 13.1% of GDP in 1992 to 7.5% in 1993. That 5.6 percentage point cutback in the deficit reflected a 2.8 percentage point shrinkage of revenues (from 50.7% of GDP to 48%) and an 8.4 percentage point shrinkage of expenditures (from 64% of GDP to 55.4%).

The 1993 budget. The officially balanced budget for 1993 reflected the government's attempt to control expenditures while simultaneously introducing a major tax reform. Given that the estimated underlying deficit in 1992 was 13.1% of GDP (including transfers from the federation), the 1993 budget implied a major adjustment effort. Cuts equivalent to about 10% of GDP were made in almost all expenditure categories, the largest coming in transfers to households (3% of GDP), other current expenditures (5%), and investment (2.5%). The cuts were intended to more than compensate for the expected revenue losses associated with the administrative difficulties accompanying introduction of a value added tax and the reform of personal income and profit taxation.

Revenue projections and performance. Revenues were well below projections in virtually all tax categories in early 1993, with the exception of income taxes on wages.[5] Administrative difficulties with the new VAT were partly to blame, but the primary reasons seem to have been the difficult financial position of enterprises and the slowdown of economic activity in 1992. The continuing contraction in economic activity manifested itself in enterprise tax arrears equivalent to Sk 14.5 billion in the first quarter of 1993, almost Sk 8 billion of it on payroll taxes, which finance the social insurance funds. The agricultural sector alone was responsible for Sk 3.6 billion of payroll tax arrears. By the end 1993, tax arrears had risen to Sk 18 billion.

The government moved quickly by mid-year to identify further fiscal measures (equivalent to 2.5% of GDP for the second half of 1993, or 5% on an annual basis) to contain the deficit and hold down inflation. This fiscal tightening, supported by a Systemic Transformation Facility loan from the IMF, was intended to hold the overall fiscal deficit to 6.7% of GDP, though in the end the deficit came in at 7.5%. The VAT rates were raised, as were excise taxes (6% increase) and property taxes (25% increase). Changes in social security legislation were expected to generate revenues equivalent to 1% of GDP. To cut spending even more, social expenditures were targeted more narrowly, and investments and subsidies were cut back, generating savings equivalent to 1.5% of GDP.

---

5 Revenues from excises and profit taxes are also well below projections, possibly a reflection of the contracting tax base and, given the high rates of taxation, growing evasion. The one bright spot is the higher than expected revenues of budgetary and subsidized organizations, which appear to be using their greater financial autonomy to charge fees for services. However, in aggregate terms, this will have little impact because of the small amounts involved.

Box 1.3: The New Tax System

A fundamental tax reform had been planned for Czechoslovakia for 1993. When the federation split up, both new republics decided to proceed with the tax reform on January 1, 1993. Since 1989, taxes on turnover, profits, wages, and payroll had been gradually replacing the old system of predominantly discretionary taxes used to extract surpluses from state-owned enterprises. The 1993 reform was designed to replace the numerous turnover taxes with a value-added tax and to introduce personal income and corporate profit taxes. The payroll is to be replaced by contributions from employees and employers to four social insurance funds: pensions, health insurance, sickness, and employment (Box 1.2).

Value added tax. The decision to adopt a value added tax (VAT) was driven by the desire for compatibility with the EU and by the attractive economic characteristics of the tax, such as neutrality, efficiency, and coverage of the services sector. The basic VAT rate is 23%, with a lower rate of 5% for food, energy, medicines, and paper products. An extensive public information program preceded introduction of the tax, to familiarize businesses with the new system. Despite these efforts, there was some confusion in the early stages. As revenue shortfalls became apparent in mid-year, the top rate was raised to 25% and the bottom rate to 6%.

Income taxes. The June 1992 law on direct taxes replaces six different laws on the taxation of corporate and personal income. The new uniform corporate profit tax rate of 45% replaces previous profit taxes of 40% for joint ventures, 50% for agriculture (which makes mostly losses), and 55% for all other corporations. The government also proposed to use tax incentives to attract foreign direct investment, despite widespread evidence that such incentives have little impact at the margin. The personal income tax is 15% up to an annual income of Sk 60,000; thereafter it rises progressively to a rate of 34% for income of Sk 1.08 million, with a marginal rate of 47% for income above that. Deductions are permitted for dependents (up to four children), the disabled, and charitable contributions. Interest and dividend incomes are taxed through a withholding tax of 15% to 25%.

Social insurance funds. A 50% payroll tax is used to finance four social insurance funds to pay benefits to pensioners, the sick, and the unemployed. Employers pay 38% of the tax, employees 12% (as a percentage of base wages). The pension fund takes the largest share (26.5%), followed by health insurance (13.7%), the sickness fund (5.6%), and the unemployment fund. These social funds were intended to operate independently as self-financing funds, but they will continue to be part of the budget for accounting purposes in the near term. Expected shortfalls in revenues will have to be met by the budget. (Operations of these funds are discussed in more detail in chapter 5.)

These measures made fiscal sense in the short run, but in the longer run, as the tax base grows, lower rates may be appropriate. Tax revenues as a share of GDP are extremely high in the Slovak Republic compared to OECD countries (Table 1.4). Slovakia relies far more on taxes on goods and services and on corporate income and far less on personal income taxes than do OECD countries on average.[6] The high tax rates needed to generate these revenues and to compensate for lower collection efficiency create economic disincentives. The 50% payroll tax creates a clear bias against hiring. Similarly, in an economy where firms are likely to finance of their investment through retained earnings, the corporate profit tax may create disincentives to capital formation.

---

6   VAT collections in Slovakia in the first year of implementation were 8.1% of GDP, higher than the OECD average. Slovakia's success in VAT implementation was due in part to a high import to GDP ratio (62%), which implies that a substantial share of VAT revenues are collected at the border.

Table 1.4: Revenue Statistics of Slovakia and OECD Countries
(percentage of GDP[b])

Country	Total tax revenue	Tax on goods and services	VAT Share	Tax on corporate income	Tax on personal income	Social security contributions	Tax on payroll and work force[a]	Tax on property
Australia	30.1	8.5	-	3.8	13.4	-	1.7	2.7
Austria	41.0	13.3	8.7	1.5	8.2	13.7	2.5	1.1
Belgium	44.3	11.3	7.2	3.0	13.6	15.1	-	1. 2
Canada	35.3	10.4	-	3.0	13.5	4.6	-	3.1
Denmark	49.9	16.5	9.1	2.1	26.0	1.2	0.3	2.2
Finland	38.1	14.4	8.8	1.6	17.6	3.0	-	1.5
France	43.8	12.6	8.3	2.4	5.2	19.2	0.8	2.2
Germany	38.1	9.7	5.9	2.1	11.2	13.8	-	1.2
Greece	33.2	15.0	8.1	1.5	4.4	10.5	0.6	1.1
Iceland	33.8	18.7	-	1.0	8.2	0.9	1.1	2.7
Ireland	37.6	16.7	8.1	1.3	11.9	5.4	0.5	1.8
Italy	37.8	10.2	5.3	3.8	10.1	12.5	0.2	0.9
Japan	30.6	3.9	1.0	7.5	7.6	8.5	-	3.1
Luxembourg	42.4	10.3	5.9	7.5	9.9	11.1	-	3.5
Netherlands	46.0	12.0	7.5	3.5	9.7	18.9	-	1.7
New Zealand	40.3	13.0	8.1	3.6	18.5	-	0.7	3.3
Norway	45.5	16.5	8.7	2.4	12.5	12.4	-	1.3
Portugal	35.1	15.8	7.0	1.4	4.9	9.2	-	0.5
Slovakia	40.0	14.0	8.2	6.5	4.3	12.7	-	11.1[b]
Spain	34.4	9.9	5.6	3.0	7.9	11.9	-	1.3
Sweden	56.1	13.5	7.6	2.1	22.0	14.7	1.8	1.9
Switzerland	31.8	5.9	-	2.1	10.6	10.4	- ·	2.7
Turkey	29.0	7.1	4.7	2.4	6.7	4.5	-	0.6
United Kingdom	36.5	11.3	6.2	4.5	9.7	6.4	-	4.6
United States	30.1	4.9	-	2.6	10.7	8.8	-	3.1
Unweighted average								
OECD total	38.4	11.7	5.5	2.9	11.4	9.0	0.4	2.1
OECD Europe	39.7	12.7	6.5	2.6	11.1	10.3	0.4	1.8
EU	39.9	12.6	7.0	3.0	10.4	11.3	0.2	1.9

Note: OECD data are for 1989; Slovak data for 1993.

[a] Payroll taxes (as a proportion of payroll or as a fixed amount per person) that are not earmarked for social security expenditure. In Slovakia, all payroll tax revenues are earmarked for social security contributions.
[b] Including a road tax amounting to 0.4% of GDP.

Expenditure performance. Social sectors dominate expenditures, a reflection of the communist legacy of large social transfers (Table 1.5). Pensions, at 17% of total government spending (10% of GDP), are the single largest expenditure category; an aging population and a very low retirement age—fifty-seven years for women and sixty years for men—account for the large size. Other social benefits account for 21% of government spending (12% of GDP). Any attempt to reduce spending will clearly have to include further cuts in social spending and better targeting of programs to meet the expected increased demand as unemployment rises and incomes fall.

Table 1.5: Actual Government Expenditures, 1993 (billions of current koruny)		
Item	Amount	Percentage of GDP
Total expenditure	189.0	55.4
Investment	18.1	5.3
Subsidies to enterprises	16.2	4.7
Agriculture	8.7	2.5
Other current expenditure	154.7	45.4
Unemployment benefits	1.8	0.5
Employment programs	1.1	0.3
Pensions	32.7	9.6
Other transfers	13.7	4.0
Social assistance	3.1	0.9
Education	8.0	2.3
Health	15.7	4.6
Debt service	12.5	3.7
Source: Slovak authorities.		

Subsidies take another large bite from the budget, amounting to 8.6% of total spending and 4.8% of GDP. Agriculture absorbs about half of all subsidies, mostly to compensate farmers who are cultivating poor-quality land;[7] subsidies for heating, railways, and urban transport account for the rest. Agricultural enterprises are also major culprits in the network of interenterprise and tax arrears. Agriculture's financial weakness stems in part from the burden of bad loans associated with liberalizing input prices but not output prices. Nevertheless, agriculture's dependency on budgetary transfers must be reduced in the long run.

Public investment accounted for 9.6% of spending and 5.4% of GDP in 1993. About 70% of investment funds go to sectoral and general purpose support of budgetary organizations (mainly transport, telecommunications, and education) and subsidized organizations (mainly health facilities). The remaining 30% goes to specific projects, most of them in agriculture. Only one manufacturing enterprise received public investment funds in 1993. Most investment spending is for completing ongoing activities rather than for new initiatives.

---

7   Such subsidies amounted to Sk 4.8 billion in 1991 and Sk 3.6 billion in 1992. Further subsidies for "stabilization and intensification" amounted to Sk 2.2 billion in 1991 and Sk 1.9 billion in 1992.

Expenditures have generally been kept under control, although there were some overruns in 1993. The Ministry of Finance monitors revenues and expenditures daily and informs government entities monthly on their net position. With the exception of social benefits, pensions, health care, defense, foreign affairs, and a few other programs, each entity is permitted to spend no more than 7% of its annual budget allocation each month (less than one-twelfth its annual allocation). Any overage must be made up the following month. Although this system helps keep the official deficit at a reasonable level, there is growing evidence that it has also generated government arrears. Without explicit policy measures to reduce spending, this system of expenditure controls acts simply as a warning signal—and sometimes even contributes to the breakdown of financial discipline in the economy.

Most of the expenditure adjustment in 1993 came out of the capital budget (including extrabudgetary projects). Capital spending went down by 5.6% of GDP, compared to 2.1% for social expenditures and 0.6% for subsidies. The cuts in public investment are a worrisome sign for the sustainability of the adjustment. For one thing, many extrabudgetary projects in 1992 were one-off expenditures (particularly the Sk 8 billion spent on the Gabcikovo dam), so that the estimated deficit of 13.1% of GDP in 1992 overstates the structural budget deficit for that year and thus the implied fiscal effort needed for 1993. For another, the large cuts in capital expenditures are symptomatic of the difficulty of finding room to make more cuts on the current side, cuts that will be needed in 1994 and thereafter to ensure macroeconomic stability.

Monetary Policy: Credibility and Crowding Out

Establishing Credibility

Following the breakup of the federation in December 1992 and the dissolution of the monetary union in February 1993, the most important objective of the Slovak monetary authorities was to establish credibility for the new currency so that currency-holders would convert their old Czechoslovak koruna (Kc) into the new Slovak koruna (Sk). The monetary authorities used indirect and direct monetary instruments to curb expectations of a devaluation and inflationary pressures. Credit auctions were relied on to inject liquidity into the banking system and to establish market rates of interest. In addition, the National Bank of Slovakia (NBS) used its rediscount facilities to offer a limited amount of funds to

Figure 1.6

Monetary Base and Net Foreign Assets
(In billion of Sk)

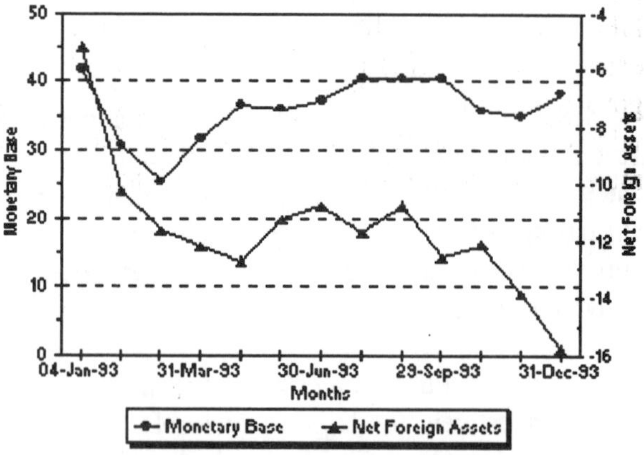

Source: National Bank of Slovakia.

banks that lent to agriculture and export activities, and it used the lombard facility to provide emergency credit to banks. In early 1993, the NBS found it necessary to introduce direct monetary instruments in the form of bank credit ceilings to prevent imprudent risk-taking by banks with large non performing loans in their portfolios.

In the wake of the external trade shock following dissolution of the federation, expectations of a devaluation of the new currency led to a large loss of foreign reserves in early 1993. In February 1993, when the currency union was dissolved and currency-holders were asked to convert their old koruny into new Slovak koruny, many people decided to convert into foreign currency instead, causing a sharp drop in currency in circulation and in NBS's net foreign assets (Figure 1.6). In the first quarter of 1993 broad money fell in both nominal terms (3.3%) and real terms (13.5%), while net foreign assets of the banking system declined by some US$120 million; they fell by an additional US$45 million in the second quarter. The substantial drop in real broad money in the first quarter was partially reversed later in 1993, as the monetary authorities worked to stabilize expectations of a devaluation and establish credibility in the new currency. Real broad money increased 1.6% in the second quarter, declined 2.9% in the third, and increased 10.9% in the fourth. Overall, it declined 5.3% in real terms in 1993 (compared with a drop of 4.1% in real GDP).

Crowding Out

The NBS's decision to stabilize expectations about devaluation by controlling the expansion of base money was undermined by pressure on NBS to finance the budget deficit. The government's inability to reduce the large fiscal deficit overnight and the absence of well-developed financial markets for treasury bills resulted in reliance on the NBS to finance the deficit. The NBS's total credit to government (the sum of net credit plus purchases of treasury bills) increased from Sk 22 billion in early January 1993 to Sk 38 billion in April (Figure 1.7). This rapid increase in credit to the government stimulated a further fall in net foreign assets.

When the currency union was dissolved, the stock of base money was reduced by more than the amount converted into foreign exchange or bank deposits between early January and February 4, 1993. Because that was equivalent to reducing NBS's liabilities,[8] NBS was able to use these extraordinary profits to expand credit to the government in the first quarter of 1993 without too great an effect on base money—and while maintaining confidence in

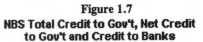

Figure 1.7
NBS Total Credit to Gov't, Net Credit to Gov't and Credit to Banks

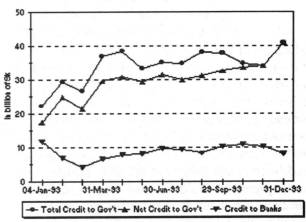

Source: National Bank of Slovakia.

---

8   The authorities may have overestimated the stock of Slovak currency in the opening balance sheet of the National Bank of Slovakia. In that case, the NBS profit would have been at the expense of the National Bank of the Czech Republic. However, there is no strong evidence that this might have been the case.

the new Slovak koruna.[9] By the second and third quarters of 1993, however, the budget and the enterprise sector were exerting stronger pressure on NBS to loosen monetary policy and expand credit.

Government intervention in credit auctions and the treasury bill market in the second half of 1993 exerted additional pressures on the NBS to loosen monetary policy. In May 1993, in an attempt to lower interest rates and make credit more accessible to the productive sectors, the NBS suspended credit auctions, relying on the low interest rate rediscount facility as the main instrument for making liquidity available to banks—especially the rediscount of bills of exchange for the agriculture and export sectors. Banks began to rely primarily on NBS credit, which was less expensive than using deposits. The mobilization of real deposits slowed, and financial resources for lending, particularly to private enterprises, began to dry up. The NBS responded by restoring the credit auctions in November 1993 as the primary channel for injecting liquidity into the banking system.

When the government set a ceiling on treasury bill prices in June 1993 and fixed yields at about 12%, private investors and banks became reluctant to hold treasury bills. The NBS was thus compelled to finance an increasing proportion of the fiscal deficit. From December 1992 to June 1993, before the price and yield controls, the government raised the equivalent of 1% of GDP from the banking system through the sale of treasury bills; over the period December to August, however, the government became a net repayer to the banking system, to the tune of about 0.1% of GDP. The government lifted the ceiling in November 1993.

Net domestic assets in the banking system increased by some Sk 59 billion in nominal terms in 1993, but declined by 4.2% in real terms. The composition of the assets changed, however, with net credit to the government and the National Property Fund rising by Sk 34.6 billion, for a real increase of 25%, and net credit to nongovernment increasing by Sk 24.4 billion, for a real decline of 11.8%. In this manner, the entire Sk 25 billion budget deficit was financed by credit from the banking system. A smaller budget deficit would have freed resources for the nongovernment sector, while maintaining the same underlying monetary expansion consistent with macroeconomic stability.

Prices, Wages, and the Exchange Rate

Despite rapid liberalization of prices, inflation has been kept in check through tight monetary policy and, under the Czechoslovak Federation, small budget deficits (Figure 1.8). Price liberalization began in 1990 with the elimination of retail food subsidies and increases in the prices of gasoline and diesel fuel. More extensive liberalization began in 1991, when the coverage of price regulation was scaled back from more than 85% of turnover to 15% in January and to about 6% by the end of the year. In 1992, rents and prices were liberalized on a variety of municipal services and on gasoline, coal, water for industrial uses, and metals. The introduction of the VAT in January 1993 led to a one-time 8.9% upsurge in prices, which then fell back to a 1% to 2% a month increase, for a cumulative inflation rate of 25% for the year. Following each phase of price liberalization in Slovakia, inflation has subsided quickly, as prudent demand management policies and wage restraint have avoided a wage-price spiral.

---

9   Although the reduction in currency in circulation was attributed to the decision by currency-holders to deposit their currency in banks, evidence indicates that the amounts deposited was not sizable. Bank deposits between the end of December 1992 and the end of January 1992 increased by Sk 2.4 billion. However, the currency deposited in banks is not counted as currency extinguished nor as part of the NBS's extraordinary profit.

Wages have responded with a lag to price increases, reflecting the social consensus among employers, employees, and government—ratified through tripartite agreements—on targeted levels of real wage reductions. After the massive price liberalization of 1991, real wages fell almost 30% (labor productivity fell 8% that year). There was some recovery in 1992 as real wages rose 9%, but part of the gain was reversed in 1993, when nominal wages increased by 18.3% but real wages declined by 3.8%.

The former Czechoslovak koruna was devalued twice during 1990, cutting its value in half. At the end of 1990, the commercial and tourist exchange rates were unified and fixed to a basket of five convertible currencies at a rate of Kcs 28=US$1.[10] Full "internal" or current account convertibility for business purposes has been in effect since January 1991. Though all export receipts must be surrendered to commercial banks and only a few enterprises are permitted to have foreign exchange accounts, the NBS meets all foreign exchange needs through the commercial banking system. All enterprises are free to engage in foreign trade and to remit profits and dividends. Individuals were granted a foreign exchange allowance for foreign travel of Kcs 7,500 in January 1992.

Following dissolution of the federation, NBS reserves fell to very low levels. Capital flight was heavy in late 1992 and early 1993, as Slovak citizens put their savings in foreign currency in anticipation of a devaluation. In response, the government introduced a number of

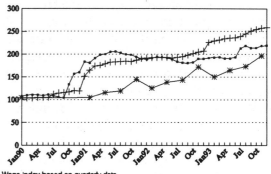

Figure 1.8: Indices of Exchange Rates and Wages (average 1989 - 100)

Note: Wage index based on quarterly data.

Source: National Bank of Slovakia and Slovak Statistical Office.

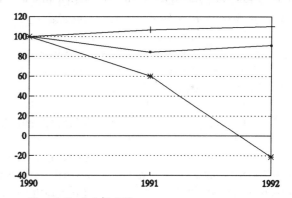

Figure 1.9: Indices of Industrial Unit Cost and Profit (1990 - 100)

Source: Slovak Statistical Office.

---

10   The basket consisted of the currencies of Austria, Germany, Great Britain, Switzerland, and the United States. The Slovak government is considering moving to a two-currency basket. The Czech government has shifted to a basket based 65% on the German mark and 35% on the U.S. dollar.

exchange controls[11] and restricted commercial banks'access to foreign exchange held by the NBS.[12] The NBS's reserve position improved slightly, but the situation was not tenable, and on July 12, 1993, the government devalued the Slovak koruna by 10%.

Devaluation has had a major impact on unit costs in the enterprise sector. Real unit labor costs in industry fell by 21% in 1991 as a result of the sharp decline in real wages. Profitability did not rise, however, because labor costs account for only 17.5% of unit costs, and input costs such as raw materials and energy had risen by 10% following dissolution of the CMEA. In 1992, as industrial productivity continued to fall (by about 4%) and real wages rose modestly, unit labor costs rose 16%, with adverse consequences for profitability (Figure 1.9). The 10% devaluation in mid-1993 helped restore competitiveness to earlier levels. The real effective exchange rate of the koruna (based on relative consumer prices of Slovakia's trading partners) has appreciated slightly since its all-time low at the end of 1990. As of end of 1993, the Slovak koruna had appreciated 3% over its mid-1992 level (as evidenced by calculations of the real exchange rate using a CPI-based price which does not diminish competitiveness).

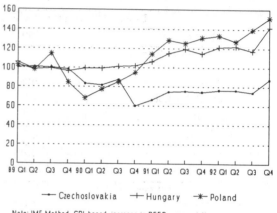

Figure 1.10
Real Effective Exchange Rate Index, 1989-92
(1989 = 100)

Note: IMF Method, CPI-based, increase in REER = appreciation
Source: World Bank data.

Slovakia's real exchange rate is quite competitive compared to that of many of its neighbors (Figure 1.10). The average gross dollar industrial wage in the Slovak Republic is about 40% below Hungary's and 25% below Poland's. Now that the country has devalued, market access is the key to improving its external position. Exports would be an important engine for recovery, particularly at a time when domestic demand is stagnant and trade volumes have collapsed. However, if quota restrictions in export markets impose binding constraints, the gains from devaluation will be minimal.

Restructuring for Recovery

With its skilled and competitively price labor force, strong manufacturing tradition, and proximity to European markets Slovakia's medium-term prospects are favorable. But there are about a dozen countries in Eastern Europe and the former Soviet Union with similar characteristics. What makes Slovakia different is, first of all, its tradition of macroeconomic prudence. Inflation has remained low,

---

11   For imports in excess of Sk 1 million (US$35,000), down payments to suppliers are limited to 15%. For consumer goods, a three-month credit is required as well as a two-week advance deposit of the local currency equivalent. For capital goods, suppliers' credits (of one- to five-year maturity depending on import value) are required. These restrictions are similar to those introduced by Czechoslovakia in 1990 and gradually removed in 1991.

12   Banks' access to NBS's foreign exchange depends on their reaching a certain minimum foreign currency exposure as a percentage of their capital. This limit was raised from 15% to 35% in early February 1993.

particularly by regional standards, and there has been a massive adjustment to lost fiscal transfers from the former federation. Slovakia is far more advanced in privatizing state enterprises than are its neighbors (with the exception of the Czech Republic), with almost half its state-owned enterprises and banks now in private hands. Unemployment is also lower than in most neighboring countries (Table 1.6). Moreover, Slovakia is closer to many wealthy markets—only 60 kilometers separate Bratislava and Vienna, for example—than are most transition economies. The country's strategic position in the European gas pipeline network is also important as a source of substantial transit fees. And Slovakia's foreign debt is relatively small, implying that prudent financing of the transition is a viable alternative.

Table 1.6: Comparative Experience of Transition Economies, 1990-93				
Indicator	1990	1991	1992	1993
GDP Growth Rate				
Albania	-10.0	-27.7	-9.7	11.0
Bulgaria	-9.1	-11.7	-7.7	-4.0
Czech Republic	-1.2	-14.2	-7.1	0.0
Hungary	-4.3	-10.2	-4.4	-1.5
Poland	-11.9	-7.6	1.5	4.0
Romania	-7.3	-13.4	-15.1	1.0
Slovakia	-2.5	-14.5	-7.0	-4.1
Slovenia	-2.6	-9.3	-6.5	-0.5
Unemployment rate				
Albania	8.6	10.6	25.8	40.2
Bulgaria	1.4	12.0	15.0	16.5
Czech Republic	0.8	4.1	2.6	3.5
Hungary	1.6	7.5	12.2	12.2
Poland	6.3	11.8	13.5	15.7
Slovakia	1.6	11.8	10.4	14.4
Slovenia	4.7	8.2	11.6	14.5
Inflation Rate				
Albania	0.0	35.5	225.9	85.1
Bulgaria	23.8	338.5	77.2	45.2
Czech Republic	9.6	56.6	11.1	20.8
Hungary	28.9	35.0	23.0	22.5
Poland	585.8	70.3	43.0	35.5
Slovakia	10.4	61.2	10.0	23.0
Slovenia	551.1	117.7	198.7	33.0

Source: World Bank data.

But all these advantages are not enough. Like all successful small open economies, Slovakia will have to find its niche in the world market. The strategy described in greater detail in the chapters that follow relies on enabling the growing private sector to find the opportunities that will generate sustainable growth in the future. But there are a number of risks. Slovakia is a new country with limited institutional capacity to implement a complicated reform progra in sectors (such as steel, chemicals, aluminum, and armaments) in which the in other countries and high levels of protection. Thus far, private sector in foreign, has been limited. There is also a risk that unless economic reco difficult to maintain the social consensus for reform.

Which of these influences will have the greatest impact depends on the reform path Slovakia chooses: a reform program based on accelerated restructuring, which will have fiscal consequences in the near term but should enable a stronger and more rapid recovery (the reform case), or a program based on slower progress, in which restructuring is piecemeal, subsidies remain high, large fiscal deficits persist, and external financing is limited (the downside case). Each scenario has implications for real GDP, inflation, the current account balance, and the budget deficit (Figure 1.11).

The reform scenario assumes continuing success in macroeconomic stabilization, good standing with the IMF, and successful implementation of the structural reforms outlined in chapters 2-5 of this report. The costs of restructuring are assumed to remain severe in the near term and are likely to lead to higher budgetary expenditures in some categories. Although there are projected gains in efficiency from better targeting of social spending, the expected rise in unemployment would swell the costs of severance payments, social assistance, and unemployment benefits. As restructuring proceeds, certain liabilities of state-owned enterprises will be assumed by the government, and expenditures associated with orderly closure are expected. As insolvent enterprises are liquidated, their liabilities to the banking system will have to be written off and may be replaced with assets such as bonds to improve the banks' capital adequacy. The costs of recapitalizing banks affected by bad loans are assumed to be phased out over time. Overall, despite improvements in tax administration, these steps will result in a fiscal deficit of 4% of GDP in 1994-95.

In the downside scenario, budget deficits are higher because restructuring efforts are postponed. The deficits grow even larger over time, as does the gap with the reform case, because of the accumulation of structural problems. Subsidies to enterprises are maintained or even increased as enterprises continue to muddle through and become more inefficient. Unemployment benefits are less burdensome than in the reform case, however, because labor shedding occurs more slowly. The public sector's share of GDP remains higher (over 50%), in contrast with the reform case.

Under the reform scenario, the efficiency gains from the restructuring efforts should lead to an increase in output by 1995. Unemployment would decline, expenditures on unemployment and social assistance would fall, and retraining programs should result in greater labor flexibility. As liquidation and reorganization are completed, government subsidies to enterprises, for both current and investment spending, are projected to decline, and budget expenditures would increasingly be concentrated in infrastructure investment and better-targeted social benefits. Although tax rates are projected to decline, the recovery and growth of output would lead to a larger tax base that will generate higher revenues. Thus, the fiscal deficit is projected to decline significantly by the end of the decade. In addition, continued prudent monetary policy would contain inflation in the medium term.

As Slovak firms exploit their comparative advantage and as stronger demand conditions develop—and trade restrictions on Slovak goods remain unchanged or are relaxed—real exports are projected to grow by about 4%. Investment is projected to increase in the late 1990s, most of it originating with private firms. Also, improvements in investment productivity in the medium term, mainly in the private sector, will allow for higher GDP growth. Financial sector reforms will increase the mobilization of domestic savings and help direct them to the most productive investments. As government borrowing from the banking system falls, the share of credit to the private sector will increase. Rising real wages, falling unemployment, and continuing improvements in the productivity of investment would accommodate higher growth of private consumption.

23

Figure 1.11: Reform and Downside Scenarios to the Year 2000

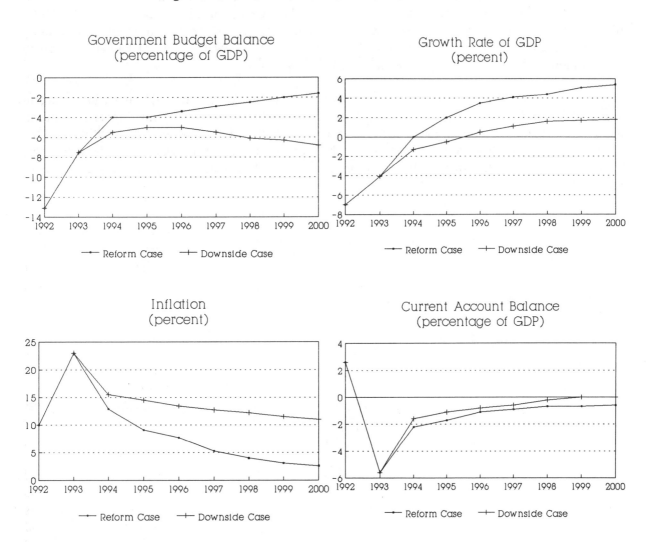

Source: World Bank staff projections.

By the end of the decade, average real growth of GDP would reach 5.7% a year. Industry would re-emerge as a leading source of growth in the late 1990s, the service sector would grow in relative terms, and agricultural productivity would increase with privatization and reorganization of the agricultural cooperatives. Foreign investors would be attracted to industrial subsectors with high export growth potential as competitive wages and exchange rates are maintained. Imports are projected to increase, to support restructuring and the investment needs of the rapidly growing private sector. The current account is expected to remain in deficit, but the external accounts are projected to improve in the long term.

Substantial inflows of gross medium- and long-term capital are needed under the reform scenario to finance more imports, to meet higher repayment obligations, and to permit a buildup of foreign reserves to cover two to three months of imports. Total external debt is expected to rise moderately, with accelerating GDP and export growth keeping the country in a comfortable position to repay its debt. The debt service ratio is projected to peak at 10% in the mid-1990s and to fall gradually thereafter. Improvements in the policy environment are expected to attract higher levels of foreign investment. Gross disbursements of official creditors (including the World Bank, the IMF, and the G-24) are assumed to be higher during the restructuring period, with private commercial creditors increasing their exposure thereafter. In the downside case, however, lower levels of external financing lead to monetization of the deficit, and inflation never falls below 10%.

By the turn of the century, per capita incomes would be some 25% higher in the reform case than in the downside case with delayed restructuring. The productivity gains, higher investment, and greater capacity to import goods and technology under more favorable external conditions in the reform scenario contribute to an upward shift in the economy's long-run growth path. The gains from launching a major restructuring effort now appear to be substantial, arguing strongly for a more aggressive reform effort.

CHAPTER 2: THE FINANCIAL SECTOR

Successful transformation of the economy requires an efficiently functioning financial system that handles resource mobilization efficiently, allocates financial resources to viable economic activities, provides a broad range of services to depositors and businesses, and imposes financial discipline on loss-making enterprises. The ability of the financial system to finance viable new private sector initiatives will be critical to Slovakia's economic growth as enterprises restructure, nonviable operations are liquidated, and the state enterprise sector contracts. Despite some decisive steps since 1990 that have begun to produce positive results, the banking system is still beset by structural problems that prevent it from becoming a dynamic force in a market economy. The weakness of key institutions and the lack of an enabling financial infrastructure remain important obstacles to an effective financial system.

Because the financial system is dominated by banks, the analysis focuses on changes in the way that banks function after three years of reform, looking particularly at the characteristics of the banking system and the impact of financial reform on intermediation. The major components of the initial phase of financial reform are in place: a legal and regulatory framework for banks, including accounting and bankruptcy laws; market-established interest rates; and liberal entry procedures, to provide the basis for a competitive environment. Two of the three main banks have been partly privatized, and attempts have been made to resolve the pervasive problem of bad loans. Many institutional and structural problems remain, however, and an agenda for further reform would include strengthening existing institutions; restructuring and privatizing the last of the large state-owned banks, the Slovak Savings Bank (SSB); and creating an environment that encourages diversification of products, services, and types of financial institutions.

The Structure of the Financial System

Banks are by far the largest component of the financial system. The only other financial activity to speak of is the insurance industry, with assets that are only 7% those of the banking system.

Banking System

Prior to 1990, Statni Banka Československa (SBCS) was both the central bank and the only commercial bank in Czechoslovakia. Because resources were allocated to enterprises on the basis of central plans, banks performed primarily budgetary and accounting functions. Two savings banks (one in each republic) collected household savings and placed deposits with SBCS, net of lending to consumers —mainly for subsidized housing. Československa Obchodni Banka (CSOB), which operated in both republics, handled foreign exchange transactions for the government and enterprises.

In 1990, this monobank system was converted into a two-tier banking system. The SBCS became exclusively a central bank and banking system regulator. All its commercial banking functions, including loans to enterprises and cooperatives, were transferred to three newly created banks: Komerčni Banka (KB) in the Czech Republic, Všeobečna Úverová Banka (VUB) in the Slovak Republic, and Investični Banka (IB) operating in both republics. The savings banks and CSOB were given universal banking licenses, and entry was liberalized. New banks and branches of foreign banks soon sprang up. Rules were established to guide the activities of banks and other financial institutions and the supervision and enforcement functions of SBCS. As important, changes in the environment sector began to make enterprises more responsive to market signals. To start with, enterprises were given greater autonomy in decision-making. A significant number of enterprises and banks were partly privatized through the voucher scheme. New accounting laws were introduced for both banks and enterprises, and a bankruptcy law became effective in June 1993. In this new environment, banks are expected to make independent, prudent lending decisions.

New entry and privatization. From two banks in 1990 the banking system grew to seventeen banks in Slovakia by December 1993, plus nine branches and six offices of foreign banks (Table 2.1). Following the first wave of privatizations, the ownership structure of the banking system changed substantially. More than half of the equity of VUB and Investična a Rozvojova Banka (IRB, which assumed Slovakia's shares of IB's assets in 1992) was transferred to the private sector through vouchers (including the 3% of shares reserved for restitution of former owners). The National Property Fund holds the rest. Since it also holds the shares set aside for restitution, it has de facto majority ownership of both VUB and IRB. A capital increase by IRB in 1993 diluted the government's stake in the bank to 34%. The Slovak Savings Bank (SSB), the large state-owned savings bank, may be included in the second wave of privatization, although the government would maintain control and majority ownership under the proposed structure of share ownership.[1] Also still wholly owned by the state are Konsolidačna Banka Bratislava (KBB),[2] which holds some nonperforming loans transferred from VUB, and Slovenska Zaručna Banka (SZB), a small bank that issues guarantees to small and medium-scale businesses. The remaining banks are owned by the domestic private sector and foreign institutions (Table 2.2).

Table 2.1: Growth of the Banking System, 1990-93 (number of banks)				
Ownership	1990	1991	1992	1993
State-owned	2	3	2	3
Locally-owned	-	1	3	6
Some foreign ownership	-	1	3	8
Total	2	5	8	17
Branches and offices of foreign banks	-	-	-	15
Source: National Bank of Slovakia.				

---

1   The proposed plan would distribute shares as follows: 48% to the National Property Fund, 20% to institutional investors (enterprises), 15% to voucher privatization, 10% to the National Insurance Company, 4% to employees, and 3% reserved for restitution.

2   KBB was created in January 1993 and absorbed the Slovak accounts held by Konsolidačna Banka (KON).

Table 2.2: Ownership Structure of Banks, December 1993 (percent)			
Bank	Domestic private	State	Foreign
Všeobečna Úverová Banka	49.0	51.0ᵃ	0
Slovak Savings Bank	0	100.0	0
Investicna a Rozvojova Banka	66.0	34.0ᵃ	0
Slovenska Zarucna Banka	0	100.0	0
Credit Lyonnais	10.0	0	90.0
L'udová Banka	7.0	0	93.0
Postova Banka	87.0	0	13.0
Prva Stavebna	35.0	0	65.0
Tatra Banka	55.0	0	45.0
Eight others	100.0	0	0

a   Includes 3% reserved for restitution.

Source: National Bank of Slovakia.

Concentration. Concentration is high in the commercial banking system (Table 2.3). The deposit market is dominated by SSB and VUB, which as of the end of 1993 together shared some 88% of the deposit market, SSB accounting for about 53% of total deposits and 90% of household deposits. VUB's deposits, which come mainly from its borrowers, the state-owned enterprises, accounted for about 35% of total deposits in the banking system. VUB also accounted for 38% of total loans in the banking system and shared the bulk of loans to state-owned enterprises with IRB and KON. Four banks—VUB, IRB, KON, and SSB—accounted for 75% of the loan portfolio in the banking system. More than 50% of VUB's liabilities were accounted for by deposits of other banks, primarily SSB, which in 1992 redeposited more than 60% of its deposits with other banks.

Table 2.3: Structure of the Banking System, December 1991, 1992 and 1993 (percent)									
	Share of assets			Share of loans			Share of deposits		
Bank	1991	1992	1993	1991	1992	1993	1991	1992	1993
VUB	46.0	39.1	32.1	48.2	40.9	37.8	28.5	25.9	35.0
SSB	39.4	40.5	30.0	14.7	20.1	19.3	58.9	60.3	52.8
IRB	14.1	12.8	9.0	16.3	14.3	19.3	7.6	7.0	6.6
Others	0.5	7.6	28.9	20.8	24.7	30.6	5.0	6.8	5.6
Total	100.0	100.0	100.0	100.0	100.0	100.0	100.0	100.0	100.0

Source: National Bank of Slovakia.

Despite these high levels of concentration, changes in banking system stocks show that some transformation has occurred (Table 2.4). VUB's loan portfolio shrank in 1992 and 1993, as a significant portion of new lending issued from the new banks and SSB, which has assumed the full spectrum of commercial banking activities. Thanks largely to SSB's increased lending, mainly in the small-privatization process, the share of loans to private entrepreneurs increased from 7.7% in 1991 to 18.1% in 1992 and 36.4% in 1993, while that of state enterprises and cooperatives dropped significantly. A similar shift has occurred in the structure of deposits. Households' share of deposits has changed little, perhaps because of a shift to private sector deposits as entrepreneurs use their own savings to finance their ventures. Borrow-back ratios show that the household sector is a significant net lender, while enterprises and cooperatives are net borrowers. At 6.0 in 1992 and 4.3 in 1993, borrow-back ratios for enterprises and cooperatives are relatively high—the ratio was 1.7 in Hungary in 1990. For enterprises and cooperatives, the increase in the ratio is correlated with the deterioration in their liquidity and profitability (see chapter 3).

Table 2.4: Loan and Deposit Structure, December 1991, 1992 and 1993								
	Share of loans			Share of deposits			Borrow-back ratio		
Sector	1991[a]	1992	1993	1991[a]	1992	1993	1991[a]	1992	1993
Enterprises/ cooperatives	82.5	67.5	46.9	21.1	14.0	13.7	4.70	6.04	4.26
Entrepreneurs	7.7	18.1	36.4	6.9	9.9	14.1	1.34	2.29	3.22
Households	9.2	11.3	11.6	54.3	54.3	55.6	0.20	0.26	0.26
Others[b]	0.6	3.1	5.1	17.7	21.8	16.6	0.04	0.18	0.38

[a] A major reclassification of sectors in 1993 dropped cooperatives from the enterprise sector.
[b] There is a large increase in the unclassified category from 1991 to 1992.

Source: National Bank of Slovakia and World Bank staff estimates.

The banking system in Slovakia has relied heavily on deposits as a source of funds. Its loan to deposit ratio in 1993, was 1.25, compared with 1.70 for Hungary in 1990. Deposits accounted for 46.7% of total liabilities and equity in Slovakia at the end of 1993, loans for 58.4% of total assets, and own-funds for 10.6% of total assets. Refinancing from the central bank (excluding the inherited redistribution credits) accounted for only 1.5% of banking system assets in Slovakia at the end of 1993, (Table 2.5 shows the consolidated balance sheet of the banking system as of December 31 for 1992 and 1993).

Table 2.5: Banking System Balance Sheet, December 31, 1992 and 1993 (Sk billion)					
Assets	1992	1993	Liabilities	1992	1993
Loans	235.9	260.8	Deposits	188.6	208.9
Short term	64.4	66.8	Demand	69.4	69.3
Medium term	44.5	41.4	Term	26.2	33.8
Long term	92.7	95.8	Savings	93.0	105.8
Category 23[a]	26.6	26.0	Redistribution credits	33.6	33.6
Category 24[a]	7.7	30.8	Refinancing	11.3	6.4
Other	75.9	n.a.	Other	58.9	n.a.
Required reserves	9.7	10.6	Own funds	29.1	47.6
Total	321.5	n.a.	Total	321.5	n.a.

[a] Category 23: loans are overdue less than three months; category 24 loans are overdue more than three months

Source: World Bank staff estimates.

Insurance Sector

The insurance sector, the other major component of the financial system, has assets worth only about 7% of those of the banking system. Total insurance industry assets as of the end of 1992 were about 7.5% of GDP (U.S. insurance company assets were 26% of GDP in 1990). Slovenska Statni Poistovna (SSP) was the only insurance company until 1989. Since then five new institutions have entered the field, but SSP still commands more than 90% of the market. The insurance industry in Slovakia is not yet a major player in money and capital markets. Total investments, loans, and deposits of the insurance industry accounted for only 7.5% of domestic credit in Slovakia in 1989 (the comparable figure for U.S. Life insurance companies was 16%). Furthermore, the industry's investment activities are mainly in the form of deposits with banks.

Financial Intermediation

The National Bank of Slovakia (NBS) uses a variety of channels for its financial intermediation operations: redistribution credits, refinancing auctions, rediscounts, lombard credits, and emergency credits (as of July 1993). NBS credits account for about 10% of the liabilities of the banking system. Seventy-six percent of its credits are the redistribution credits incurred in the breakup of the monobank SBCS. These credits, which carry interest rates of 8% to 10%, in effect "financed" the assets that were transferred from the books of the monobank to the commercial banks. After a brief suspension between May and November 1993, the NBS has restored credit auctions as the major instrument for injecting liquidity into the banking system, but with more stringent rules on participation. To avoid distress bidding, banks not in good standing are not permitted to participate in the auctions. NBS has also begun currency swapping and open market operations as a means of providing short-term liquidity to the banking system. Rediscount and lombard credit facilities, previously provided at below-market rates, will now be at prices linked to the auction rate.

Banks are required to maintain minimum reserves at the NBS. In 1991, reserve requirements were 8% on deposits and earned 4% interest. As part of the tightening of monetary policy in October 1992, reserve requirements were increased to 9% for demand deposits and 3% for term deposits (over three months), with no interest paid. These reserve requirements are a tax on deposits and result in higher intermediation costs, though they are not excessively high given the country's tight fiscal situation. Once the budgetary situation improves, the government should consider paying interest on reserves.

Flow of Funds

The flow of financial funds is an indicator of the volume of financial savings generated by households, government, enterprises, and the external sector and is a measure of the strength of financial intermediation. In general, a sector registers positive net savings when its total volume of financial savings is greater than its volume of bank loans; when the reverse is true, the sector has negative net savings.[3]

An examination of the flow of funds in Slovakia in the first half of 1993 shows a low level of savings by the household sector and large absorption of financial resources by the government (Figure 2.1).[4] Although the household sector accounts for most of the savings, savings are small by international standards and relative to the total

Figure 2.1

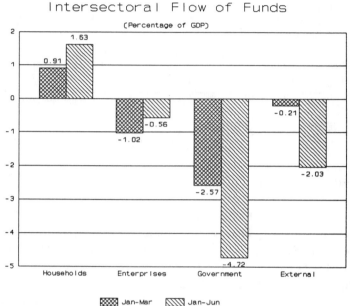

Source: National Bank of Slovakia and World Bank staff estimates.

demand for funds. One reason could be the uncertainty stirred up by the breakup of the federation and the dissolution of the monetary union, which may have encouraged a shift out of domestic currency; the fall in NBS's foreign exchange reserves provides some evidence for this argument. The negative real interest rates on savings deposits might also have discouraged saving. The large negative savings of the government sector is explained by the fiscal deficit and the heavy reliance on domestic finance.

The enterprise sector shows moderate negative net savings, contrary to the pattern in other countries in the early stages of transition, when enterprises are commonly strong net borrowers from the banking system. A breakdown of the net financial savings components of enterprises indicates that they increased their bank deposits by an amount similar to their gross borrowing, presumably to build up

---

3   To limit the distortionary effect of the sharp reduction in currency in circulation in early January 1993, estimates of the flow of financial funds start with the end of January 1993.

4   The estimates in Figure 2.1 were calculated using the monetary survey and are subject to a certain degree of error because available data are still subject to frequent revisions. Although the sum of financial flows for the four sectors should add up to zero, it does not because of unclassified assets such as the "other items."

liquidity. Again, uncertainty may have contributed to a reluctance to invest or banks may have rationed credit by offering it only to borrowers with liquid collateral such as bank deposits, which could explain the simultaneous increase in enterprise borrowing and deposits. Meanwhile, external savings fell sharply, reflecting NBS's loss of foreign exchange reserves and the difficulty of attracting foreign finance under conditions of uncertainty.

Credit Allocation

Banks are under pressure to accelerate their transformation from passive dispensers of credit to professional bankers accountable for their credit decisions. Banks are now required to adhere to established performance criteria through capital adequacy regulations, and new accounting rules require them to provision for nonperforming loans. However, since classification of loans does not reflect a standardized assessment of asset quality, provisions do not necessarily reflect the true risks associated with loan recovery. Banks are audited under international accounting standards, and international auditing firms review their financial statements and internal controls. The prospect of future reorganizations and liquidations of several enterprises under the new bankruptcy law means that banks need to review their current exposure and critically examine additional lending. Finally, the emergence of new banks is bound to increase competitive activity.

In 1992, there were signs of a fundamental shift in bank behavior—a move to cut back lending to state enterprises and to increase lending to the private sector. The poor financial condition of state enterprises and their uncertain prospects led to a re-evaluation of lending strategies by banks, especially by VUB. Its loan portfolio in 1992 showed a decrease in nominal terms in its exposure to state enterprises, a reversal of its lending practices in 1991, when loans to state enterprises rose 32% (many of them for activities that proved unviable; see chapter 3). Provisioning rules combined with stricter audits forced banks to show the impact of bad lending decisions in their financial statements. As the accounting rules for enterprises improve the accuracy of financial reporting, the state of banks' loan portfolios will become more transparent. All these changes contribute to more prudent lending decisions.

At the end of 1990, loans to state enterprises in Slovakia totaled Kcs 120 billion. By the end of 1992 (before the first wave of privatizations), total exposure of the banking sector to state enterprises in Slovakia remained at the same level in nominal terms (Kcs 129 billion), despite a 15% expansion of overall bank lending. Nearly all the increase in nongovernment lending was to the private sector. The share of private entrepreneurs in commercial bank loans rose from 7.7% at the end of 1991 to 18.1% at the end of 1992 and 36.4% in 1993 (Figure 2.2). Small privatization loans by SSB represented more than half the loans to the private sector as of the end of

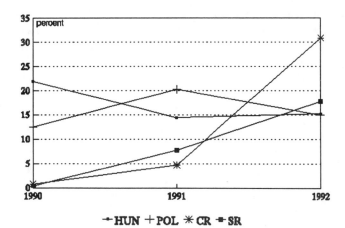

Figure 2.2: Comparison of the Share of the Private Sector in Total Bank Credit, 1990-1992

-•-HUN +POL ✳CR -■-SR

Source: World Bank staff estimates.

1993. However, the rapid expansion in SSB's lending activity has raised concerns over the deterioration of its asset portfolio. VUB had about 18% of its portfolio in the private sector in 1992, double the share of the year before.

Interest Rates

Interest rates were not used to allocate credit prior to 1990. Until the third quarter of 1990, interest rates were relatively stable, averaging 6% a year for long-term loans to state enterprises and 1% to 3% for housing. Deposit rates ranged from 0.5% for enterprises to 5% for time deposits of households. Average interest rates for loans increased to 15% a year during the first quarter of 1991, as inflation accompanied the country's early economic transformation measures. At the beginning of 1991, the maximum lending rate was set at 24%, irrespective of term (computed on the basis of the discount rate plus a maximum allowable margin). The ceiling was dropped to 17% in September 1991 and eliminated in mid-1992.

Average lending rates have been below the ceiling and positive in real terms except in the first half of 1991. The fixed rates of long-term loans negotiated during the period of low rates may account for the downward slope of the term structure for interest rates. It is difficult to determine what real interest rates have been because of the high variability in the annual inflation rate. With an inflation rate of 10% in 1992, average real lending rates for the year range from 3.0% to 6.9%, not high for the risk situation in Slovakia. For 1993, real interest rates are negative if the annual inflation rate is used but positive (except during January-March, when the introduction of the VAT resulted in a one-off increase in inflation) if an estimate of the expected inflation rate is used, based on the annualized monthly inflation rate of the previous, current, and following month.

Table 2.6: Interest Spreads for Short-Term Lending and Deposit Rates, by Sector, 1992-93 (percent)				
Item	Q4 1992	Q1 1993	Q2 1993	Q3 1993
Short-term average lending rate	15.40	17.53	18.28	17.86
Short-term average deposit rate	8.05	10.35	10.61	11.39
Short-term average spread	7.09	7.18	7.67	6.47
Private Sector				
Short-term lending rate	15.31	16.59	17.39	17.46
Short-term deposit rate	7.47	8.63	10.47	10.88
Interest spread	7.84	7.96	6.93	6.58
Enterprises				
Short-term lending rate	15.11	17.91	18.75	18.08
Short-term deposit rate	7.55	10.21	11.93	13.32
Interest spread	7.56	7.70	6.82	4.76
Households				
Short-term lending rate	13.87	10.79	11.82	9.87
Short-term deposit rate	8.24	10.40	10.38	11.07
Interest spread	5.63	0.39	1.44	-1.20
Memorandum items:				
Cost of reserves	1.25	1.12	1.56	1.42
Reserve requirement	-	8.50	8.50	8.50
Auction rate	-	13.20	18.40	16.70
Source: National Bank of Slovakia and World Bank staff estimates.				

The structure of interest rates in Slovakia has sometimes discouraged efficient financial intermediation. NBS's decision to suspend credit auctions and offer funds to banks through the low-cost rediscount facility gave banks little incentive to attract deposits or to use interbank market resources. At the end of June 1993, a bank could borrow from the NBS at 9.5%, while it would have had to pay 12% on deposits or 16% to borrow on the interbank market. Banks were further encouraged to borrow from the NBS because those funds are not subject to reserve requirements. In addition, interest rates on the interbank market were sometimes higher than banks' lending rates, yet commercial banks continued to borrow on the interbank market because most of them have no branch network. This structure of interest rates can be explained by the concentration in both markets. The Slovak Savings Bank is the only supplier in the interbank market, and a few large banks such as the VUB and IRB dominate the lending market. Although large banks with an extended branch network or access to the NBS's low-cost funds might be able to survive in this environment, new banks with a small deposit base and a small number of branches could not compete.

The structure of the banking system—its high concentration in the state enterprise lending market—and the household deposit market—the impact of bad loans, and the non-interest-bearing reserve requirements all tend to put upward pressure on interest spreads. Interest spreads on short-term lending and deposit rates are on the high side compared with rates in countries with efficient banking systems, although the spreads are declining overall and are converging across state and private enterprise sectors (Table 2.6). The spreads were between 6% and 8% during 1993.

Regulation and Financial Infrastructure

Banking Sector

The Central Banking Act and the banking law of December 1991 constitute the legal basis for the new banking system (Box 2.1). The banking law defines the activities of banks and their regulation and affirms the requirement for compliance with the antimonopoly law and the accounting law. All mergers and breakups must be approved by the banking authorities. There are also provisions governing insider trading and limitations on lending to major stockholders and employees. These laws were made applicable in Slovakia after the breakup of the federation, although they are under review. Regulations covering capital adequacy, liquidity, large exposures, connected lending, and foreign exchange operations were issued and made effective in mid-1992 and are currently in force in Slovakia.

Under the federation, the state was the guarantor of deposits of the state-owned banks. Currently, there is no national deposit insurance, although a law is expected to be prepared jointly by the NBS and the Ministry of Finance. Household deposits, most of them held by the state-owned Slovak Savings Bank, will continue to benefit from implicit government protection, however.

The payments and clearing system which is owned jointly by NBS (majority owner) and the banks seems to work efficiently. Payment orders are executed within three working days. There is ample room for expansion of the system, which currently handles 150,000 transactions a day. A clearing fee of Sk 1.50 is charged per transaction. Connecting bank automated systems and the clearing system could result in further efficiency gains.

Since 1993, banks have been required to follow international accounting standards, which most had already been doing for two years ago. NBS has to approve each bank's external auditor; most of the major banks use well-known international firms. Enterprises are also required to follow similar standards. The quality of financial information on enterprises is still poor, however, and it will take time to establish adequate systems of accounting, auditing, and financial disclosure. There is also a dearth of qualified local accountants and auditors.

Box 2.1: Central Banking and Commercial Banking Acts

The Central Banking Act covers the enforcement of banking regulations. The National Bank of Slovakia can impose fines of up to Sk 5 million, require corrective measures to resolve an unsatisfactory situation, order the termination of certain activities, withdraw a bank's license, or introduce enforced administration, which may involve restrictions on credit and deposit-taking activities.

The Banking Act stipulates a gearing ratio for assessing the capital adequacy of the bank. NBS has a risk-weighted formula that meets international standards. Banks were required to have a minimum capital adequacy ratio of 6.25 percent by the end of December 1993 and 8 percent by the end of 1996. Quarterly reports on capital adequacy must be submitted to NBS.

Rules on liquidity focus on prudent liquidity management practices such as diversification of funding sources, designation of responsibilities for liquidity management, and money market and bond trading activities. Commercial banks must maintain liquidity in Slovak and foreign currencies. Banks are required to establish measures for effective liquidity management, including an information system that provides a breakdown of the assets, liabilities and off-balance sheet commitments by maturity and by liquidity grade of assets and the nature and commitment grade of off-balance sheet items. Banks are required to submit quarterly liquidity (assets and liabilities by maturities) reports to the central bank.

Commercial banks are obliged to submit monthly reports to NBS on the credit exposure of debtors representing 10% or more of the bank's capital. Credit exposures to a single borrower cannot exceed 25% of the adjusted capital of a commercial bank, and the sum of credit exposures to the ten largest debtors cannot exceed 230% of the bank's adjusted capital. Banks are required to maintain an information system for monitoring credit exposure and can stipulate limits on certain economic sectors or geographic locations. A bank's own regulations on exposure limits must be approved by the banking supervision board. Banks are required to reduce any inherited exposures that exceed the new limits to 40% by the end of 1993 and 25 % by the end of 1995.

Banks may not enter into transactions with their major shareholders or members of the banks' supervisory boards or statutory bodies if such transactions would limit the banks' activities with other clients. Loans and payments to such insiders must be approved by the board of directors. The maximum exposure for major shareholders or other bank insiders is 20% of the bank's capital. There are restrictions on the amount of unmortgaged credit granted by banks to their employees.

NBS has issued a prudential regulation defining the standards by which assets are to be classified for provisioning purposes. The asset classifications are based primarily on past-due status. Classification A loans are in good financial standing, classification B loans ("nonstandard assets") are overdue by more than thirty days, classification C loans ("doubtful assets") are overdue by more than 90 days, and classification D loans or ("bad assets") are overdue by more than 360 days. NBS has issued recommendations to banks to set aside specific reserves equal to 20% of nonstandard assets, 50% of doubtful assets, and 100 percent of bad assets.

Investments of a participative nature are not allowed to exceed 25% of the bank's capital. Banks can acquire capital interest up to 10% of a company's capital. Banks must seek NBS approval for acquiring ownership interest in another bank. Transfers of more than 15% of a bank's basic capital to a company must be approved by NBS. Market shares on savings deposits and commercial and consumer credits may not exceed 30 %.

Banks can sell foreign exchange to the NBS on an unlimited basis. Banks whose foreign exchange position (foreign exchange liabilities less foreign exchange assets) is more than 25% of the their capital may buy foreign exchange from NBS up to the amounts that would bring their foreign exchange position to 25%. Banks are required to submit their daily foreign exchange positions to NBS.

The central bank's supervision responsibilities (under the Banking Supervision Department) include licensing and compliance. The Banking Supervision Department has a staff of thirteen but needs twice that number. Its six examiners cannot hope to meet the supervision requirements of a growing banking sector. The shortage of people with banking experience makes recruitment difficult. An Institute for Banking Education has been established to provide training in banking skills. It receives guidance on its curriculum from a Council for Banking Education, made up of representatives from NBS, the banks, and academia.

Currently, supervision is limited to off-site examinations, which are important for monitoring trends in the banking sector and for detecting emerging problems. Through a new system of routine regulatory reporting by commercial banks, the department receives daily foreign exchange reports, monthly financial statements, reports on prudential regulations, and special reports on lending to stockholders. These examinations can serve as an early warning system and can be used to direct the very limited capacity for on-site inspection to areas where the need is greatest. On-site supervision is crucial for assessing the quality of loan portfolios and identifying institutional weaknesses. Procedures are being developed for on-site supervision, with external advisory assistance. A recent report by the Banking Supervision Department provides a preliminary set of rules for on-site examinations, which include evaluation of license conditions and business activities since establishment and assessment of capital structure and financial statements.

A sound system of banking regulation is in place; future efforts should focus on strengthening supervision capacity, especially for on-site supervision. Until then, outside assistance will be needed. External auditors are now required to review the reports submitted by banks and to conduct annual audits. Special quarterly studies could be requested, such as analyses of control deficiencies in specific banks or reviews of bank portfolios. For banks with severe problems, the Supervision Department may need to intervene in the bank in some manner; twinning with an experienced foreign banker until the bank is on sound footing again may also help.

Insurance Sector

The Slovak Insurance Law of 1991 provides for regulation of the insurance industry by a supervisory body, currently housed within the Ministry of Finance. Entry has been liberalized, bringing the number of firms from one to five and increasing the urgency for expanding supervision capacity. Investment rules stipulate limits on certain investment areas, but supervision capacity is virtually nonexistent. Efforts are under way to review the rules and regulations covering insurance operations and to make them more coherent. The following areas should be covered by the review:

- Chartering and licensing of companies and agents, including minimum capitalization for insurers and competency requirements for agents.

- Approval of contract forms, to exclude ambiguous language and prevent unfair or deceptive practices.

- Regulation of reserve liabilities to maintain adequacy by prescribing the basis for calculating minimum reserves (mortality table to be used, interest rate assumptions, and valuation method) and, indirectly, to control the premium charged to the consumer.

- Regulation of investments and establishment of standards for assessing the prudence of investments decisions.

- Solvency monitoring through review of periodic financial statements and on-site surveillance.

- Organization of a capable insurance regulatory unit.

Securities Market

The privatization program has given rise to large but unsophisticated securities market. Citizens with little investment experience have suddenly become stockholders, creating an environment ripe for market manipulation and fraud. The poor information infrastructure makes matters even worse. An obvious case can be made for securities regulation, but success depends on being able to implement regulation effectively.

Securities regulation is currently handled by the Ministry of Finance, but should strengthened and possibly moved to an independent body. The initial focus of securities regulation should be on registration and uniform requirements for information disclosure. Both equity and debt instruments should be available, including short-term commercial paper traded in the money market. Credible sanctions should be established and imposed to discourage fraud and market manipulation. Licensing of brokers and dealers should be based on clear and open criteria. Self-regulation should be encouraged through associations or the stock exchange. Fees and the pricing of securities should be left to the market.

Other Regulations

Laws governing commercial activities have several deficiencies that affect financial institutions. The laws on the use of movable goods (inventories, receivables, and securities) as collateral—as well as such supporting institutional arrangements as registration, conflict adjudication, and enforcement—do not adequately protect the rights of lenders, who are therefore reluctant to accept movables as collateral. The rights of mortgage or collateral holders during bankruptcy reorganization also need to be clarified. A related concern is whether the courts and legal, accounting, and auditing professionals will be adequate to handle the initial high volume of bankruptcy cases expected.

Issues in the Financial Sector

Bad Loans in Bank Portfolios

Bad loans, although they reflect a loss of resources that has already occurred and not the current efficiency of the banking system, continue to be a problem to the extent that they distort incentives. Overdue loans increased from 1.9% of outstanding loans in the banking system in 1991 to 21.8% in 1993. It is possible that the major banks, which still have considerable market power, could increase interest spreads to pay for the cost of bad loans, thus effectively imposing a tax on both depositors and good borrowers. Problems of adverse selection and moral hazards also arise. The need to secure higher spreads leads to adverse selection, a problem exacerbated by the lack of risk-evaluation skills and poor information, while expectations of government bailout create a moral hazard situation by encouraging banks to engage in excessively risky lending. Poor auditing and supervision enable banks to continue to finance insolvent enterprises to prevent them from going bankrupt, a situation that would make transparent the true size of the bad loans in bank portfolios. Debtors, for their part, are kept afloat through artificial means, delaying the restructuring of enterprises and complicating the privatization process. While improving bank solvency through retained earnings is desirable, it should occur in a competitive environment where effective supervision insures that retained earnings strengthen the banks' capital base, rather than pay for dividends or other current expenditures.

In 1990, a significant portion of VUB's working capital loans to enterprises was restructured (preferential interest rates and extended repayment) and transferred to KON. VUB and KON now share the same clientele, with VUB holding the investment loans and the remainder of the working capital loans. The inability of enterprises to pay loans thus affects both VUB and KON. In 1991, National Property Fund bonds were issued to VUB to replace certain loans and improve its capital adequacy ratio. These loans were also written off the enterprise's balance sheets. In effect, the financial positions of VUB and the enterprises were restructured, with the National Property Fund absorbing the cost. This initiative was intended as the final bailout preceding privatization of VUB and the enterprises. The value of the loans transferred to KON and loans replaced with bonds was equivalent to about 35% of the inherited portfolio.

There are two alternatives for dealing with the remaining problem of bad debt: a centralized program in which a workout agency consolidates the loans and implements a top-down solution, and a decentralized program in which banks and enterprises negotiate a solution. Ideally, the resolution of the bad debt problem should involve cleaning up the banks' balance sheets, strengthening their financial position, and writing down the debts of enterprises to a level they can service with their operating cash flow. The decentralized approach requires the right environment for effective financial restructuring, including adequate financial resources and skills for banks and an appropriate legal and procedural framework for bankruptcy, conciliation, and reorganization. Whichever the approach chosen, there are likely to be fiscal costs involved in the resolution of the bad debt problem since banks will probably not be able to cover the entire cost out of future earnings.

In the event that bank's capital is seriously impaired after provisioning for bad loans, there may be a need for recapitalization to reduce the risk of perverse behavior and to prepare the banks for further privatization. There are several ways of increasing banks' capital. One is to accompany capital injections with the sale of equivalent government bonds to the bank and then allowing banks to increase retained earnings by keeping the spreads high; another is to swap loans for bonds. To ensure that the bad debt problem does not recur, reform is needed in other areas as well, especially in privatization and institutional development.

Role of Banks in Enterprise Restructuring

Finding the right solution to the problem of bad loans is important not only for improving bank operations but also for accelerating enterprise restructuring and thus economic growth. Previous efforts to deal with bad loans did not provide proper incentives for restructuring. Fundamental reform in the enterprise sector was impeded by the absence of adequate information, a workable bankruptcy law, and staff skilled in workout procedures. To be successful, any action on bad loans must be linked to parallel reforms in the enterprise sector.

Identifying firms that are value subtracting and should be liquidated and distinguishing them from overindebted but otherwise profitable firms that should undergo financial restructuring is not easy. For one thing, the necessary financial information is lacking. For another, any assessment would have to look into the future to evaluate viability under a changed structure of industries and relative prices. Institutional mechanisms are not available for identifying troubled enterprises and working out a solution or for establishing who will bear the cost. Privatization throws in the added complication of whether the government has an obligation to bail out the stockholders if the problem in an enterprise or bank is essentially an inherited one.

Banks need to be involved in the restructuring process because of their current exposure to the enterprises. In addition, banks have the information about their customers and the capability to monitor enterprise performance that are needed for making decisions on additional lending. But the positive contribution that banks could make to the restructuring process could be undermined by several other factors. If a bank's current level of provisions is inadequate, the possibly negative impact of enterprise restructuring on the bank's own financial position creates perverse incentives. Weakness in bank governance could allow banks to stray from commercial principles, especially since the National Property Fund is a major stockholder in both banks and enterprises. The lack of supervision capacity eliminates one source of checks and balances in the process. Expectations of government bailouts encourage imprudent risk taking.

Banks could have a greater influence on enterprise restructuring if certain reforms were put in place: realistic provisioning policies, more effective supervision, recapitalization, privatization, implementation of the bankruptcy law, and establishment of related institutions for market-based workouts. In the short run, banks would have to protect their claims by requiring collateral coverage for their loans or imposing certain covenants, such as target ratios and prior approval for certain enterprise actions. In addition, banks should establish better information flow from enterprises and develop analytical and workout capabilities. To eliminate conflict of interest, the National Property Fund should divest its holdings in banks.

Privatization of Banks

Privatization of banks should improve their performance and behavior, resulting in increased economic efficiency through better mobilization and allocation of resources. For that to happen, however, privatization needs to be accompanied by improved governance, incentives, and competition. The current privatization plan for SSB needs to be revised to eliminate or reduce government participation and increase competition in the market for deposits. As it stands, it will not result in private sector control of the bank. In the case of VUB, the National Property Fund's stake should be privatized. The major concern with respect to IRB is the treatment of several loans to enterprises that are considered to be strategically important to the government. Options include explicit government guarantees and removal of the loans from IRB's balance sheet. Increased capital requirements for IRB should come from the private sector.

Structure and Competition Policy

The underlying strategy for increasing competition in the financial sector is to open the market to all eligible institutions and to enforce the antimonopoly law. New entrants have already increased the number of banks and insurance companies in Slovakia over the past few years. While breaking up the large banks—VUB and SSB—provides a quick solution to the structural problem of the banking system, VUB's weak portfolio would simply be spread across smaller banks. On the other hand, breaking up SSB might simply replace its monopoly with several smaller banks with the same market power over smaller geographical areas.

Any top-down solution to the problem of financial structure should be approached with caution since there is no guarantee that a competitive structure would result. Competition from other banks has already reduced VUB's share of the lending market; the privatization of many state enterprises would change the dynamics of enterprise lending and provide even more opportunities for other banks to bid for VUB's clientele. SSB's share of the deposit market remains very high, however, and a case can be made for restructuring SSB before privatization. But that would be a complicated process, especially if many operational systems, such as computing, are centralized.

The long-term solution to the structure problem is a competitive environment that encourages diversification of financial products, services, and institutions the establishment of enabling infrastructure. The development of a bond and commercial paper market would provide enterprises with more options for raising funds and offer competition to the banking system. The need for a legal and regulatory framework for these financial markets and for enabling institutions (such as a securities and exchange commission) would have to assessed.

Financial Reform Agenda

Further financial sector reform should focus on strengthening existing institutions, reducing SSB's monopoly, and creating an environment that encourages diversification. In addition to developing restructuring programs for each institution, some specific recommendations are:

- *Upgrade supervision.* A full-time foreign adviser has been hired to assist the Banking Supervision Department. Bringing in additional foreign supervisors for a period of two to three years would further strengthen supervision capacity and allow local supervisors to learn from them. The role of international accounting and auditing firms in providing reports to the Supervision Department should also be studied. A supervision strategy should be developed for each bank that focuses on areas of weakness and risk. Anticompetitive behavior and imprudent risk taking deserve special scrutiny. Outside the banking sector, consideration should be given to the creation of an independent securities and exchange agency and the restructuring of insurance regulation and supervision.

- *Invest in information capital.* Lack of information is a major constraint to the effective allocation of financial resources. The new accounting and auditing law should provide a good starting point for developing financial information. More detailed financial and operating information should be required for companies issuing securities, and the financial statements of public companies should be readily available from a government agency such as an independent securities and exchange office. Government measures to encourage development of information capital are partly linked to the regulatory framework: regulation of banks, insurance, and securities should require the preparation and dissemination to the public of adequate financial information.

- *Design further measures to encourage financial market development.* Three areas could be reviewed. First, the instruments that the NBS uses for monetary and liquidity management should not distort prices or discourage the creation of markets. The resumption of credit auctions in November 1993 was an important step in the right direction. The few remaining facilities that allow banks to borrow from the NBS at below-market rates (such as for agriculture) should be discouraged. NBS would then focus on credit auctions and the money market as the mechanisms for managing liquidity. Second, the legal framework and supporting institutions should be strengthened. Laws relating to movables should be reviewed, and the capacity to handle commercial and bankruptcy cases should be improved rapidly. Third, the regulatory framework and supervision capacity for issuing securities should be developed to encourage diversification of financial instruments and the emergence of nonbank financial institutions involved in the issuance of securities. A comprehensive securities law should be considered.

CHAPTER 3: PRIVATE SECTOR DEVELOPMENT

The enterprise sector in Slovakia faces three challenges: commercialization, private sector development, and restructuring. Commercialization means a shift from an administrative to a market-based economy, requiring decentralization of decision-making, greater attention to marketing and finance, and a retooling of management. Private sector development involves a shift away from predominant state ownership through privatization, promotion of new firms, and the faster growth of private firms than state firms. Restructuring means a shift of resources out of low or negative value-added activities. What distinguished the former Czech and Slovak Republic from most other economies in transition was its relatively advanced technological base, proximity to industrial market economies, and an emphasis on rapid privatization of both small and large enterprises. What distinguishes Slovakia from its former federal partner is, mainly, a greater need for restructuring.

Production has fallen dramatically over the past few years as the enterprise sector has tried to adjust to changing conditions. Output in industry fell by almost one-third from 1989 to 1992. Much of the decline reflects the collapse of old trading arrangements and the fall in external demand for traditional Slovak goods such as armaments and heavy machinery. Compounding the damage has been the buildup of bad loans and interenterprise arrears, with effects that have spread through the financial and enterprise sectors. In addition to the recommended reforms of the financial system (chapter 2), the key recommendation for private sector development is to face these challenges at the level of individual enterprises. More specifically:

- *The endorsement of current programs* is an acknowledgement that substantial reform has already taken place and that much of the painful but necessary restructuring and privatization is already past. If sustained, these reforms should contribute to a turnaround in overall economic performance.

- *The call to clear the remaining obstacles to enterprise development* reflects assessments that growth will stem mainly from the entry of new private firms and the expansion of old ones and that private firms are restrained by a slew of micro-level nuisances. Chief among these nuisances are lagging privatization of land, regulatory red tape, weak enforceability of contracts (including debt collection), and fears of policy instability. Shortcomings in enterprise governance and in some elements of further plans for privatization are also a concern.

- *The warning against massive state-led restructuring* is prompted by the sorry record of such efforts in other countries, which have left many companies in long, confused, and expensive receivership. Serious problems are already brewing in the current National Property Fund-dominated framework. The National Property Fund ought to be treated as a transitional instrument of privatization, with limited restructuring exposure and no long-term control.

Recent Developments in the Enterprise Sector

Two outstanding changes in the enterprise sector are the explosive growth of private firms —and the concomitant decline in public sector employment—the result of both large-scale new entries and the mass privatization program, and the widespread financial distress of enterprises and banks (chapter 2).

Before the "Velvet Revolution," the enterprise sector was dominated by state-owned enterprises. Private entrepreneurs were frozen out of most sectors, prices were controlled, trading and investment ties with market economies were discouraged, and private property had relatively little protection. Today, far fewer sectors are reserved for the state, prices have been liberalized, barriers to foreign trade have been lowered, and there is little fear of direct expropriation. Thanks to deregulation and rapid privatization, the private sector in Slovakia has grown quickly (Table 3.1). The number of registered private firms almost doubled during 1992, and their share of output increased from 15% to 21%. There were also more than 320,000 self-employed entrepreneurs not registered as firms, a 60% jump in one year.

Table 3.1: Growth of the Private Sector, 1991-93 (percent)					
	December 1991		December 1992		December 1993	
	Public	Private[a]	Public	Private	Public[a]	Private[b]
Number of enterprises	2,392	9,436	2,540	18,485	2388	23,972
Share of output	85	15	78	22	73	27
Employment	75	25	70	30	68	32

a Includes enterprises owned by municipalities.
b Excludes cooperatives.

Source: Slovak Statistical Office.

Much of the new entry occurred in services (Table 3.2). By the end of 1992, trade and repair services accounted for 44% of all private firms and 24% of the self-employed. Real estate engaged 16%-17% of both private firms and the self-employed; transport and communications, 4%. Another 4% of the self-employed and 3% of private firms provided food and lodging.

Private sector involvement in manufacturing and construction is increasing as well. At the end of 1992, 2,300 private firms (12%) and 57,000 self-employed people (19%) were engaged in manufacturing, and 1,300 private firms (7%) and 62,900 self-employed (21%) in construction. A significant number of nominally self-employed manufacturers and builders are said to work for someone else but to list themselves as self-employed to avoid social security taxes. Employment in public enterprises dropped by half, from 1.2 million people in 1990 to 620,000 at the end of 1993. These changes have been driven by the privatization program as well as by the startup of new enterprises.

The potential for further private sector development, particularly of small businesses, is excellent in nearly all sectors. The Slovak economy, like most formerly socialist economies, tends to be top-heavy in large firms. It needs more small private businesses that can respond more flexibly to changes in demand, to rush jobs, and to small orders. There is also great potential for expanding private sales to Western Europe. Proximity to developed European markets, low wages, and a relatively skilled work force beg for more subcontracting arrangements, with Slovak firms producing components to Western firms' specifications. Other prime candidates for expansion are tourism in the Tatra mountains and consumer services to neighboring Austrians.

Table 3.2: Ownership and Activities in the Enterprise Sector, December 31, 1993 (number of enterprises)					
Sphere of activity	Private	Cooperative	Joint Venture	Public[a]	Total
Agriculture, forestry, fisheries	189	1,026	26	230	1,471
Mining	153,226	5	10	32	62
Manufacturing	28	226	576	755	82
Utilities	1,845	2	3	49	2,508
Construction	8,693	161	204	298	12,313
Commercial and services	549	152	3,177	291	602
Catering and housing	15	16	71	68	42
Transport and communications	188	1	10	16	325
Finance and insurance	748	6	53	1,364	2,615
Research and development	1,741	185	617	78	632
Other commercial activities	419	119	193		238
Other	-	27	94		138
Total	17,656	1,926	5,034	2,285	26,901

[a] Includes enterprises owned by municipalities.

Source: Slovak Statistical Office.

Privatization

The "large" and "small" privatization programs undertaken by the former Czechoslovak Federation have been the driving force for bringing medium- and large-scale enterprises into the private sector.   By quickly purging most state ownership from the once-monolithic economy, with minimal restructuring, the intention was to lock in reform momentum and speed economic revitalization.

Large Privatization

Various privatization methods were used, with primary emphasis on a novel scheme: auction for special privatization coupons (vouchers), distributed widely and equally among the citizenry. Coupon privatization appealed for its combination of transparency, equity, and perceived boost to household wealth.   More standard methods included direct placements, cash auctions, and competitive tenders.   Liquidation is another method of privatizing assets.

Privatization was to take place in two "waves," depending on an enterprise's readiness. Many of the more complex privatizations—such as energy, health services, and agriculture—were postponed to the second wave.   Of 2,744 enterprises included in the first wave in Czechoslovakia (as inventoried in November 1991), 751 were Slovak and had a book value of Kcs 167 billion.   Coupon privatization and direct sales were the predominant methods of privatization.

Privatization was intended to be a four-step process (Figure 3.1). First, each enterprise would submit a privatization project to its sectoral or "founding" ministry. Competing projects could also be submitted from outside. Each project specified the assets to be privatized and their book value, the privatization method to be used, the conditions and terms of payment, and the implementation schedule. Second, the founding ministry would select a project for review by the Ministry of Privatization and oversee any required revisions. Third, after the Ministry of Privatization accepted a project, the enterprise was typically converted into a joint-stock company

Figure 3.1: Privatization is a Four-Step Process

ORGANIZATION OF PRIVATIZATION

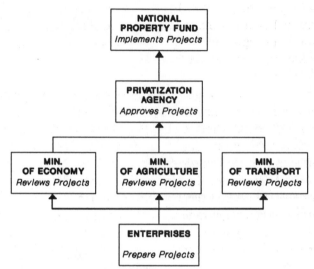

Source: Slovak authorities.

wholly owned by a new state agency, the National Property Fund.[1] Fourth, the National Property Fund would implement the privatization and provide governance to the enterprise during the transition.

Each enterprise entering the second wave of privatization must complete an environmental survey. The survey must address ongoing and past pollution and be cleared by the local representative of the Ministry of Environment or by the central ministry in important cases. In the past, the government placed responsibility for cleaning up pollution on the new private owners. Recently, the Ministry of Environment proposed that quantifiable environmental liabilities be reflected in an enterprise's price at the time of privatization. A cleanup agreement would also be concluded at that time based on the findings of the environmental survey of the firm. Hidden or subsequently detected environmental liabilities are to be assumed by the state. For this system to work, environmental audit methodologies need to be further developed, acceptable pollution standards agreed on, and staff trained to perform the audits. This will be crucial for attracting private investors (particularly foreigners) to purchase enterprises, particularly in environmentally risky sectors such as chemicals.

Coupon privatization. In Slovakia, most enterprises were transferred to citizen owners through the coupon scheme. Booklets of coupons worth 1,000 points were printed and distributed through a network of registration centers in the winter of 1991/92. Each adult Czechoslovak citizen was entitled to purchase one booklet, at a fee equal to about one week's average wages. In terms of average book value of assets purchasable for coupons, each booklet was projected to be worth about six months' average wages. Each citizen purchasing coupons received an identification code, which was written on each coupon. Coupon trading was prohibited until the privatization was completed. However, citizens were allowed to sign over management of their coupons to Investment Privatization Funds, which had emerged on their own. These funds were legally established as joint-stock companies and operated like

---

1   The National Property Fund may also sell assets of state-owned enterprises without first converting the enterprise into a joint-stock company.

mutual funds. The largest funds were run by commercial banks, savings banks, and insurance companies. The Investment Privatization Funds enabled the less informed to defer to the more informed, without relinquishing their stakes. Interest in the scheme intensified when some of the funds promised one-year returns of 1,000% or more on coupon books and made loans against coupon book collateral. Ultimately, 8.5 million people (of an eligible Czechoslovak population of about 10.5 million), including 2.6 million from Slovakia, registered for coupons.

The original deadlines for submitting privatization proposals were extended two months to allow for more competitive proposals. The first auction round thus slipped from January to May 1992, and the last round was not completed until late December 1992 (Box 3.1). A more recent problem has been the delay in issuing stock shares to winning bidders, which has delayed secondary trading. Complaining of Slovak government tardiness in settling interrepublican arrears, the Czech government temporarily suspended the distribution; some Czech politicians even called for cancellation. The Slovak authorities challenged the Czech accounting and also stressed that seizure of private property to pay government debts contradicts the principles of the Velvet Revolution. Eventually, the Czech authorities relented and began to issue the withheld shares. Considering the setbacks to large privatization experienced in other countries, the stumblings have been relatively minor.

Box 3.1: Bidding Rules under Coupon Privatization

Equity in each enterprise to be privatized in the first wave was divided into shares nominally worth Kcs 1000 each in book value and initially priced at 33.3 points. Given the huge uncertainties about the real valuation and market demand, the coupon auctions proceeded in several rounds. In the "zero round," points could be transferred to the Investment Privatization Funds. Thereafter, the following allocation principles applied:

- When not all shares were demanded (undersubscription), bidders received their shares at the asking price, and the remaining shares were offered in the next bidding round at a lower price.

- Where oversubscription was less than 25%, citizens received all the shares they directly bid for, while the demand of the Investment Privatization Funds was prorated to clear the market.

- Where oversubscription exceeded 25%, all shares were offered again in the next round at a higher price.

To discourage "wait and see" tactics, the government reserved the right to terminate the auctions with some points left unused. After the auctions were completed, stock certificates would be sent to the winning bidders. The new owners would select boards of directors, to supervise the restructuring at their enterprises.

Note: For a more detailed analysis of coupon privatization, see N. Shafik (1993) "Making a Market: Coupon Privatization in the Czech and Slovak Republic," Policy Research Working Paper 1231, Central Europe Department, World Bank, Washington, D.C.

Other privatization methods. Almost a third of state companies in the first wave were privatized through standard methods, mainly direct sales to predetermined owners. However, such companies tended to be smaller than those privatized through coupon vouchers, commanding less than 8% of the book value of public enterprise assets. Total sales proceeds in Slovakia were about Sk 14.5 billion. Domestic investors acquired about 59% of the property under direct sales, paying 5% below book value on average. Foreign investors bought the remainder, but tended to pay almost twice the book value, reflecting their focus on more attractive firms. By spring 1993, the first wave of large privatizations was nearly complete, an impressive accomplishment in its scale, its relative smoothness, and its speed.

Impact on governance. In a market economy, active owners of enterprises play two complementary roles. As capitalists, they supply capital and collect profits on their investment. As governors (directors), they choose top managers, set general ground rules, approve the business strategy, and monitor compliance. Capitalists provide the resources, while directors set the strategic orientation and managers conduct day-to-day operations. Capitalists can be created with a stroke of the pen, but governance must be cultivated. The nominal owners may lack either the incentive to govern effectively, as in the case of small shareholders in a large firm, or the information needed to do so.

In the current transition, setting appropriate ground rules for management basically means corporatization. Most noncommercial activities should be terminated or transferred to special-purpose government agencies, and management should be steered toward maximizing an enterprise's net worth and given the autonomy to do so. The first wave appears to have given corporatization a major boost, although less through privatization than through the preparations for it. Drawing up privatization projects forced managers to view their enterprise in a different light, while the prospect of new profit-oriented owners has helped shake them out of old routines.

While it is still too early to judge the effect of privatization on governance (especially coupon privatization), anecdotal evidence suggests that management in enterprises privatized in the first wave is anticipating investor behavior and taking steps to secure its position. In the process of privatization, some enterprises have transferred control to lower levels of management by setting up holding companies with small separate subsidiaries. In a limited number of cases, enterprises transferred their social assets to local municipalities. Supervisory boards of some enterprises have reportedly raised management salaries, and many firms have started debt collection efforts, either through the courts or with the help of newly created private debt collection and factoring firms. A secondary market for interenterprise debt is beginning to emerge.

The first wave of privatization has been fairly effective at preserving or reestablishing large owners. One category of large owner is the Investment Privatization Funds, which arose more or less spontaneously. Collectively, they controlled over 70% of the coupons in the first wave and purchased a corresponding proportion of the shares sold for coupons. They are the dominant private owners of enterprises in Slovakia. Other large private owners have been created through restitution or sale to foreign firms. Individual citizens have very small holdings, but the emergence of shareholder associations could increase their voice in enterprise governance.

By far the single largest owner of enterprises is still the National Property Fund (NPF). As of September 1993, NPF owned all or part of 517 companies (Table 3.3). NPF has sold all of its shares in forty companies, but still controls 3% of the shares in companies that were set aside in a restitution fund for compensating previous owners. NPF owns a majority of shares (including restitution fund shares) in some 101 companies. The remaining companies can be said to be under the control of private owners. The largest companies in which the NPF owns a majority of shares include VUB (50.8% ownership), the Slovak Insurance Company (52%), Slovnaft (oil, 80%), Benzinol (oil distribution, 97%), Nafta (gas, 55.2%), Trnavske Automobilove (50.1%), Zavod SNP (aluminum, 72%), and Slovakofarma (chemicals, 80.9%). The extent and desirability of long-term strategic stakes by NPF in these and other firms is under review; its involvement is likely to be reduced by the government.

Table 3.3: Inventory of Companies in Portfolio of National Property Fund, September 1993 (number of enterprises)					
Book value of equity (sK million)	Completely privatized (no NPF ownership)a	Majority privatized (NPF ownership less than 47%)a	Partially privatized (NPF ownership greater than 47%)	Not privatized	Total enterprises
Less than 10	1	42	6	5	54
10 to 30	5	92	9	7	113
30 to 50	6	48	2	12	68
50 to 100	13	91	14	13	131
100 to 300	12	74	15	6	107
300 to 1,000	1	54	3	3	61
1,000 to 10,000	2	14	4	1	21
More than 10,000	0	1	1	0	2
Total number of enterprises	40	416	54	47	557
Share of enterprises (%)	7.2	74.7	9.7	8.4	100.0
Total book value of equity (Sk million)	6,366	93,683	28,902	7,012	135,963
Share of total (%)	4.7	68.9	21.3	5.2	100.0
Book value of NPF stake (Sk Million)	0	20,950	20,390	7,012	48,352

a   NPF also controls 3% of shares held in the restitution fund.
Source: National Property Fund.

The NPF has three main roles. It is:

- The primary institution responsible for implementing privatization.
- The owner, on behalf of the government, of enterprise that have been converted into joint-stock companies but not transferred to private ownership.
- The custodian of the proceeds from the sale of state assets.

The NPF is an agency created by law and responsible to the Slovak Parliament. It is supervised by a nine-person presidium, with members elected by Parliament for five-year terms. The presidium appoints an executive committee of NPF and employees to conduct the day-to-day business of the fund. A board of trustees plays an ombudsman role, reporting to Parliament and investigating any shortcomings in NPF's operation. As part of an effort to depoliticize the NPF and eliminate the government's role in appointing NPF officers, an amendment to the privatization law passed in March 1994 stipulates that all board members are to be appointed by Parliament. "Constitutional officials," such as ministers and members of Parliament, cannot fill these positions.

NPF does not have the resources necessary to carry out a large privatization program using standard methods. With a staff of only about sixty-five people—it plans to expand to about 200 —the NPF relies primarily on financial advisers to carry out auctions or tenders. Most of these advisers are from local financial institutions, which lack the experience to attract foreign investors. Since March 1992, tenders of sixty-one companies were initiated but only about four were completed. The NPF is receiving some technical assistance from the EU-Phare program and other international agencies but probably needs even more.

NPF is a relatively passive owner, as a matter of policy and because it lacks the staff to supervise the 557 enterprises in which it has shares. NPF is represented on the boards of only about 120 enterprises; forty of its staff sit on these boards. Staff from other ministries represent the government's ownership interest in enterprises that are considered strategic. It is reported that the board members appointed by NPF tend to follow the lead of board members from the Investment Privatization Funds. The official objective of the NPF as owner is primarily commercial: to maximize the value of the shares that it owns in these companies. Considering NPF's limited ability to supply board members and the risk that they might have a social or political agenda, it is probably best that the NPF play a passive role in corporate governance, leaving active involvement to private owners such as the Investment Privatization Funds.

The law spells out how NPF, as custodian of the proceeds of privatization, may use these funds. They are to be used primarily to cover the cost of privatization; pay for the debts of enterprises scheduled for privatization, including an option to cover certain environmental liabilities; and provide capital to banks (this latter is risky, and could imply a renationalization). The NPF also guaranteed the debts of enterprises privatized in the first wave for a period of one year. It may also guarantee loans to strategic enterprises—those in which the NPF owns more than 34% of the shares on a permanent basis.

The proceeds of privatization are often viewed as a source of funds to help meet the government's financial needs and the capital requirements of enterprises and banks. As in other transition economies, funds for such purposes are in extremely short supply. There is a danger of overcommitting the proceeds of privatization by making guarantees or other promises that the NPF cannot meet. By one estimate, the NPF will have received about Sk 14 billion by the end of 1993 from the sale of assets and enterprise shares in the first wave of privatization and from small-scale privatization; as of August 1993, it had spent more than Sk 10 billion. About Sk 4 billion was spent to recapitalize the banks. Another Sk 1.5 billion was used to write off debts of large enterprises prior to privatization. It is unclear what portion of the proceeds has been committed through guarantees. Thus, it is important that the NPF maintain accurate accounting statements that include the liabilities that may arise from its provision of guarantees. NPF intends to have a detailed audit conducted to present a clearer picture of its financial position.

The Investment Privatization Funds. The Investment Privatization Funds (IPFs) are the largest and most important private owners of enterprises in Slovakia. Unlike mutual funds or investment trusts in many other countries, the IPFs play an active role in corporate governance. The ten largest IPFs control about one-quarter of the shares offered in the coupon scheme. A typical large fund has 200,000-500,000 shareholders, owns shares in more than a hundred companies, and has a staff of about fifty. Legally, these funds differ little from joint-stock companies, with a board of supervisors elected by the shareholders at the annual meeting. The founders of a fund—for example a bank—appoint the initial board of supervisors and hire an investment company to manage the fund's portfolio. The investment company receives an advisory fee of no more than 2% of the value of the fund's assets. An important question for the new board of supervisors elected at the first annual meeting is whether to continue to employ the same investment company, which in most cases is affiliated with the founding institution.

The objective of the funds should be to increase the value of their shareholdings in Slovak companies. The investment company advising the fund on its portfolio has an incentive to increase the value of shares because its fee is linked to the value of the portfolio and because the new board of supervisors may decide to hire a different investment company. The IPFs are similar to holding companies rather than to the diversified investment funds common in Western Europe or the United

States. Though many of the IPFs had intended to follow the model of these diversified mutual funds or investment trusts as passive owners of corporations, most now realize that the only way to ensure that the value of their shareholdings increases is by taking an active role in corporate governance.

Although the IPFs appear to be having a favorable impact on enterprise governance, further progress in improving the quality of governance is being hindered by the weak information base and the shallow pool of managerial experts. In problem cases, the new owners have little choice but to remind the current management that the ground rules have changed and to give incumbents three to six months to adjust their behavior. These constraints should ease over time. More worrisome is the quality of governance within the IPFs, since their representatives on enterprise supervisory boards are essentially agents of other owners, the numerous small private stockholders in IPFs.

Because this type of fund is rare in other countries, there are no regulatory models to follow. Slovakia is to a large extent pioneering in the development of this regulation, and considerable effort should be devoted to the task. The role of these funds will evolve as the Slovak economy changes during the transition, and no one can say now what their ultimate role should be. Thus, there is a substantial risk in forging too far ahead of experience with regulations that stifle the ability of funds to meet emerging needs. For example, current regulations that emphasize limits on how much the funds may invest in a particular company (Act No. 248 limits a fund's shareholding in any one company to 20%) are likely to restrict the ability of the funds to influence the activities of the enterprises that they own. Though IPF supervision and control of enterprises may not be perfect, it is preferable to no supervision, and there is little evidence that such strict controls are needed or that the funds are not playing a useful and productive role in the economy.

The regulation of investment funds should emphasize disclosure of information about operations to the shareholders who own the funds and to the appropriate government ministries. Public scrutiny is the best method of regulating their activities. Thus an important regulatory issue is whether the funds should be required to disclose any financial or business connections of its senior managers, board of supervisors, or management company that might constitute a conflict of interest. For example, is the fund using a broker to buy and sell shares who is affiliated with the investment company that is managing the fund's portfolio? Compulsory annual audits by an internationally recognized accounting firm could help uncover irregularities in the funds' operations.

To discourage insiders' use of IPFs for bailouts, IPFs should not be allowed to invest in their own corporate founders. It is reported that some large enterprises established IPFs in order to maintain control of their enterprise. For example, employees of an enterprise could be given or loaned the money for coupons on the understanding that the coupons would be invested in the fund founded by the enterprise. Another concern is that the large funds founded by banks may become the primary owners of the banks. Though ownership of banks by daughter IPFs is expressly forbidden by law, a legal dodge allows bank ownership (of up to 10%) by "granddaughter" IPFs belonging to bank subsidiaries. Thus, in the case of VUB, a daughter investment company owns several IPF granddaughters that are themselves shareholders in VUB, the grandparent company (Box 3.2).

Box 3.2 VUB Kupon: Profile of an Investment Privatization Fund

VUB KUPON, an Investment Privatization Fund, was founded by Všeobečna Úverová Banka, the largest bank in Slovakia, in November 1991, with an initial capital of Sk 1 million. It is managed by VUB Invest, an asset management company to which VUB Kupon paid Sk 14 million in management fees in 1992. During the pre-round of the coupon privatization, VUB Kupon collected over 500 million investment points from 531,419 holders of investment coupons who became shareholders of this stock company. In five bidding rounds, VUB Kupon acquired stakes in 238 privatized companies. With a total nominal value of shares in its portfolio of Sk 12 billion, VUB Kupon is the largest Privatization Investment Fund in the Slovak Republic and the fourth largest in the territory of the former Czech and Slovak Federal Republic.

The fund's portfolio is concentrated in only a few industrial sectors: chemicals (15%), engineering (22%), energy (12%), and metallurgy (9%). Nearly half of its investments are in large shareholdings in seventy enterprises (35 Slovak and 35 Czech), including VUB. VUB Kupon is potentially able to exercise strong corporate governance in these seventy enterprises.

VUB Invest, the asset management company, was founded in September 1991 as a wholly owned subsidiary of VUB, with capital of Sk 33 million. Its young management team prepared the business plan with the assistance of VUB, and a foreign consulting company specialized in emerging securities markets. To encourage investors to contribute their coupons to the fund, VUB made loans to the shareholders in VUB Kupon, with shares as collateral, and further proposed to buy back the shares at a guaranteed price equal to about 1,200% of the administrative fee charged to the investors for obtaining coupons (coupon books). Preliminary stock market prices of the underlying shares in the enterprises suggest that this guaranteed price is not excessive.

Small Privatization

Over 9,300 small shops in Slovakia, or about 80% of the total, were privatized during the first two years of the privatization program, a remarkable and strikingly visible achievement. The privatized shops offer an abundance of previously unavailable goods and services that have literally changed the face of the country. The privatizations of small shops generally received strong popular support, though support from current shop employees was mixed, since they were denied preferences in purchase (unlike the case in most transition economies) and feared losing their jobs (over 20% did). Still, the privatization procedures were relatively straightforward and transparent, and no one is seriously arguing for a reversal. The small privatizations have reinforced economic reform elsewhere in the economy, partly because of the services the small shops provide to other sectors and partly because the small privatizations have expanded the ranks of the reform-minded middle class.

About a third of small shops were returned to the original owners or their descendants. Another third, mainly service outlets on the ground floor of large apartment blocks, were leased for two years (sometimes longer), pending privatization of the apartment block. The remaining third, usually shops built by state enterprises, were sold directly to buyers, some with and some without the attached land. Sometimes the owners or leaseholders were required to purchase inventory and equipment at book value, and in some cases they had to pledge to continue the current line of business for a stated period. Most of the small shops remaining in state hands were slated for inclusion in the second wave of privatizations, either in a bundle with the large enterprises they are affiliated with or as free-standing stores.

The small privatizations yielded proceeds of Kcs 14.2 billion, or slightly more than the proceeds from the first wave of large privatizations. Because the period for paying off inventories was not specified, about Kcs 1 billion in bills remains outstanding. Buildings had to be paid for within thirty days. Most purchases were financed thorough loans from the Savings Bank (Sporitelna). The Savings Bank, which was required to extend the loans, tried to reduce its risk by demanding that borrowers put up personal property (such as vacation houses) as collateral.

The Second Wave

The second wave of privatization will include most of the productive enterprises remaining in state hands. As in the first wave, privatization projects are being submitted by management and competing bidders to the supervisory ministries (mainly the Ministry of Economy, but also the Ministries of Transport and Telecommunications and of Agriculture). The proposals are screened and sent on to the Ministry of Privatization, which prepares the project for privatization through the National Property Fund.

The second wave is likely to prove more difficult than the first because some of the more difficult cases were intentionally deferred to the second wave and because of a change in the approach to privatization to remedy what some Slovak officials saw as shortcomings of the first wave of privatization:

- Too great a preference for coupon privatization over other standard methods that result in stronger governance.

- Too low a priority on attracting new domestic and foreign capital.

- Inadequate attention to specific sectoral characteristics and restructuring needs.

The previous government's plan, September 1993. In September 1993, the previous government established the principles that were to guide its new privatization strategy. To foster the emergence of a class of domestic entrepreneurs with a stronger hand in managing enterprises, standard privatization methods were to be used exclusively for medium-size and smaller enterprises (book value of less than Sk 250 million), which accounted for about 15% of the book value of enterprises to be privatized in the second wave (Table 3.4). Coupon privatization was to be used only to transfer a minority stake to coupon holders in large enterprises (value greater than Sk 250 million). A majority of shares in large enterprises were to be reserved for eventual sale using standard methods of privatization. The goal was to allow a large foreign or domestic investor to buy a controlling block of shares in these companies even though that might take longer than coupon privatization.

The main standard method to be used was public tenders, with investment and employment pledges given priority over price. Public auctions were to be used only when the chief consideration was revenue. In exceptional cases, when competition was impossible or too costly to organize, a sale was to be negotiated directly with a predetermined buyer. Capital thresholds were to be lowered by permitting more sales at prices below book value and by extending the opportunities for installment purchases. The government was also inclined to encourage banks to provide financing for purchases, by having the National Property Fund guarantee loans.

Table 3.4: Value of Enterprises in the Second Wave of Privatization, September 1993			
Book value of equity or net worth (Sk million)	Number of enterprises	Total value per category (Sk million)	Share of total value (%)
Standard privatization			
Less than 25	81	1,118	0.6
25 to 50	75	2,866	1.5
50 to 100	83	5,814	3.0
100 to 250	126	20,229	10.3
Subtotal	365	30,027	15.4
Standard privatization plus minority voucher privatization			
250 to 500	86	30,056	15.3
500 to 1,000	37	26,166	13.3
More than 1,000	31	109,844	56.0
Subtotal	154	166,066	84.6
Total	519	196,093	100.0
Source: The Ministry for Administration and Privatization of the National Property of the Slovak Republic.			

Installment sales involve substantial risk. In effect, the National Property Fund must act as a lending institution and determine whether a buyer is likely to make the installment payments. If the downpayment is too low, speculative bidding may lead to unrealistically high prices. If the business is profitable, the buyer may be able to make the installment payments. If not, the buyer loses only the small downpayment and ownership reverts to the National Property Fund. Even worse, a buyer may have no intention of making the installment payments but seeks to strip the enterprise of any valuable assets and then turn back an empty shell to the National Property Fund. Loan guarantees are also fraught with risk. It may be that neither the National Property Fund nor the banks adequately review the qualifications of the buyer or monitor management of the enterprise.

Relying on standard methods has one potentially serious shortcoming: doing so may substantially slow the pace of privatization since there is no detailed implementation plan yet for using standard methods. If the pace slows, the government's reform credibility may erode. Pressure may intensify for the state to restructure enterprises before privatization to make them more profitable and to close large loss makers. Though legal, organizational, and possibly financial restructuring may boost interest in an enterprise, experience in other countries demonstrates that large expenditures on physical restructuring rarely pay off.

Wishing to maintain a rapid pace of privatization, the government announced that it intended to privatize one-third of all enterprises still with majority government ownership by the end of 1994. To meet this goal, the government would probably have been forced to rely more on coupon privatization than its September 1993 policy would suggest. The government announced that the second wave of coupon privatization was to begin by the end of the third quarter of 1994, with an initial target sale of shares with a book value of Sk 45-70 billion.

The current government's plans, March 1994. The government that came to power in March 1994 announced a new approach to privatization. First, voucher privatization will receive equal standing with other privatization methods, and the government is working hard to launch the second wave of voucher privatizations by September 1994. Though discussions are still under way about the exact amount of assets and number of enterprises to be included, indications are that it would involve some 180 enterprises with assets of about Sk 70-80 billion. There is also discussion about including some Sk 20 billion of equity in 120 enterprises from among the holdings of the National Property Fund remaining after the first wave of privatizations. The government intends to proceed with sales through standard methods in cases where discussions with strategic investors have already been initiated.

The government is considering temporarily retaining 20% to 40% of the equity in the firms including the second wave of voucher privatizations and selling these shares later to raise revenues to meet the liabilities of the National Property Fund. This approach has two weakness. For one, the fund may not be able to sell all these shares. For another, the procedure might crowd out private finance by diverting investments that might otherwise have been made in the private sector.

Constraints on the Private Sector

The main constraints to growth of the private sector are temporary restraints on private ownership and use of land and buildings; court backlogs in enforcing contracts; inadequate regulatory framework, including too much regulation of new businesses and a lack of coherent regulation for emerging capital markets; and weak infrastructure, especially poor information systems.[2] If the political will is there, most of these problems have fairly straightforward solutions.

Privatization of Land and Buildings

Recent surveys of small privatizations in the Czech Republic, Hungary, and Poland have documented a striking connection between ownership form and investment. Even an option to purchase improves investment.[3] Slovakia recognizes private land ownership rights and has been including land title as part of the assets transferred in privatization of medium-size and large enterprises. The problem lies in the significant amount of commercial office space, urban housing, and agricultural and vacant land that remain in the hands of local government authorities.

Most noticeably affected have been the small shops located on the ground floors of large office or apartment complexes. Typically, when shops were privatized, short-term leases on the retail space were passed on to the new owners, pending resolution of land title. These leases have generally been extended on a month-to-month basis, discouraging maintenance, investment, and resale of businesses to third parties. A new mechanism for the orderly conversion of short-term leases to long-term leases currently being put into place should introduce more certainty to business planning.

---

2   For results of a survey of private sector firms and an analysis of constraints, see D. Swanson and L. Webster, 1992, "Private Sector Manufacturing in the Czech and Slovak Federal Republic: A Survey of Firms," World Bank Technical Paper 230, Washington, D.C.

3   R. Frydman, A. Rapaczynski, J. Earle, A. Harding, J. Mladek, and J. Turkewitz, 1993, "Small Privatization Survey in the Czech Republic, Hungary and Poland," Joint Study of the Central European University Project and the World Bank.

The title uncertainty affects residential as well commercial occupants of urban buildings. As tenants, both groups are charged low rents—often below maintenance costs—and protected against eviction. This setup has perverse consequences: it discourages new development by reducing demand for building repair and renovation while boosting real estate prices. And by eliminating a potential source of collateral for loans, this arrangement inhibits the development of the commercial space and housing markets. More power is placed in the hands of local authorities, which deters both domestic and foreign investors. To speed the process of sorting out current titles, a new land cadastre should be created, using modern mapping techniques. All land records should be computerized, to allow for easy access for households, enterprises, and banks. Also, the process for transferring and insuring titles should be simplified.[4]

The lagging privatization of housing and agricultural land also hinders labor mobility and discourages intergenerational transfers. It is common in market economies for workers to move their residence as labor requirements shift and for pensioners to sell their house and farm land to younger families. In Slovakia, the scale of this kind of trading is unnaturally small. Freeing up the housing and farmland markets could promote labor mobility, assist in matching housing space to family requirements, and free more disposable income for pensioners.

Legislation passed in July 1993 would allow the purchase of publicly owned housing. The price would be negotiated between buyers and sellers, subject to a maximum price of Sk 4,400 per square meter of usable living space.[5] To deter speculation, windfall gains from resales when the owner is not an occupant will be subjected to near-confiscatory taxation for ten years. Opponents object that this amounts to de facto extension of rent control by rewarding tenure in state housing and penalizing its relinquishment. Nevertheless, passage of the legislation was seen as a major accomplishment, and speedy implementation is expected.

Weak Contract Enforcement

Until January 1, 1992, commercial disputes (including debt collection and enforcement) were resolved through state arbitration. Under the new commercial code, such cases became the responsibility of newly created commercial courts, and the former arbitrators became judges in the new courts. A lack of familiarity with court administration and procedures and with the commercial code itself resulted in a tremendous backlog of unresolved cases. Of the 306,000 cases admitted in 1992 (24,000 of them related to debt collection and enforcement), 174,000 were still unresolved at the end of the year. Despite some minor reforms to increase the courts' capacity, it can still take up to a year or

---

4   The current decentralized records are not completely clear, due mostly to lapses in record-keeping, and are difficult to access. Restitution claims in urban areas have been mostly resolved while agricultural land title has yet to be resolved. The disposition of common apartment property (entryways, elevators, surrounding grounds) also poses a problem, especially when some residents choose to buy and others to continue renting. At the least, condominium associations will have to be organized or management companies retained to make decisions on property management.

5   Sitting tenants would become eligible for another 30% discount after ten years, provided they do not sell the unit during that time to someone other than a family member. Minimum downpayments would be 15%, with the remainder paid in ten-year installments at zero interest. Sales to a third party would be permitted only when the tenant fails to pay rent for six months or more, and even then the seller would have to provide the tenant with alternative housing.

more to resolve a case. A related problem is the absence of enforcement capacity for debt collection: courts do not have effective mechanisms for seizing or selling debtors' assets. Debt collection has become the outstanding problem facing many businesses. Suppliers, recognizing their vulnerability, are increasingly insisting on barter or cash payment up front. While this alleviates the problem of moral hazard, it exacerbates problems of illiquidity. The government has responded by passing legislation requiring enterprises to net out their arrears through a private clearinghouse (Box 3.3).

Box 3.3: Clearing Interenterprise Arrears

In 1992, the Government appointed a private company, Fizako, to deal with the chain of interenterprise arrears. Fizako organizes registration rounds at which enterprises register their receivables (for claims over Sk 10,000)—a compulsory process since September 1993. Fizako's role is to match the data on these claims and track debt chains with the objective of clearing the interenterprise debt. The scheme should identify some of the major loss-making enterprises, which have primary responsibility for the whole chain of interenterprise arrears, and firms whose payables exceed receivables and thus may have to undergo financial restructuring or liquidation.

In one year, Fizako conducted eight rounds of voluntary registration and cleared Sk 10 billion of receivables out of an estimated stock of Sk 80-90 billion. Two compulsory rounds cleared another Sk 9 billion. As of the end of March 1994, interenterprise indebtedness was estimated at Sk 50 billion. To finance loans bridging the arrears chains, Fizako received Sk 1 billion in 1993 from the National Property Fund through Konsolidačna Banka.

A substantial part of both payables and receivables includes Czech-Slovak cross-border overdues, claims on former CMEA countries, and claims on countries against which arms embargoes were established. The outstanding debt owed to the Czech Republic by Slovak state-owned enterprises totaled an estimated Sk 35 billion at the end of 1992, 73% of it overdue as of April 1993. The Slovak Ministry of Economy recently proposed to the Czech Ministry of Industry and Trade to settle this debt.

The Slovak government passed an amendment to the bankruptcy law in June 1993 that introduced a simplified conciliation procedure. The procedure allows creditors to reach agreement on liquidation or on physical and financial restructuring plans for potentially viable enterprises. The procedure has not worked well in practice because it requires unanimity by creditors and lacks mechanisms for resolving conflicts among creditors and between creditors and equity holders. The government should improve liquidation and reorganization procedures by, among other things, permitting the intervention of a neutral, third party whose decision would be binding on all creditors and equity holders.

The government is currently in the process of reestablishing nonjudicial, binding arbitration, which would greatly improve the resolution of commercial contract disputes. It does not, however, address the backlog of pending commercial cases in the courts or the lack of effective enforcement mechanisms. These problems must be addressed by streamlining court administration and procedures, providing better training for judges in commercial law and the administration of justice, and instituting procedures for enforcing judgments. Rules for fair credit reporting are also needed, so that records of enterprise debt service performance would be available to banks and private sector agencies interested in offering enterprises credit and so that an enterprise credit rating system could eventually be set up. Finally, the Slovak Chamber of Commerce, to which all Slovak firms belong under law, should be authorized to conduct voluntary arbitration procedures for all business disputes, not just for disputes between domestic and foreign businesses as at present.

Over- and Under-Regulation

Making it easier to do business in Slovakia should be the government's first regulatory priority. The regulatory burden on new businesses is too heavy and too complex. Lack of information about the requirements is itself a barrier to private enterprise development. To receive a trade license, applicants must provide confirmation of qualifications (including certificates attesting to the lack of a criminal record and number of years of specialized education and training) and pay substantial licensing fees. Because few foreign countries have similar requirements, foreigners interested in establishing a business in Slovakia find it especially difficult to obtain trade licenses. An amendment is under consideration that would reduce many of these requirements.

Simplifying and clarifying the requirements for trade licenses and for registration of commercial businesses would also promote new enterprise development. The tremendous backlog in trade license requests arising from the requirement that all licenses be re-issued following the establishment of the Slovak Republic is starting to diminish, but the wait in urban areas is still one to two months. Inconsistent interpretation of registration requirements often results in multiple visits, repeated filings, and undue delays. Frequently, additional paperwork must be filed for environmental impact assessments, health and safety inspections, social security payments, customs, and taxes. Mistakes may be penalized by hefty fines or—perhaps worse—by being sentenced to start the process over again.

Taxes on business are numerous. Up-front taxes and fees should be reduced, to make new entry less risky. Basic tax rates include a 50% payroll tax for social insurance programs (38% from employers and 12% from employees), 25% (6% for some services) for the VAT, and 45% for the corporate income tax. Often taxes are levied regardless of whether the supplier has been paid, a requirement made the more onerous by the frequency with which payments are delayed. Foreign exchange restrictions in force at various times impose other taxes. The main results, not surprisingly, have been an increase in foreign refusals to ship without prepayments, and higher profits for cross-border banking intermediaries, most of them based in Vienna.

Instead of focusing on these problems, which could be resolved at a relatively low budgetary cost, government efforts to promote the domestic private sector stress tax holidays for new investment, guarantees, and subsidized and directed credits. The same problems afflict the promotion of foreign investment, the responsibility of the new Slovak National Agency for Foreign Investment (Box 3.4). Foreign direct investment could more readily be encouraged by adopting a one-stop assistance approach that eliminates the problems of misinformation and delays in starting businesses.

Facilitating the development of active capital markets and supporting fair competition should also be important regulatory concerns. Despite the absence of a comprehensive regulatory framework, several markets for trading shares in recently privatized companies have developed spontaneously. A nascent stock exchange has emerged, trading ten listed and more than forty unlisted companies on a weekly basis. The majority bank-owned stock market is planning to introduce twice-weekly trading. The largest volume of shares—more than eighty companies—is traded through the RM System, an over-the-counter market that emerged from the more than 190 local offices created to carry out the first wave of voucher privatizations. Trades now take several weeks to execute, but the RM System also intends to introduce daily trading by the end of the year. The joint foreign and domestically owned Bratislava Options Bourse trades forwards on shares. The Ministry of Finance, through a wholly owned joint stock company, has established the System of Company Registration of Stock Ownership (SCP), the official system of company registration of share ownership. What is needed now is legislation designed to build investor confidence, through mandatory disclosure of information by enterprises issuing shares, and to promote competition in the share-trading market. Fair competition is also essential to the development of a vigorous and dynamic private sector. A fair competition law has been drafted and will soon be presented to Parliament. An Antimonopoly Bureau has already been established. Review of intellectual property protection is also being carried out.

Box 3.4: Climate for Foreign Investment in Slovakia

Foreign investment in Slovakia totaled Kcs 6.6 billion, (US$230 million) at the end of 1992, strikingly low, considering the proximity to Western Europe and the far larger investments in the neighboring Czech Republic and Hungary. Most foreign investments were in services, and most were very small, in the range of US$3500-US$35,000. The biggest investors are Austria (US$63 million at the end of 1992), Germany (US$57 million), and the United States (US$44 million). The Netherlands, Italy, Sweden, and the Republic of Korea account for another US$11-14 million each. The largest acquisitions have been undertaken by K-Mart, which bought the largest Slovak department store chain; Volkswagen (Germany, cars); Henkel (Austria, chemicals); Molnlycke (Sweden, paper); Samsung (Korea, refrigerators); Hoechst (Germany, pharmaceuticals); and Whirlpool (Italy, washing machines). Although the base is small, growth has been rapid. In the last three quarters of 1992, foreign investment grew by 87% (US$107 million). Most of this growth reflects foreign purchases of enterprises privatized in the first wave. Bratislava hosts two-thirds of all foreign investment in Slovakia, reflecting its size and easy access.

Recent government efforts to encourage foreign investment have focused on tax holidays, credit guarantees and subsidies, and exemptions from import duties. Yet, foreign investors cite other concerns as the major problems in doing business in the country:

- Lack of reliable information on the requirements for establishing businesses.
- Burdensome legislation, excessive red tape, and delays in setting up a new company.
- Uncertainties surrounding the second wave privatization program.
- Restrictions in place in the past on the convertibility of the Slovak koruna and excessive corporate taxes.
- Lack of effective commercial law enforcement mechanisms.
- Inadequacies in the laws, regulations, and other basic institutions needed for a market economy.

Note: For a more detailed analysis of the pattern of foreign investment and the constraints, see Foreign Investment Advisory Service (1993), "Improving the Environment for Foreign Direct Investment in Slovakia," World Bank, Washington, D.C.

Weak Infrastructure

Basic telecommunications facilities are essential to the development of private, competitive enterprises. Slovakia has one phone link for every four citizens, which is more than in Hungary and Poland but far less than in Western Europe. Installation delays of several months are standard. What might be a mere nuisance to Slovak households or government agencies can be intolerable in private foreign trade. The quality is poor, which limits computer networking and access to the world's electronic highways, increasingly as important as access to physical transport routes. Planned World Bank co-financing for a substantial expansion and upgrading of the telecommunications network should improve the situation. Internal transport links do not appear to be a major bottleneck, but rail, road, pipeline, and port links with Western Europe, which were discouraged during the Soviet period, need extension and upgrading. Slovakia should be able to capitalize on its strategic location to become a transit point for east-west goods traffic as well as pipeline networks (Box 3.5).

Box 3.5: Slovakia as a Strategic Crossroads—The Case of Natural Gas

The Slovak government has suddenly become a key player in the European natural gas industry. Almost all of the gas that flows from the Commonwealth of Independent States to central and western Europe passes through Slovakia. The government needs to consider how to maximize the long-term value of this asset. The government's handling of the privatization of the transit pipeline will have a profound effect not only on its economic recovery, but also on the long-term development of the energy system in Europe. The transit pipeline now produces transit fees equivalent to nearly US$500 million a year, and its economic importance is likely to grow. Western European countries are seeking to diversify their sources and reduce their dependence on Russia, but it is almost certain that both the east-west and north-south links will pass through Slovakia. The country's potential to provide strategic storage services near the consuming centers further enhances the value of the gas transit system.

In exploring how to maximize the long-term benefits this asset can provide, the government faces several immediate decisions:

- The transit contracts with Russia must be renegotiated to provide more equitable terms for Slovak owners. If the pipeline is to be collateralized, longer-term contracts, control of pipeline access, and direct commercial links with other transporters and customers are essential.

- Will the transit system be integrated with the internal gas supply system? Foreign investors would pay a higher price for an international pipeline unencumbered by local responsibilities, but Slovakia's energy security would be reduced if it depended on another party for transportation.

- Should the pipeline system be recapitalized before privatization? The capital structure is greatly underleveraged. The government could issue debt instruments against future earnings, thus providing revenue in the immediate future.

- What will be the role of the government after privatization? The government could retain controlling interest and collect profits as a shareholder, or it could sell its equity share and tax the profits.

Slovakia's strategic location guarantees that the gas transit network will be a primary source of government revenue for the foreseeable future. Any actions should be taken with care and with a view to the long-term fiscal impact.

Enterprises in Financial Distress

Enterprise restructuring and liquidation must be accelerated. To survive in the new business environment, enterprises must reorganize, downsize their operations, shed excess labor, sell their nonproductive assets, improve the quality of their products, and find new markets. The longer adjustment is postponed, the higher the eventual costs to society: growth will be impeded by the continued misallocation of resources to nonviable operations, the private sector will be crowded out by the ever-growing financing needs of loss-making enterprises, and the banking system and other creditors will see a further rise in the losses they will eventually have to absorb. The question is how much the government should do to help resolve these underlying structural difficulties.

Many enterprises are reeling from the twin blows of the reform program and the breakdown of traditional trading arrangements. Financial distress is widespread among state enterprises and privatized enterprises. Nearly a third of the 419 state enterprises currently under the purview of the Ministry of Economy and a third of the 316 joint stock companies under partial or full National Property Fund ownership reported losses in 1992 (Table 3.5). In 1991-92, the largest losses occurred in the engineering industry, internal trade, machinery, pulp and paper, electric and electronic products, wood processing, construction, fuels, and textiles. As measured by primary insolvency, or the excess of overdue payables over overdue receivables, the worst performers are in engineering and electrical engineering, including fuels and energy and textiles. Summarized balance sheets for this group of enterprises are revealing (Table 3.6).

Ratio analysis confirms the existence of widespread financial distress. Joint-stock companies have high inventories, receivables, and payables. Debt-equity ratios are probably much higher than reported because the book value of capital may be significantly overstated under pre-1992 Slovak accounting rules and because balance sheets do not reflect overdue interest on bank loans and penalty interest on payables. The debt burden is likely to be especially high for enterprises that initiated large new investments right after the transformation in 1989. (The structure of enterprise liabilities is described in Box 3.6).

Losses are not confined to the industrial sector. Nearly all agricultural entities along the production chain are experiencing severe financial distress. Farms and farmers (public, cooperative, and private) had losses of Kcs 10 billion in 1991 and Kcs 13 billion in 1992. Food processing enterprises had losses of Kcs 5.3 billion in 1991-92. Agricultural services companies suffer because of the collapse in demand by farms and farmers for their services. In 1992, the Slovak part of the National Railway lost Kcs 1.6 billion, despite a decision to postpone Kcs 1.9 billion in depreciation charges. Road maintenance companies have been badly hit by government budget cuts for maintenance. Urban bus companies are reportedly in better financial shape, but that may be due to the large budget subsidies they receive.

Causes of Financial Distress

Industry. The collapse of the CMEA market and of the arms trade following a temporary federal government ban on arms export were the proximate causes of the financial difficulties of Slovak industrial enterprises. Adjustment to these shocks has been slow, and in some cases the response of enterprises and government has been perverse, increasing the eventual adjustment costs. Initial forced bank financing of enterprise losses and of conversion investments in key industries created enormous overindebtedness, and the subsequent financial distress experienced by a few large enterprises has been rapidly transmitted throughout the industrial and services sectors (Box 3.6). To a large extent, this transmission was the result of the inability to pay off affected enterprises, but there are also indications that the breakdown of financial discipline in a few large enterprises has generated an economywide erosion of payment discipline. The absence of adequate debt collection and enforcement mechanisms and the favorable terms of pre-1992 suppliers' credit probably encouraged enterprises to pass along their financial difficulties to their suppliers.

Agriculture. The initial losses in the agricultural sector can also be attributed largely to external shocks. The economic transformation initiated in 1990 caused real wages and domestic demand to fall. Trade liberalization subjected the sector to low-priced foreign competition, and though farm input prices were liberalized, output prices remained under government control. Liberalization of interest rates sharply raised financial costs (in 1992 alone, financial cost increased by Kcs 2.5 billion). The inefficiency of the distribution system and a severe drought in 1992 also contributed to the losses. In 1992, output prices were liberalized, and the distribution system was broken up and sold in the first wave of privatizations. Other than that, there has been little adjustment in the sector to date. Indeed, rather than encouraging adjustment, the government has responded by continuing to provide large subsidies to agriculture.

Table 3.5: Profitability of State Enterprises and Enterprises with Some National Property Fund Ownership, 1992
(Sk billion)

Summarized consolidated income	State enterprises under Ministry of Economy	Enterprises with National Property Fund ownership
Revenues		
Sales revenues	138.6	81.9
Other revenues	4.2	5.1
Subsidies	0.8	0.2
Total revenues	143.6	87.2
Costs		
Materials	87.3	60.6
Depreciation	11.6	5.9
Wages and wage-related charges	24.4	13.1
Interest expense (net)	8.2	5.4
Total costs	131.5	85.0
Gross profit	12.1	2.2
Profit-making enterprises	17.1	5.6
Loss-making enterprises	-5.0	-3.4
Taxes and penalties	9.5	3.0
Profit-making enterprises	9.4	2.9
Loss-making enterprises	0.1	0.1
Retained profit	2.6	-0.8
Profit-making enterprises	7.7	2.7
Loss-making enterprises	-5.1	-3.5
Memo items:		
Number of enterprises	419	316
Number of loss-makers	143	106
Return on sales (%)	1.9	-1.0
Return on assets (%)	0.9	-0.3
Return on capital (%)	1.4	-0.5
Subsidies as share pre-tax income (%)	6.7	9.3

Source: Ministry of Economy and National Property Fund.

Transport. Losses incurred by the railways were caused mainly by the collapse in domestic and cross-border trade and a rise in electricity prices unmet by any adjustment in transport tariffs. Transport tariffs are still regulated; not until April 1993 was the first tariff increase approved. While some adjustment has taken place (mainly labor shedding), the government has been providing increasingly large direct budget subsidies to the railways. The picture of enterprise losses and government response is very similar in urban road transport.

Table 3.6: Summarized Balance Sheet Data for State Enterprises and Enterprises with some National Property Fund Ownership, 1992 (Sk billion)		
Summarized balance sheet data	State enterprises under Ministry of Economy	Enterprises with National Property Fund ownership
Assets		
Cash	6.4	5.0
Receivables	48.4	39.1
Inventories	56.1	58.0
Fixed Assets	199.3	137.1
Other and adjustments	2.5	5.8
Total Assets	312.7	245.0
Liabilities		
Trade and other payables	35.8	22.6
Bank loans	55.2	37.9
Other	25.9	37.8
Total Liabilities	116.9	98.3
Basic capital and reserves	195.8	146.7
Memo items:		
Current ratio	1.0	1.4
Cash ratio	0.1	0.1
Ratio of total liabilities to equity	37:63	40:60
Inventory turnover (weeks)	33	50
Receivables turnover (weeks)	19	25
Payables turnover (weeks)	14	14

Source: Ministry of Economy and National Property Fund.

Enterprise response.   Enterprises initially responded to the shocks by continuing to produce for inventory. In certain sectors (arms, aluminum) large new investments were financed through forced bank lending and, more recently, National Property Fund loans and guarantees.   To preserve liquidity despite the collapse in sales, enterprises ran up overdues on their liabilities, first to the banking system and then to suppliers and the government. There are signs that these processes are coming to a halt and that enterprises are initiating the necessary structural adjustments to the changed business environment. Enterprises have started to lay off redundant workers, albeit slowly.   The rapid buildup of overdues pushed many enterprises toward up-front cash and barter payments. At the same time, to build up market share, enterprises are increasingly selling to new markets on medium- or long- term credit.   While these developments are favorable in many ways, the combination of cash purchases and credit sales is intensifying liquidity problems.

The government's response.   The government responded to the dual trade shocks by providing financial support to enterprises to cushion the impact or to finance conversion investments. In 1989, the State Bank (SBCS) started to make long-term loans to enterprises to finance conversion, and VUB provided new money for conversion and to cover enterprise losses. In 1991, the government started to issue loan guarantees for investment lending and for public investment projects.

Box 3.6: Structure of Enterprise Liabilities

The main enterprise liabilities are bank loans, interenterprise payables, and overdue tax and social security payments.

Bank credit to the enterprise sector as of end-1992 was Kcs 135 billion, one-third of it short term. Most of the long-term lending went to state enterprises during 1989-91 to finance environmental (aluminum) and reconversion (arms) investments. While some term loans (Kcs 16.2 billion at end-1992) carry direct government guarantees, most are unsecured. Some bank claims on enterprises privatized in the first wave enjoy one-year National Property Fund guarantees. Creditors have called guarantees for fifty small and medium-size enterprises privatized in the first wave, for an estimated total of less than Kcs 1 billion. Most bank loans to Slovak enterprises are held by VUB, Konsolidačna Banka, CSOB, Slovak Savings Bank, and Investični Banka. In addition, the Ministry of Finance holds approximately Kcs 12 billion of loans to foreign trade organizations, which financed losses incurred as a result of repeated devaluations of the Czechoslovak koruna and arms embargoes. Foreign banks, including Komercni Banka in the Czech Republic, also hold small claims on Slovak firms. Of total bank credit, Kcs 34.3 billion was overdue for three months or more as of the end of 1992. Banks have become increasingly reluctant to lend, even to enterprises with confirmed export orders. Thus the change in the total stock of lending to enterprises in 1992 was negative in real terms (7.9%), most notably to industry (11%). The services and construction sectors experienced a 3% increase in credit, while credit to the agricultural and mining sectors was virtually unchanged.

Interenterprise credit as of the end of 1992 for enterprises with the Ministry of Economy and the National Property Fund stood at Kcs 89 billion in receivables and Kcs 57 billion in payables, more than half of them overdue. A substantial part of both payables and receivables is cross-border: claims on former CMEA countries (estimated at around Kcs 6 billion) and on countries against which arms embargoes were established. The break up of Czechoslovakia also generated significant cross-border overdues, as enterprises in both republics wait for their governments to mutually settle claims. Other arrears (end-1992) include farms and farmers (owing Kcs 7.5 billion to suppliers of energy, spare parts, fertilizers and seeds, but with unpaid state farm claims of Kcs 2.5 billion for nonagricultural services—mainly construction and maintenance); food processing companies (owing farmers Kcs 2.5 billion, but with large claims on wholesale distributors who in turn have claims on retail shops); and railways (owing Kcs 1.3 billion to Slovnaft for oil supplies and to rail car maintenance companies, but with claims of Kcs 1.1 billion on customers, of which 50% is cross-border claims—mostly on Hungarian and Yugoslav railways). The stock of outstanding interenterprise credit increased by approximately 3% in real terms in 1992, while overdue payments on payables declined slightly (by 0.76%). Thus, the growth in interenterprise credit may already have come to a halt.

Tax and social security overdues are growing as a consequence of tight bank credit and increasing watchfulness over interenterprise credit. Of the 419 enterprises with the Ministry of Economy, only 193 paid all their taxes on time. For the industrial and services sectors, total tax arrears at the end of the first quarter of 1993 stood at Sk 14.9 billion. For the agriculture sector, tax arrears amounted to Sk 4.3 billion. At the same time, a number of enterprises are paying too much in taxes because their monthly tax payments are based on historic profits; seventy-three enterprises with the Ministry of Economy reportedly paid excess taxes of Sk 205 million in the first quarter of 1993.

The government also provided more direct support through subsidies. During 1991-92, the Slovak Republic alone provided Kcs 22 billion in current subsidies to Slovak enterprises and Kcs 8 billion in investment subsidies. Some enterprises also received indirect subsidies through subsidized energy prices. The government budgeted another Sk 21 billion in direct subsidies for enterprises in 1993 (Table 3.7). More recently, the government has started to use extrabudgetary means to channel resources to enterprises by requiring the National Property Fund to provide guarantees to individual enterprises.

Government financial support has merely postponed the necessary adjustment—including the eventual liquidation—of nonviable enterprises. In addition, the ensuing buildup of arrears and bad loans may well have pushed some enterprises into financial crisis that would have been profitable in a healthier economy with a well-functioning financial system. Few of the conversion investments initiated in 1989-91 would pass the market test of generating sufficient cash flow to repay the loans (on commercial terms) that finance them. Some enterprises are now experiencing severe liquidity problems, despite large investment subsidies. Where the investments did not succeed in rebuilding long-term viability, they must be considered sunk costs; the losses have already been incurred. Someone now has to absorb these losses, and market solutions must be found for dealing with the enterprises concerned: either further physical and financial restructuring or liquidation of nonviable activities. For enterprises that would be viable in a healthier economy, a market workout between the enterprise and its creditors is called for.

Table 3.7: Central Government Subsidies to Enterprises, Fiscal Year 1993 (Sk million)		
	Current subsidies	Investment subsidies
Industry		
Arms conversion	-	22.9
Restructuring, environment, energy (aluminum plant)	278.0	317.0
Coal mines (price support and severance pay)	561.5	-
Mineral mines and enterprises (closure)	70.7	-
Unallocated funds for restructuring	2,300.0	900.0
Agriculture		
Water resources, water treatment, and forestry	800 0	1,638.0
Price support and price subsidies	1,400.0	-
General subsidies to farmers (for feed stock, seeds)	7,000.0	-
Transport		
Railways and road maintenance	1,528.0	1,351.7
Airport reconstruction	408.0	-
Urban bus transport	1,980.0	-
Local government subsidies	-	430.0
Total subsidies	15,918.2	5,067.6
Source: Ministry of Finance		

The Role of the Government in Active Restructuring

Experience with restructuring suggests that while certain measures can have a very high payoff, others should probably be avoided unless there are new, private owners who are committed to the long-term development of the enterprise and who are prepared to assume the restructuring cost (Box 3.7). Measures that might be worth considering before privatization include:

- *Organizational restructuring*, which can appropriately be undertaken while an enterprise is in state hands. Such restructuring can include divestment of social assets (housing, schools, clinics) to local authorities (even when the assets are transferred free of charge, the enterprise will benefit by eliminating the cost of maintaining them) and divestment of other nonproductive assets or noncore business activities. Activities such as catering, transportation, and the like can be auctioned off and the services contracted out, often to groups of employees.

- *Financial restructuring,* which may be necessary to make an enterprise privatizable. In Hungary and Slovenia, for example, the state appointed specialists to estimate the amount of debt a company could bear based on its projected cash flow and to take measures to eliminate (or convert to equity) debt in excess of that amount. Financial restructuring should be done only in exceptional cases, where privatization proposals envisage breaking up a state-owned enterprise. The military equipment enterprise PPS Detva is one case in which such restructuring is probably both feasible and desirable (Box 3.8).

Box 3.7: Lessons on Restructuring from the Treuhand in Germany

While some of the achievements of the Treuhand, the agency established to oversee the privatization of state enterprises, in restructuring enterprises before privatization have been impressive, these have come at considerable cost:

- Staffing and technical assistance requirements are large. The Treuhand has some thirty staff members per hundred enterprises. In addition, enterprise supervisory board members with relevant market skills had to be recruited in the former Federal Republic of Germany.

- Restructuring and privatization costs are enormous relative to the proceeds from privatization. The Treuhand has spent about US$155 billion more on privatization and restructuring than it has received from the sale of enterprise shares and assets.

- The process takes time. The Treuhand intends to liquidate itself at the end of 1994. But, after two years of operation, there are still 2,000 enterprises (about 20% of Treuhand's original portfolio) that Treuhand has been unable to privatize or liquidate. Moreover, some privatized enterprises are coming back to the Treuhand, as the new owners find it difficult to make them viable.

A type of restructuring that should be avoided involves investments in new plant and equipment to modernize or otherwise improve a state-owned enterprise with a view to making it profitable. Where this has been tried, the results have usually been disappointing, with the subsequent privatization yielding less in returns than the cost of restructuring. For a privatized enterprise, however it may make sense for the government to provide subsidized technical assistance to the new private owners and managers to help them develop business plans that include investments for modernization and expansion. Establishing mechanisms for delivering this technical assistance should be a priority. Assistance to financial institutions to help them appraise business plans with a view to financing them may also be appropriate. The risks associated with investments should be borne by the enterprise owners and the financial institution, however, not by the government.

Box 3.8: Financial Restructuring—the Case of PPS Detva

PPS Detva was established in 1955 as a manufacturer of machines for the construction, agriculture, and defense industries. In 1965, the enterprise was incorporated into the VHJ Martin defense industry organization, but retained some independence in production decisions. By the late 1980s, Detva was producing 60% for defense, 30% construction and earthmoving equipment, and 10% special purpose tools and machines. In May 1990, the enterprise regained its independence, but lost most of its market for military production. Output dropped by 45%, and employment by 50%.

The company began to expand aggressively and to broaden its production of nonmilitary equipment. It is developing new lines of construction equipment and producing components for a variety of Western equipment producers including John Deere, Bitelli, and Hanomag-Komatsu. It is expanding exports to both east and west. Despite these positive developments, the company as a whole is bankrupt, saddled with debts and unsalable inventories related to its previous military production. One option would be to close down the whole operation and liquidate it. A better one would be to restructure the enterprise, carving out the viable operations from the nonviable and assessing a reasonable level of debt to be assumed by the new, smaller enterprise, which could then be privatized. The government would have to deal with the nonassumable debt, but it would have to do so in any event because it is still a fully state-owned enterprise.

Facilitating Market-Driven Restructuring

Though its role in direct enterprise restructuring should be limited, the government is of key importance in *facilitating* restructuring efforts, particularly through:

- Enforcing a hard budget constraint.
- Leaving debt workouts to the market.
- Drawing up policies for enterprises that will remain in state hands.
- Defining government's role as owner, regulator, and creditor of enterprises.

Enforcing a hard budget constraint. By rapidly phasing out subsidies and abolishing loans and guarantees, the government could signal to enterprises that they will have to renegotiate their debt and attract commercial financing if they want to survive.

Leaving debt workouts to the market. Another important cornerstone of government policy should be to leave enterprise restructuring as much as possible to market players. The government already subscribed to this principle in the first wave of privatization. In enterprises privatized in the first wave, creditors and equity holders have risk capital at stake, and thus an incentive to maximize the return on their investment while minimizing risk. For the remaining state enterprises, creditors and incumbent management and workers are well placed to develop restructuring plans; they know their enterprise best and might become stakeholders in the process of restructuring and privatization. The government as an equity holder in both partially privatized and state-owned firms should assume a passive role.

Viable business propositions need a capital and debt structure that makes them financially viable. An enterprise with too much debt and too little capital needs financial restructuring. For market-based debt and equity financing to develop, the normal ranking of different classes of creditors (secured, senior, junior, subordinated) and equity holders (preferred, common) should be respected as much as possible. Violation of this principle would retard development of the capital market by eroding confidence.

A menu of options is generally used to maintain the ranking of creditors and equity holders in debt workouts. A menu approach may also accommodate different creditor and shareholder preferences that can be honored without violating their relative ranking. The most commonly used options are debt restructuring (changing the maturity or terms of a loan), debt forgiveness of all or part of a loan), debt buybacks (a debtor buying back debt at a discount), debt-equity-swaps, and new loans. There are numerous other financial instruments that can be used in a debt workout, but a good workout does not have to be complex or sophisticated to be successful. There may be some merit, however, to encouraging an outcome that leaves an enterprise with at least some debt. Because debt needs to be serviced regularly, it subjects companies to financial discipline in a way that an all-equity-company, which has to pay dividends only when it makes a profit, does not experience. In judging restructuring and privatization proposals, the government ought to keep this consideration in mind.

Drawing up policies for enterprises remaining in state hands. Despite all its best efforts to foster market-based enterprise restructuring and privatization, the government will not be able to avoid taking responsibility for the restructuring and liquidation of all enterprises. Some already privatized companies may fail to work out market solutions, and creditors might call in their government or National Property Fund guarantees. Paying out the guarantees would make the government the de facto new owner of the company. The government also may regain ownership of a company's equity if it fails to pay its taxes.

The government should encourage bottom-up restructuring initiatives by workers and managers in the context of privatization; such initiatives will relieve the government of responsibility for having to undertake the necessary restructuring itself. If such initiatives are not endorsed, the alternative would be for the government to retain ownership of firms that cannot be sold at any price. Realistically, the government will have to retain ownership of some state enterprises whose management is passive or uncooperative. For these enterprises, the government will have to assume responsibility to reprivatize or liquidate them. An efficient, out-of-court mechanism will be needed for liquidating enterprises that allows assets tied up in these firms to be quickly released for alternative uses. Although the government has slated over one hundred enterprises for liquidation, the process is slow, and only a few liquidations have been completed. The government may have to engage the assistance of external institutions such as investment banks for enterprises that are to be reprivatized to ensure speedy divestiture. To reduce the risk of political pressure on the government to postpone liquidation and to resume providing direct budget support, sunset provisions could be put in place calling for the automatic liquidation of any enterprise not privatized or reprivatized within a certain period.

Defining the government's role as owner, regulator, and creditor. As owner, regulator and, frequently, an important creditor, the government can facilitate adjustment and restructuring by addressing a number of important problems:

- *Government claims.* As a creditor by virtue of overdue tax and social security contributions, the government may simplify debtor-creditor negotiations by developing a policy of standard treatment of its claims. Such a policy would remove uncertainty for other creditors and equity holders about the government's willingness to match their concessions.

- *Interenterprise arrears.* There is merit in netting out interenterprise credit. Many suppliers incurred claims early in the transformation process, before they had any way of knowing which firms were bad credit risks. These old claims might be legitimate candidates for a netting out exercise. Netting out, when it occurs in the context of a government policy that ensures subsequent restructuring and privatization, may simplify market-based debt workouts. Thus far, the Slovak government's approach to netting out has avoided some of the pitfalls of such schemes in other countries (Box 3.3).[6]

- *Environmental liabilities.* There is a need to clarify the legal responsibility for environmental clean-up costs. Contingent environmental liabilities should be brought onto the balance sheet and included in debt workouts. For enterprises still to be privatized, the government has agreed that the buyer is responsible for clean-up costs identified at the time of privatization, but that these costs will be deducted from the selling price. Any environmental liabilities discovered after the assessment made at the time of privatization will be the responsibility of the government. This policy will make Slovakia far more attractive to private investors, especially foreigners. For firms already in private hands, a case-by-case evaluation will be needed. The government will also have to decide on pollution clean-up standards, whether EU standards, current Slovak standards, or some new standards. Environmental audits will be conducted prior to privatization to clarify the timing of the damage, the standards for environmental protection, and the necessary clean-up costs.

- *Social assets.* The government should develop a policy for divesting the social assets of state enterprises. These assets are often a source of losses for enterprises. In the first wave of privatization, most enterprises were privatized with all their social assets, allowing losses to continue to build up at the expense of the new equity owners. In the second wave of privatization, the government should define a policy that allows enterprises that wish to do so to pass on social assets to municipalities free of charge. Enterprises sold in the first wave that would like to divest their social assets should be given the same opportunity. The government may need to adjust the tax and revenue base of municipalities to accommodate this policy. Municipalities will get social assets that cannot be given away to existing tenants or occupants because maintenance costs exceed current rents. They will need resources to cover maintenance costs in the interim period until rents are liberalized.

- *Financial assistance for liquidation.* The government may consider providing targeted financial assistance to enterprises that will be liquidated. Such assistance could

---

6   Claims on and liabilities of individual enterprises will differ in quality (the likelihood of repayment will be higher for a claim on a good enterprise than for a claim on a bad enterprise). Thus the process may reward enterprises whose receivables, if marked to market, are worth less than their payables, and punish enterprises whose receivables are worth more than their payables. There is a risk of a netting-out exercise being used as an outright instrument to provide across-the-board debt relief to enterprises. The experiences of Romania and Russia are instructive. In Romania, the government required banks to refinance overdue payables, thus merely shifting bad enterprise debt onto the books of the banks. In Russia, the government replaced both net payables and receivables with government bonds; however, the government did not subsequently enforce its claims, but it does service the bonds it issued in exchange for receivables. One round of netting out may create expectations of another round, with enterprises anticipating such a repeat exercise by running up new arrears. In short, netting-out interenterprise credit may have potentially adverse effects on financial discipline if not carefully designed and managed.

encompass severance pay and retraining of laid-off workers and the costs of closing down operations and environmental clean-up.

- *Financial discipline.* To ensure that restructuring efforts undertaken by market players have a lasting impact, the government should take measures to strengthen financial discipline in enterprises that have been restructured. Debt collection and enforcement rules will need to be substantially strengthened.

CHAPTER 4: EMPLOYMENT AND LABOR MARKET DEVELOPMENT

The transition to a market economy has entailed major changes in the level and structure of employment. The collapse of CMEA exports affected Slovakia more than other countries in the region, because of Slovakia's greater dependence on exports to CMEA partners.[1] Major job losses have occurred in the public sector, particularly in trade, construction, and certain heavy industries. In many enterprises, managers are delaying staff layoffs by instituting involuntary part-time work or extended holidays. These delays have led to considerable labor redundancy, as evidenced by the greater decline in labor productivity in Slovakia than in other transition economies.

Unemployment has nonetheless risen rapidly, the Slovak government has made rapid progress in coping with unemployment by providing unemployment benefits and employment services. The benefits are administered by a network of 137 local employment offices, which also provide job placement services and requalification training. As enterprise restructuring proceeds, further unemployment is inevitable. If workers are to be matched with new jobs, it will be essential that actions be taken that make it easier for workers to switch jobs, including requalification training, nationwide job placement services, and privatization of housing. Unemployment should also fall as a result of policies to encourage small business development and, eventually, a reduction in payroll taxes that discriminate against hiring. Such policies will only be effective if the social safety net preserves incentives to work while protecting the truly needy. This chapter describes the recent evolution of employment in Slovakia and the measures adopted to deal with unemployment.

Labor Force Growth

Population growth has been declining almost continuously in Slovakia from 1.8% a year in the mid-1950s to less than 0.5% currently. This slowing of population growth implies a gradual aging of the population, which stood at 5.3 million people in the 1991 census, and a rising share for the working-age population (people fifteen to fifty-nine years old). Under the World Bank's current population projections for Slovakia, the share of the working-age population is projected to rise from 59.7% of the population in 1990 to 63.1% in 2005. During that period, the working-age population is projected to grow at an average rate of 0.9% a year—about twice the projected rate of population growth—a legacy of higher fertility rates in the past.

This growth in the working-age population is likely to be overshadowed by prospective changes in labor force participation—particularly of women. Labor force participation by women in Slovakia has been among the highest in the world. At the time of the Velvet Revolution, the average participation rate was virtually the same for women (83.0%) and men (83.3%). By comparison, average participation rates in 1989 were the same for men but only about 59% for women in OECD countries and 81% for men and 70% for women in Central and Eastern European countries.[2] The extraordinarily high participation rate for women in Slovakia reflects social norms that encouraged paid employment for

---

1   For example, by 1991, Slovak exports to CMEA partners had fallen by almost 30 percent from 1989 levels but still accounted for 42 percent of Slovakia's exports. In contrast, Czech exports to CMEA partners accounted for just 29 percent of total Czech exports in 1991.

2   *OECD Employment Outlook,* July 1991, Chapter 1, Table A.2.

all adults; low wages and employment-related benefits, which together provided little surplus for support of other family members; generous maternity benefits for working women; and good child-care provisions—often employer provided.

Since the start of the reforms, female labor force participation has dropped sharply, falling to 68.0% in 1992. International experience suggests that declines in labor force participation will result largely from declines in female participation. In Slovakia, the incentives for both husbands and wives to work will weaken as productivity differences lead to greater wage dispersion (allowing some families to afford a nonworking spouse), as public maternity benefits are scaled back, and as child-care facilities are privatized and their services priced accordingly. The tendency for women workers to withdraw from the labor force could be partially offset if the retirement age for women were raised—a measure that is desirable for reasons of equity and the economy.[3]

The effects of this decline are apparent in recent changes in the labor force. From mid-1990 through the end of 1992, the working-age population grew steadily at about 0.5% a year, but the recorded labor force (based on data on registered employment and unemployment) contracted at an average rate of 0.4 % a year—largely because of the effects of declining female participation. In the first quarter of 1993, however, the registered labor force increased by over 40,000 (Table 4.1). If this reported figure is accurate, it implies a significant and rapid increase in labor force participation that could be signaling a deterioration in real household incomes in line with the fall in real wages since the start of the transition.

Table 4.1: Quarterly Changes in Employment and Registered Unemployment, 1990-93 (thousands)					
Quarter ending	Employment[a]	Unemployment[a]	Labor force[a]	Unemployment rate (%)	Recipients of unemployment compensation
March 1990	2,463.7	2.7	2,466.4	0.1	0.0
June 1990	2,526.8	5.8	2,532.6	0.2	0.0
September 1990	2,520.6	21.1	2,541.7	0.8	0.0
December 1990	2,515.4	39.6	2,555.0	1.6	25.0
March 1991	2,461.5	94.8	2,556.3	3.7	61.0
June 1991	2,392.6	161.4	2,554.0	6.3	105.0
September 1991	2,311.1	244.0	2,555.1	9.6	194.0
December 1991	2,252.6	302.0	2,554.6	11.8	254.6
March 1992	2,198.0	307.4	2,505.4	12.3	147.5
June 1992	2,224.9	282.3	2,507.2	11.3	96.8
September 1992	2,239.7	266.1	2,505.8	10.6	87.8
December 1992	2,247.2	260.3	2,507.5	10.4	87.3
March 1993	2,242.5	306.1	2,548.6	12.0	108.3

[a] Including women on maternity leave.
Source: Slovak Ministry of Labor, Social Affairs, and Family.

---

3   The normal age of retirement is sixty years old for men and fifty-seven years old for women. Women with children may retire up to two years earlier.

Another change in the composition of the labor force is in the share of working people older than the normal retirement age. That share dropped from 7.5% of the labor force at the end of 1990 to 5.5% at the end of 1991 and 1.8% at the end of 1992, according to the December 1992-February 1993 household labor force survey of the Slovak Institute of Statistics. The decline reflects the tendency of restructuring enterprises to make their staff cuts first among those who are eligible for retirement. This group's share in the labor force is likely to remain negligible for the immediate future.

Characteristics of the Labor Force

The Slovak labor force constitutes a major source of comparative advantage for the economy. It is both highly skilled and highly competitive. Labor costs in Slovakia are less than one-tenth as high as in many of the OECD countries (including Austria), and are one-third the level in Greece, the least-cost European member of OECD (Table 4.2).

Table 4.2: Hourly Nonagricultural Labor Costs in Slovakia and Selected Comparator Countries	
(U.S. dollars)	
Country	Average hourly labor cost
Austria	18.31
France	19.23
Greece	4.19
Ireland	5.34
Netherlands	22.78
Slovakia	1.40

Note: Figures for countries other than Slovakia are average nonagricultural labor costs to employers (including payroll taxes and benefits). The figure for Slovakia is based on the average gross private sector wage as reported by the Ministry of Labor, plus the employer's 38% contribution under the new social insurance programs.

Source: Slovak Ministry of Labor, Social Affairs, and Family; ILO, *Yearbook of Labor Statistics, 1992.*

Education

The educational attainment of the labor force in Slovakia compares favorably with that in the most advanced OECD countries (Table 4.3). It is higher than in several OECD countries (Austria and Italy) and many Central and Eastern European countries. Slovakia's education system is well developed at all levels. A striking feature of the system is the very high share (83% in 1990/91) of secondary enrollments in vocational or technical specializations, a distribution reflecting an allocation process in the command economy favoring industrial technology. The quality of education and training programs is generally high, although there are some deficiencies. The most important is that preservice vocational education and training is offered too early and in too narrowly defined occupational specializations, limiting subsequent job flexibility and job mobility. Another problem that will need to be dealt with is the disintegration of the former enterprise-based apprenticeship training programs, a casualty of the precarious financial situation of most enterprises.[4]

Table 4.3: Educational Attainment of the Labor Force in Slovakia and Selected Comparator Countries (percentage distribution)				
Country (year)	Basic or less	Vocational	Secondary	Higher
Austria (1990)	28.8	57.8	6.3	7.1
Bulgaria (1990)	44.6	15.8	30.0	9.6
France (1989)	35.3	46.0		14.6
Greece (1989)	52.6	35.3		11.4
Hungary (1990)	38.4	23.1	26.9	11.6
Ireland (1989)	26.8	55.5		17.5
Italy (1990)	26.6	66.2		7.2
Netherlands (1989)	12.6	61.3		19.7
Poland (1988)	34.2	29.5	27.9	8.4
Romania (1990)	35.8	31.4	24.0	8.8
Slovakia (1993)	13.5	41.5	32.4	12.6

Source: Slovak Institute of Statistics (household labor force survey data); data for other countries from Nicholas Barr et al., *Labor Markets and Social Policy in Central and Eastern Europe: The Transition and Beyond*. Oxford University Press, forthcoming.

Wages

Under the command economy in Czechoslovakia, wages were among the most compressed of any country, reflecting social norms rather than embodied human capital and the relative scarcity of specific skills.[5] Wages were liberalized in 1990, though an excess-wage tax was imposed until December 1992 to control costs. In most enterprises, wages are now set by tripartite (firm, employees, government) collective bargaining. Wages are otherwise subject to the general minimum wage—currently, Sk 2,450 (US$ 82) per month—and to a schedule of occupation- and industry-specific minimums set by the

---

4   "Education and Training in Czechoslovakia," 1991, Birks, Sinclair, and Associates, March; and "Czech and Slovak Republics, PHARE Labor Market Restructuring Programme, Strategic Review of Vocational Education and Training, Draft Policy Statement," 1993, Birks, Sinclair, and Associates, in consultation with the Institute for Educational Research, Bratislava, and the Research Institute for Technical and Vocational Education, Prague, January.

5   Luis A. Riveros, 1991, "Wage and Employment Reforms in Czechoslovakia: A Policy Analysis"; and Richard Jackman and Michael Rutkowski, 1993, "Labour Markets," in Nicholas Barr et. al., *Labour Markets and Social Policy in Central and Eastern Europe*: The Transition and Beyond. Oxford University Press, forthcoming.

Ministry of Labor. Though there are no longer any legal or tax constraints on maximum wages, the withdrawal of subsidies has imposed a binding financial constraint on wages for most enterprises.

Real industrial wages fell by almost 30% in 1991 as newly liberalized prices rose rapidly early in the year. Wage hikes and more modest price growth the following year allowed a partial recovery of real wages by 10.9% between March 1991 and December 1992 (Table 4.4). On balance, however, real wages remain below the level at the start of the transition, and wages are very low in absolute terms—equivalent, on average, to US$179 a month. Wage dispersion is beginning to emerge, with average real wages increasing 76% over the period in the banking and insurance sector and 27% in budgetary and subsidized organizations—mostly schools and hospitals—and falling by more than 11% in agriculture. The two sectors with the highest average wage increases during the period were also the only sectors with gains in employment, suggesting that wages are beginning to perform their labor allocation role (Table 4.4).

Table 4.4: Average Monthly Wages and Employment, March 1991 and December 1992						
	Average monthly wage (1992 Kcs)			Employment (thousands)		
Sector	March 1991	December 1992	Percentage change	March 1991	December 1992	Percentage Change
Public enterprises, more than 25 employees						
Agriculture	5,125	4,542	-11.4	305	234	-23
Industry and energy	5,296	5,283	-0.2	733	574	-22
Construction	5,194	5,464	5.2	161	117	-27
Transport and communications	5,317	5,201	-2.2	95	79	-17
Trade	4,648	4,750	2.2	160	111	-31
Banking and insurance	5,944	10,440	75.6	10	17	+70
Other services	5,240	5,663	8.1	92	76	-17
Sectorwide	5,197	5,307	2.1	1,557	1,208	-22
Public enterprises, fewer than 25 employees	na	na	na	6	10	+67
Public budgetary and subsidized organizations	4,588	5,802	26.5	406	443	+9
Private sector (estimated)	na	7,000	na	60	400	+667
All sectors	5,230	5,800	10.9	2,029	2,062	+2

na is not available.
Source: Slovak Institute of Statistics, and Ministry of Labor, Social Affairs, and Family.

Unemployment

Open unemployment first appeared early in 1990. Initially very small, it grew exponentially to about 300,000 by the end of 1991, then subsided slowly through most of 1992 before rising again to more than 300,000 early in 1993 (see Table 4.1). Unemployment benefits began to be paid in December 1990 and rose steadily through the end of 1991. They declined sharply thereafter as a large number of long-term unemployed exhausted their eligibility for benefits. The number of people receiving unemployment benefits rose again at the start of 1993 as the number of newly unemployed exceeded the number of people whose benefits had expired. There is evidence that the private sector is absorbing a growing number of the labor force (see Table 4.4), although registered unemployment rates remained more or less unchanged through 1992 and 1993, the early stages of enterprise restructuring in Slovakia. Further unemployment is likely as enterprise restructuring proceeds.

Gender, Education, and Regional Differences

The most complete information available on the characteristics of the unemployed comes from the new quarterly household labor force survey. (For problems with unemployment data from other sources, see the appendix at the end of this chapter.) Unemployment rates vary significantly with educational attainment (Table 4.5). They are highest for both men and women at the lowest level of educational attainment (no formal schooling). Unemployment rates are strikingly low for university graduates, particularly for men (2.7%). Graduates of secondary-level technical diploma programs, which include specialized training in fields such as nursing, have the next lowest unemployment rate—about 8% for men and women—lower than graduates of other technical and vocational programs, including the numerous apprenticeship programs. There is no difference in overall unemployment rates between men and women, but there are some large gender differences in unemployment rates for particular educational categories. Among elementary school graduates and general secondary school graduates, unemployment rates are conspicuously lower for women than for men. It is difficult to attribute a cause to any of these findings without further information on each category of graduates.

Regional differences in unemployment rates are substantial, with rates ranging from 20% in Rimavská Sobota to 4% in Central Bratislava. In general, the highest rates of unemployment are in the south and southeast, and the lowest in central Slovakia. Unemployment rates are below average in the larger cities (such as Bratislava, Banská Bystrica, Martin, Košice, and Zilina), though the absolute numbers are high. Economic diversification in the larger cities makes them less vulnerable to plant closures than smaller communities dominated by a single employer. Agricultural communities have also been affected by the reduction of agricultural subsidies.

The persistence of large regional differences in unemployment is a symptom of labor immobility. Contributing factors include housing market rigidities, the local focus of job information available at most employment offices, and, in some cases, excessively generous social benefits.[6] Remedies to improve labor mobility include housing privatization, better labor market information on job prospects nationwide, rationalization of social benefits, and measures to ensure that pensions are portable.

---

6   The 1991 Employment Act stipulated that unemployment beneficiaries could refuse a job offer and continue to receive unemployment benefits if suitable housing was not available. This provision has been interpreted generously, although a proposal is under development to tighten this provision.

Table 4.5: Unemployment Rates by Educational Attainment and Gender, First Quarter, 1993 (thousands)			
Educational attainment	Employment	Unemployment	Unemployment rate (%)
No schooling			
Male	0.4	1.0	71.4
Female	0.4	1.7	81.0
Elementary			
Male	113.7	43.0	27.4
Female	158.7	38.7	19.6
Skilled			
Male	462.4	63.8	12.1
Female	205.8	32.7	13.7
Skilled with diploma			
Male	48.7	8.7	15.2
Female	17.8	4.2	19.1
Secondary technical			
Male	115.7	13.3	10.3
Female	63.2	10.4	14.1
Secondary technical with diploma			
Male	231.3	21.1	8.4
Female	287.4	25.5	8.1
Secondary general			
Male	26.1	6.4	19.7
Female	50.4	5.3	9.5
University			
Male	153.6	4.3	2.7
Female	105.3	6.6	5.9
Total			
Male	1,152.9	161.6	12.3
Female	889.0	125.2	12.3

Note: Skilled refers to graduates of technical and vocational programs, including apprenticeship programs.
Source: Slovak Institute of Statistics, household labor force survey.

Duration of Unemployment

As of the first quarter of 1993, most unemployment for both men and women was either very recent (less than three months) or of one to two years duration (Figure 4.1).[7] Some 11% of unemployed men and 20% of unemployed women described themselves as having been unemployed for longer than two years. One of the practical implications of the duration of unemployment is eligibility for unemployment benefits, which expires after six months. After that, the unemployed are eligible for a variety of social benefits and social assistance.

---

[7] Female employees on maternity leave, who numbered 148,000 in the first quarter of 1993, are not counted among the unemployed.

Under the socialist system, employment was guaranteed and the state assumed responsibility for meeting the welfare needs of all citizens, so personal savings were unnecessary—and opportunities for personal savings and investment were virtually nonexistent. Under a market economy, personal savings could eventually provide a buffer against income loss from all sources, including long-term unemployment. But right now, few people have any personal savings to draw on, and the unemployed depend on unemployment and related benefits to meet their welfare needs. Since almost 60% of the unemployed have been unemployed for longer than six months, the adequacy of social benefits for the long-term unemployed is a major issue (chapter 5).

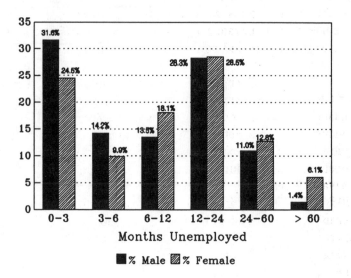

Figure 4.1: Duration of Unemployment First Quarter 1993

Months Unemployed
■ % Male ▨ % Female

Source: Institute of Statistics, quaterly household labor force survey.

Causes of Unemployment

Although the prevailing impression is that virtually all recent job losses are the result of restructuring, more than 40 percent of the unemployed interviewed in the household labor force survey—42% of unemployed men and 41% of unemployed women—reported that they had lost their jobs for other reasons, including personal and health reasons.[8] The details of the job losses for this group merit further investigation to determine, for example, whether features of the social benefits programs may have impaired work incentives.

Employment and Productivity

Although the decline in employment since the start of the transition has been significant, at just over 3.0% a year (see Table 4.1), it would have been far greater were it not for the dynamism of the private sector in making up for some of the jobs lost in the public sector. Using indirect techniques that rely on new enterprise registration and tax data to capture data on small private enterprises, which are missed by the quarterly enterprise surveys, the Institute of Statistics has estimated the evolution of employment in public and private sector enterprises over the past two years (see Table 4.5). (Because they are derived from different sources, these data are not comparable to the official employment and unemployment registration data in Table 4.1.) These data provide a useful first view of the recent growth of private sector employment. Between March 1991 and December 1992, public sector employment is estimated to have declined by 16%

---

8   Job loss from restructuring is defined as job loss due to termination of business activities or to redundancy.

most of it in small enterprises, to have increased almost sevenfold (from about 60,000 to about 400,000).[9] More than three-fourths of estimated private-sector employment is self-employment (single-person ventures), distributed roughly equally in industry, construction, commerce, and other services.[10] A critical question is whether private sector employment will grow fast enough in the future to reduce the unemployment rate and offset further—inevitable and desirable—reductions in employment in public sector enterprises and newly privatized enterprises.

Changes in the composition of public sector employment reflect, above all, the collapse of CMEA trade, particularly in industrial and chemical products, but also the first steps toward more balance in the composition of output and employment, away from the bias in favor of heavy industry and against services. Between March 1991 and December 1992, the trade sector lost the largest share of public sector jobs, experiencing a decline of 31% (Table 4.4). This decline reflects the privatization of most retail shops during the period and should be offset by an equivalent growth of employment in private retail trade. Employment in banking and insurance, though small in absolute terms, grew by 70%. Employment in small public enterprises also grew significantly but remains negligible in absolute terms. Employment in budgetary and subsidized organizations—mostly schools and health facilities— increased slightly (for reasons that are not clear). Employment in industrial enterprises, the largest category of employment, contracted at the same rate as overall enterprise employment. Within industry, the greatest absolute declines in employment occurred in machine tool manufacture, consumer products, and chemicals (Ministry of Economy data).

Using declining labor productivity as a rough indicator of the labor redundancy that results when labor shedding by enterprises does not keep pace with the output declines associated with restructuring shows less labor shedding in Slovakia in 1991 than in some other transition economies (Table 4.6).[11] With the exception of mining and metal refining, all industries have experienced falling

---

9   Public sector employment is defined as employment in central government, budgetary organizations, and subsidized organizations. These figures also include employment in the enterprises privatized during the first wave of the coupon privatization scheme, because the data series had not yet been adjusted to account for the change in status. These figures appear to exaggerate the importance of private sector employment growth in relation to public sector job loss. In particular, the series shows total employment as essentially the same in December 1992 and March 1991, whereas registered employment fell by 215,000 during that period (Table 4.4).

10   *OECD Employment Outlook,* July 1992, Table 6.4.

11   This is a useful, but crude measure of labor redundancy that ignores such considerations as nonconstant returns to scale, changing technology, and changes in factor proportions and average productivity resulting from changes in relative factor prices. (The merits of alternative measures of labor redundancy are discussed in Jan Svejnar and Katherine Terrell, 1991,"Reducing Labor Redundancy in State-Owned Enterprises," Policy Research Working Paper 792, World Bank, Urban Development Department, Transport Division, Washington, D.C., October.

labor productivity (Table 4.7).[12] The declines have been especially severe in the machine tool and consumer appliance subsectors, which account for almost half of industrial-sector employment.[13]

Table 4.6: Changes in Output, Employment and Productivity in Selected Transition Economies, 1990 and 1991 (percent)					
	Bulgaria	Romania	Hungary	Poland	Slovakia
Change from 1989 to 1990					
GDP	-11.8	-7.4	-3.3	-11.6	-2.5
Employment	-6.1	-0.2	-2.0	-3.6	-0.1
Labor productivity	-5.7	-7.2	-1.3	-8.0	-2.4
Industrial output	-16.8	-19.0	-9.2	-24.2	-2.7
Industrial employment	-8.2	-0.5	-8.8	-4.7	-2.0
Industrial labor productivity	-8.6	-18.5	-0.4	-19.5	-0.7
Change from 1990 to 1991					
GDP	-17.0	-14.0	-10.0	-9.0	-14.5
Employment	-14.5	-11.6	-6.0	-5.5	-7.9
Labor productivity	-2.5	-2.4	-4.0	-3.5	-7.9
Industrial output	-27.8	-18.7	-19.0	-11.9	-26.8
Industrial employment	-16.9	-9.5	-8.8	-7.0	-7.8
Industrial labor productivity	-10.9	-9.2	-10.2	-4.9	-19.0

Source: World Bank staff estimates based on data from the Slovak Institute of Statistics; and *OECD Employment Outlook*, July 1992.

There is evidence that managers of many enterprises are delaying layoffs as long as possible. In some enterprises, employees are placed on involuntary part-time status or extended holiday because there is not enough work to occupy them productively full-time. Other enterprises are operating at half capacity, their employees working on alternating half-time shifts. For some potentially viable enterprises, these reduced working hours can be viewed as a temporary solution, but they may simply be delaying the restructuring of enterprises that could be made viable. For enterprises with no prospects of viability, delays in shedding labor slow the reallocation of labor to more productive activities, prolong a paternalistic model of the enterprise that is inappropriate to a market economy, inhibit the emergence of a work ethic in which earnings are related to productivity, and are a more costly alternative to other forms of support for the unemployed.

---

12   Total employment in industrial enterprises under the responsibility of the Ministry of Economy numbers 570,000, accounting for virtually all of industrial output.

13   Compared to the labor force necessary to produce the 1992 level of industrial output at the average labor productivity of 1990. While this estimate could overstate labor redundancy by failing to account for possible staffing rigidities involved in shrinking production, it may understate redundancy to the extent that recent technological progress allows lower labor inputs, and production in 1990 already embodied a certain amount of labor redundancy.

Table 4.7: Changes in Industrial Output, Employment, and Labor Productivity, 1990-1992 (percent)			
Industry	Change in output 1990-92	Change in employment 1990-92	Change in productivity 1991-93
Energy	-23.0	-7.3	-15.7
Mining and metal refining	-27.8	-33.2	+5.4
Chemicals	-32.1	-18.8	-13.3
Wood products	-21.1	-5.6	-15.5
Consumer appliances	-43.4	-14.7	-28.7
Machine tool manufacture	-47.5	-20.8	-26.7
Electrical and electronics	-57.6	-43.1	-14.5
Building materials	-25.1	-20.2	-4.9
Total	-34.7	-20.6	-14.1

Source: Slovak Ministry of Economy.

Employment Policies and Programs

Virtually all economic policies and programs that affect the level and composition of national output also affect employment. In addition, a broad range of policies and programs affect employment directly, by making it more (or less) costly for employers to hire and fire employees, or by helping job seekers find jobs. Such measures include restrictions on hiring and firing workers, payroll taxes (which raise the cost of labor to employers), and social benefits, which may create a disincentive to work.

Unemployment Insurance

Because some unemployment is inevitable in a market economy, a program of budget-funded unemployment benefits was created in the Czech and Slovak Federation in December 1990, and a national network of offices was established to administer the benefits. Initially, the program was far too generous. All unemployed workers who had been employed at least twelve months during the previous three years were eligible for benefits at 90% of prior wages (without a specified ceiling) for the first six months and 60% for a second six months.[14] Unemployed people who did not meet this employment requirement but had recently completed school, military service, maternity leave, or officially sanctioned child care were also eligible to receive benefits.

---

14   These are more generous than benefits in some OECD countries in several respects. For comparisons of unemployment insurance programs in the OECD countries, see *OECD Employment Outlook, July 1991*; and Daniel S. Hamermesh, 1992, "Unemployment Insurance: Goals, Structure, Economic Impacts, and Transferability to Developing Countries," World Bank Discussion Paper, Washington, D.C.

Concerns about the cost of the program and its possible disincentive effects led to three successive amendments. In January 1992, benefits were reduced to 60% of prior wages (to a maximum of Kcs 3,000 per month) for a total of six months. As an incentive to seek requalification training, benefits were raised to 70% of prior earnings for the unemployed who were pursuing such training. Training benefits are not limited to the same six-month duration as regular unemployment benefits. The Ministry of Labor recently proposed tighter eligibility criteria to control costs in a period of rising unemployment. The replacement rate would be lowered to an average of 55% of prior earnings for regular unemployment beneficiaries and for those on training. The conditions under which beneficiaries could refuse job offers and continue to receive benefits would also be made stricter. A related issue is whether flat benefits ought to be introduced. Unemployment benefits in 1992 ranged from Sk 1,000 to Sk 3,000 a month, reflecting the extreme compression of wages in the past. With such a limited range in benefits, the additional cost of administering variable benefits may not be justified. A switch to flat benefits might be more efficient, unless public acceptance of the employment insurance scheme depends on earnings being related to benefits.

Unemployment benefits were initially financed from the general budget. In January 1993, payroll taxes began to be collected in preparation for financing benefits under a compulsory national unemployment insurance program. Employers are required to pay 3% of each employee's salary and to withhold 1% for unemployment insurance contributions. The self-employed are required to pay 4% of their earnings. Since January 1994, unemployment insurance contributions have been paid into a new employment fund to cover the cost of active and passive employment programs. Total payroll taxes for social program—including contributions to the employment fund and the new health insurance and social insurance programs—come to 50% of gross wage earnings, 38% in employer contributions and 12% in employee contributions. Such a high rate of taxation could be a significant deterrent to employment creation, even though much of the employer's contribution is no doubt shifted to employees. A tax that is more neutral in its effects on factor allocation, such as an income or value added tax, might be a preferable source of financing for unemployment benefits.

Some consideration ought to be given to whether unemployment benefits and training should continue to be provided entirely under an insurance format. In general, insurance financed by individual contributions is desirable to encourage a sense of individual responsibility in providing for personal risks, but there are limitations to the applicability of insurance programs. Insurance is appropriate for risks with an observable probability distribution that can be used to define appropriate benefits and contributions. If risks are not known, benefit and contribution levels cannot be set to ensure that revenues will equal costs over time. In the case of unemployment, the risks may be known for frictional or cyclical unemployment, but not for the transitional unemployment associated with major restructuring. To reflect this difference, a program could be established with insurance financing of benefits for frictional unemployment, however defined, and budget financing of benefits for the higher, transitional unemployment expected during economic restructuring. This approach would probably allow payroll taxes to be lowered as well, reducing their employment disincentive effect (see below).

At current contribution and benefit rates, the employment fund is projected to run a sizable surplus within a few years, with the amount varying according to three alternative assumptions about the time path of unemployment, GDP growth, and inflation. The different assumptions affect the timing, but not the outcome of continuing surplus. This finding suggests that the contribution rate is too high in relation to benefits, but the employment fund has not, in fact, run a surplus since its introduction in January 1994.

The number of people receiving unemployment benefits, which is normally limited to six months for any episode of unemployment, rose along with unemployment until the end of 1991 (see Table 4.1). The number of beneficiaries declined sharply in early 1992, as the eligibility period for many beneficiaries expired. It began to rise again at the start of 1993 as newly dismissed workers became eligible for benefits.[15] The number of beneficiaries will continue to rise so long as the number of people newly unemployed exceeds the number of unemployed who have exhausted their benefits, a likely eventuality in a period of rising unemployment.

In 1992, outlays on unemployment benefits totaled Kcs 1.7 billion and outlays on requalification training programs, Kcs 3.8 billion. The 1993 budget included Sk 3.0 billion for both unemployment benefits and requalification training. The Ministry of Labor projected that Sk 2.7 billion or more would be required for unemployment benefits alone, leaving just Sk 0.7 billion for requalification training. The joint budget allocation for unemployment benefits and requalification training effectively treats these expenditures as substitutes, though experience suggests that they are complements. Budgetary neglect of requalification training may undermine the government's efforts to deal with the expected rise in unemployment.

Different programs are needed for the long-term unemployed, that is, those who have exhausted their unemployment benefits and those who were never eligible for unemployment benefits. The Ministry of Labor, Social Affairs, and Family administers a vast, diverse program of social benefits. Some of the benefits, such as family allowances, are available to virtually everyone; others are targeted to the poor, the handicapped, or groups with special needs. In many respects, these programs are essentially a continuation of those available under the former system, when categorical benefit programs of various kinds rather than personal earnings were the main source of household well being. In a market economy, personal earnings and personal savings should play that role, so the objective of social benefit programs should be to assist groups with special needs, such as the long-term unemployed and the disabled. The government has begun to target some categories of benefits, but income ceilings have been set so high that few people are excluded. As incomes rise, targeting should become more discriminating, however.

Hiring Incentives and Labor Mobility

Under ideal economic conditions, productive factors (including labor) would be fully utilized in their most productive roles. Government regulations and other restrictions on employers account for some of the real-life departures from this ideal. One example is the complex registration requirements and other restrictions on establishing new businesses (described in chapter 3). Because new businesses—all initially small—are the most dynamic source of output and employment growth, government policy should encourage such initiatives by minimizing the bureaucratic hurdles to business startup.

Restrictions on dismissing employees may also impede employment creation. Employers must give three months notice before dismissing an employee and two months of severance pay. Collective bargaining agreements may raise the severance pay requirement by another three months or

---

15   In January 1993, there were 50,000 newly eligible unemployment beneficiaries and 25,000 whose benefit period was exhausted—a net increase of 25,000. The net increase was progressively less in February and March 1993.

provide for tradeoffs between advance notice requirements and additional severance pay. Although economic theory suggests that policies that restrict firing also discourage hiring, that does not appear to be the case in Slovakia. Many managers consider loyalty to employees in the form of job stability to be an important management objective. In fact, self-imposed objectives of employment protection appear to affect management behavior far more than statutory restrictions. The importance of this objective could diminish over time as increasingly stringent terms for commercial borrowing and stockholder demands for profitability reduce managers' discretion in retaining employees who are no longer needed for current production. Once the process of labor shedding is well under way, provisions relating to severance pay should be re-examined to see whether they inhibit the free movement of labor. For now, enterprises need to proceed apace with the dismissal of redundant workers, while providing concentrated assistance with labor redeployment and relying on the social safety net to provide for the interim welfare needs of displaced workers and their dependents.

Active measures are also needed to improve labor mobility. The free movement of workers is particularly important as Slovakia searches for an internationally competitive production niche. Finding this niche will take time, as competing countries succeed one another in producing complementary goods and services and as productive technology evolves. The unconstrained movement of workers from one job to another will be critical in supporting this evolution. This process can only occur gradually, as housing markets become more flexible and housing more readily available, as personal incomes rise, and as people adjust to increased occupational and regional mobility. Changes in education and training will also be needed to provide a longer period of general education and training as a basis for improved receptivity to training throughout a worker's professional life. The current emphases on early training prior to one's first job, a model poorly equipped to deal with technological change and other aspects of economic succession, needs to be redirected to more in-service training and other forms of adult training.

Employment Services and Training

The large-scale labor displacements accompanying the economic transition and the ease of labor movement necessary under a market economy call for more dynamic employment services than those provided in a command economy, which offered little choice in initial job assignment and little occupational mobility thereafter. Slovakia has developed an impressive network of local employment offices since the start of the transition. These offices dispense both passive services in the form of unemployment benefits, job placement services, and job counseling and active services in the form of requalification training for unemployed job seekers and job stimulus programs. Few private job placement agencies are yet in operation, but that is certain to change.

There are now 146 district and subdistrict employment offices, with 2,865 staff, most of them university graduates. Offices in the larger district centers are well equipped, with computer-based records of job vacancies and profiles of job seekers in the district. At the current level of unemployment, this implies an average staffing ratio of one employment officer for 131 unemployed job seekers, about twice the case load of OECD employment officers. The Ministry of Labor plans to increase staffing and improve the quality of employment services by offering national and local labor market analysis, job counseling, and other job placement skills. Providing labor market analysis and job counseling on a national scale is especially important. The large regional variations in unemployment clearly indicate a need for interregional labor mobility and for national job placement services to support it. At a minimum, information on job prospects throughout Slovakia should be developed and made available to all employment offices. Eventually, employment offices throughout the country should be linked in a computerized system for listing job vacancies and job applicants.

Of all the active programs carried out by the employment offices, the most effective is requalification training.[16] Most job placements of the unemployed—155,000 of 177,000 placements in 1992—involve requalification training, often with skills supplementation to qualify job applicants for existing jobs, a formula found to facilitate the re-employment of displaced workers in other countries. Training, organized jointly by the employment offices, employers, and training institutions, is dispensed in short flexible courses lasting one week to three months. Training is provided under contract through public and private training institutions. Requalification training is an important complement to the job placement services of the employment offices, and the cutback in resources for requalification training in the 1993 budget constitutes a serious threat to the government's ability to deal with unemployment. Adequate financing should be provided to maintain requalification training at an appropriate level. To keep costs in line, eligibility for unemployment benefits during retraining should be restricted and monitoring should be improved.

Other active employment promotion efforts include a public works program ("publicly useful work"), a subsidized program for job creation in enterprises and self-employment ("socially purposeful jobs"), and financial assistance to enterprises to pay part of employees' salaries during a period of reduced working hours due to restructuring. In addition to these programs ran by the Ministry of Labor, the Ministry of Economy administers a program to support job creation through the promotion of small and medium-size enterprises.

Most of these employment programs involve both a subsidy component and an informational component—for example, on how to set up a small business. The informational component is generally useful and cost-effective, particularly because experience with private enterprise is still so scarce. The costs of the subsidy component are generally too high, however, especially at a time of fiscal austerity. The subsidy costs are often higher than the costs of providing unemployment benefits and social assistance. They subsidy often amount to almost as much as it would cost to pay workers for two years at the minimum wage (net of social contribution)—and this for a job that may not be genuinely additional and sustainable.

Appendix: Labor Force Data and Surveys

Official information on the structure and evolution of employment and unemployment in Slovakia is available from two main sources. The first is registration data from employers' reports on numbers of employees and from job applicant records compiled and reported monthly by the employment

---

16   In a theoretical sense, training decisions are subject to the same profitability considerations that govern other investment decisions. Individuals would seek training to the extent that the benefits of training (in the form of enhanced earnings) exceed the costs of training (including income foregone); firms would provide training for their employees to the extent that productivity gains exceed training costs. But the form in which training is provided throughout the world differs very much from this abstract ideal. Government plays an important role in training in virtually all countries, either as provider or as financier. In Slovakia, as in other countries, government involvement in training is justified as an instrument for promoting equity and efficiency in a situation of market imperfection (pervasiveness of training externalities, absence of collateral to secure human capital investments).

offices of the Ministry of Labor, Social Affairs, and Family. The second is from quarterly surveys of all budgetary and subsidized organizations and private enterprises with more than twenty-five employees. These sources provide an unsatisfactory view of the size and structure of employment and unemployment. Only the job applicant records supply any information on the educational qualifications and work experience of job seekers. None of the sources provides information on employment in small private enterprises (with fewer than twenty-five employees), which is expected to remain the most dynamic source of employment growth.   Until recently, there was no household labor force survey—the main source of information on employment and the labor force in most OECD countries.

The current definition of unemployment in Slovakia reflects this situation and tends to understate actual unemployment for several reasons. Unemployment is defined as the number of job seekers registered in employment offices and not reported as employed. People reporting as little as one hour of paid employment in the prior week are registered as employed.[17] People who seek employment through means other than the state employment offices or who fail to register in the employment office are not counted as unemployed. Though unemployed job seekers are required to re-register with the employment office every two weeks as a condition for receiving unemployment benefits or social assistance, a substantial number of the unemployed do not register.[18] Because the newly unemployed are not eligible for unemployment benefits during the period—normally two months—covered by severance pay, there is little incentive for them to register until the severance pay period has expired and they become eligible for unemployment benefits.[19] Similarly, under conditions of high long-term unemployment and few job vacancies, there is also little incentive for the long-term unemployed to re-register.   Women on long-term maternity leave—currently 146,000 women, or 13% of female labor force—are treated as employed, rather than as temporarily out of the labor force; counting this group would boost the overall unemployment rate from 11.2% to 15.1%. Another important source of understated unemployment is the slow rate at which enterprises have reduced their work force as output has been scaled back during restructuring.

To provide better information on the numbers and characteristics of the employed and the unemployed, the Slovak Institute of Statistics launched a new quarterly household labor force survey. The first quarterly survey was carried out through a national sample in December 1992 through February 1993. Results from this survey are the basis of several of the tabulations presented in this chapter. As with any survey, it will take time to establish whether the results accurately reflect national trends, but

17   Most OECD countries define unemployment through household survey information as the number of people who are currently not employed and are actively seeking work in any of a variety of ways. Under Slovak law, eligibility for registration at employment offices is limited to people who are "not employed or self-employed, nor in the process of being systematically trained for a profession or a vocation, and who, on the basis of a written application, personally seek employment through mediation of a regional employment office."

18   The results of the first round of the new household labor force survey show that 60,000 unemployed people —more than 20% of the total surveyed unemployed—were not currently registered with their local unemployment office.

19   There is, however, an incentive for the unemployed to register promptly with the employment offices since the introduction of the national insurance programs for pensions, health care, sickness benefits, and unemployment benefits because the government makes contributions on behalf of the unemployed only if they are registered.

the survey approach in principle provides a more complete picture of labor market developments because it covers employment of all kinds, including employment in small private enterprises. It also provides information on the age, sex, and educational composition of employment, which is not collected in the enterprise surveys. Once the validity of the survey is established and the efficiency of the process for generating survey findings is confirmed, it ought to become the official basis of employment and unemployment because of its fuller coverage of labor market developments.[20] Registration data will continue to provide important detail on regional patterns of employment and the impact of active employment measures. And because registration data are reported monthly, they will generally provide more timely feedback on current employment trends.

---

20   There are some anomalies in the findings of the first-round survey results which should be resolved, including the discrepancy between the 226,000 unemployed reported as registered job seekers in the Institute of Statistics survey and the 260,000 who were listed as registered job seekers in December 1992 in the records of the Ministry of Labor, Social Affairs, and Family.

CHAPTER 5: SOCIAL BENEFITS

Slovakia has an extensive and overlapping system of social support programs, with wide coverage and generous benefit levels. Social spending accounts for 37% of total government expenditures and nearly 25% of GDP, much of it for social transfers such as pensions and child allowances. A major concern is how to reduce the high levels of social transfers while still ensuring a minimum standard of living for individuals at risk of poverty.

The current structure of social programs is costly in fiscal terms and to the economy more generally. It creates an incentive structure that promotes withdrawal from the labor force by offering generous inducements for early retirement and extended maternity leave. It promotes collusive behavior between employees and employers, as evidenced by high levels of sick leave and a rising incidence of disability pension claims. The high payroll taxes (50% of gross wages) required to support the new insurance programs increase the marginal cost of labor and promote the development of an informal market for labor. Reducing the level of social spending would have several salutary effects. It would avoid the adverse fiscal and monetary repercussions of social fund deficits, improve labor market efficiency by lowering payroll taxes, and improve Slovakia's prospects for a successful transition to a market economy by strengthening the incentives to work.

This chapter suggests several measures to reduce program expenditures now and over the long term. Recommendations include cost-containment measures for pension programs, health insurance, and social assistance that are likely to improve microeconomic efficiency while maintaining an acceptable level of benefits in the short run. Pension programs receive close attention because of their importance to current and future expenditures. Prominent among measures to contain soaring pension costs are raising the retirement age and reducing pensions for early retirement. Indexing the minimum pension to changes in the cost of living would provide protection against poverty for the lifetime poor. Making employers and employees bear more of the cost of sickness benefits would reduce the incentive to collude, improve efficiency, and reduce expenditures. In health care, tighter regulation and monitoring, with incentives designed to mitigate the collusion problems inherent in a third party-payment system, would be instrumental in containing costs.

Over the longer term, three areas require close attention:

- *Development of an effective program of social assistance.* An effective program of means-tested social assistance is needed for people whose income is below the minimum welfare level. The "Law on a Living Minimum," adopted by the Federation of Czech and Slovak Republics in October 1991 and revised in February 1992, defines minimum household incomes to meet basic consumption requirements. The amounts established in this law go well beyond the basic necessities, but it could serve as a framework for more closely targeted social assistance in the future. As personal incomes in Slovakia grow and social assistance programs provide a reliable safety net, other social benefits that are no longer needed, such as universal family allowances, should be phased out. The social insurance program, which is projected to run a surplus under certain assumptions, should be kept under review for the desirability of reducing the contribution rate.

- *Development of a multitier program for retirement support.* The new public pay-as-you-go social insurance system now provides the only source of retirement income for workers. The move to a market economy suggests a shrinking role for government and an expanding role for the private sector in pension savings and investment. The mandatory public pension program should not be allowed to crowd out supplementary private pensions for people who desire them. Short-term measures to reduce benefit levels and tighten eligibility criteria, by allowing for reduced payroll taxes to finance the public pension program, would leave room for the development of a private pension and insurance market. A well-functioning financial market, in which the government plays an important regulatory and informational role, is also a prerequisite to the development of a private pension market. Regulatory measures to ensure pension fund solvency and portability are particularly important.

- *A cost-effective health system.* Preventive health care and basic health services should take priority over expensive procedures to care for a few high-risk groups. The country needs to strengthen primary and community health care, public health and health care management training, and private health care providers. Tight budget-capping mechanisms and an effective regulatory framework are needed to contain costs.

Financing the Social Insurance System

Slovakia's system of social transfers to protect against poverty and income loss has three components:

- Insurance programs to protect against short-term income loss from unemployment and sickness and long-term income loss from permanent disability, retirement, death of a family member, and lengthy illness.

- Poverty alleviation programs such as means-tested social assistance in the form of cash benefits for people with incomes below a specified minimum and services for specific categories of the poor, such as institutional care for the elderly.

- Other means-tested benefits for poor families with children.

The Czechoslovak Federation introduced some social sector reforms in 1991 as part of the transformation program. More recently, the Slovak government has established new insurance programs for health, pensions, unemployment benefits (chapter 4), entitlement programs and workmen's compensation and restructured other benefits into two categories: state social entitlement programs (both means-tested and universal benefits to compensate for specific sources of income loss) and social assistance (both general and specific compensation for loss of income). To contain fiscal costs, the government reduced the social sector budget for 1993. At the same time, to make social insurance programs more transparent and to encourage a sense of individual responsibility for them, the budgetary finance of pensions, health care, sickness benefits, and unemployment benefits is being replaced with insurance-based funding.

Social Insurance Funds

The new insurance funds for pensions, health care, sickness, and unemployment are financed through employer and employee contributions (Table 5.1). Taken together, these contributions total 50% of base wages—a substantial amount. Contributions are temporarily being collected by the Ministry of Finance and transferred to the respective insurance funds; eventually, contributions will go directly to each fund. This transitional arrangement is intended to permit an assessment period, to establish whether contribution rates are adequate to cover the costs of each program. The health insurance fund is receiving close attention because a new fee-for-service system for compensating health service providers was instituted at the time the new contribution schedule went into effect. Experience elsewhere shows that such systems of reimbursement can lead to rapid expansion of services and costs unless there are appropriate safeguards.

Table 5.1: Contribution Rates for Social Insurance (percentage of base wages)			
Fund	Employer	Employee	Total
Pensions	22.6	5.9	26.5
Health	10.0	3.7	13.7
Employment	3.0	1.0	4.0
Sickness	4.4	1.4	5.8
Total	38.0	12.0	50.0
Source: Ministry of Finance.			

For the first quarter of 1993, actual revenues for the social insurance funds averaged 9% to 15% less than budgeted (Table 5.2), while expenditures were close to projections, except for the employment fund. At that pace, the four funds would have run an aggregate deficit of Sk 23.8 billion for 1993. This deficit is considerably less than the Sk 37 billion that the National Insurance Corporation had projected would be needed in transfers from the state budget to all four social insurance funds, but far more than the Sk 1 billion in spending that the Ministry of Finance had programmed for the pension and sickness funds.

Table 5.2: Expenditure and Revenue of Social Funds, January - March 1993 (percentage of budgeted amounts)		
Fund	Actual expenditure	Actual revenue
Pensions	23.1	11.0
Health	24.3	10.5
Employment	17.3	16.5
Sickness	23.0	13.8
Source: Ministry of Finance.		

Fund Management

Proper management of the social insurance funds will be critically important for achieving social protection and fiscal stability. As long as the state budget provides sufficient resources, the National Insurance Corporation, which is to take over responsibility for managing the funds, can be directed to hold down costs while ensuring that benefits reach those most in need. (No date has yet been set for separating the funds financially from the state budget.) The pension and sickness funds, which have long been managed by a predecessor organization of the National Insurance Corporation, present the fewest management problems. Far more problematic is the health insurance fund. Its financial requirements could balloon dramatically following the privatization of some health facilities, the introduction of a new system of payments to providers, and increased costs of such key imported products as pharmaceuticals and medical equipment. Outlay estimates for 1993 vary from Sk 14 billion to Sk 24 billion (between 4.2% and 7.3% of projected GDP), a strikingly large range.

The creation of the social insurance funds has clearly increased the transparency of the financing of social insurance expenditures. What remains to be seen is whether the state budget will allocate financial resources in the amounts planned. Many governments with independent pension and benefit systems have accepted the legal obligation to pay into the funded programs, but have frequently failed to make the payments. If fiscal stringency results in failure to pay the stipulated amounts, deficits in the social funds would constitute another form of fiscal imbalance. Keeping expenditures in line is essential to fiscal stability.

Expenditure Reduction

The government proposed measures to reduce social expenditures from 24.8% of GDP in 1992 to 21.2% of in 1993. The largest cuts were in health care services and employment programs; the social assistance budget was frozen at the 1992 level (Table 5.3). Though expenditure controls are clearly needed, cuts need to be assessed in terms of their effect on the poor and on the underlying causes of the growth in social program spending.

The level of social assistance budgeted may not be sufficient to meet the basic needs of the poor. Social assistance spending in 1992 was double the amount budgeted for the year, largely because nearly half of the unemployed who exhausted their eligibility for unemployment benefits in 1992 received social assistance that year. That pattern is likely to be repeated. Higher unemployment, lower unemployment benefits, and further restructuring and layoffs should swell the number of social assistance claimants in 1993 and 1994. Moreover, if low rates of economic growth persist, most of the current recipients of social assistance are likely to continue to claim benefits.

The government's expenditure reduction strategy also does little to address the underlying causes of rising social expenditures or to root out inefficiencies or negative incentives in current programs. For example, payments are more attractive for disability pensions than for unemployment benefits, and incentives for early retirement lead to premature departures from the labor force. Health insurance programs encourage health care providers to expand services and raise prices, but the effect on health status is not evident. Costs of the social insurance system are bound to rise, particularly in periods of low output growth, unless fundamental reforms are put in place.

Table 5.3: Social Program Expenditures, 1992 and 1993 (Sk billion)		
Category of spending	1992 Actual	1993 Budget
Education[a]	6.0	7.4
Health	15.9	14.8
Pensions[b]	28.0	30.0
State benefits	9.5	9.2
Sickness benefits	3.8	5.3
Employment and unemployment programs	4.3	3.0
Social assistance	2.4	2.4
Total	69.9	72.1
Social spending (% of)/GDP	24.8	21.2

Note: Some inconsistencies arise from different treatment of inflation adjustments and expected health care costs.

a. Education spending (probably large) by ministries other than the Ministry of Education are excluded.
b. Includes allowances for 1992.

Source: Ministry of Finance and National Insurance Corporation.

Pensions

Unlike other Central European economies—Poland and Slovenia, for example—Slovakia did not experience a dramatic rise in pension expenditures in the first few years of economic transformation (Table 5.4). Pension spending rose slowly, from 7.7% of GDP in 1989 to 8.2% in 1991. Decomposition of the growth of pension expenditures between 1989 and 1991 reveals that pension spending did not increase as much as would have been expected by the sharp rise in the number of pensioners and unemployed over this period, because of the failure to fully index pensions for inflation.[1]

---

1   The analysis decomposes pension spending as a share of GDP into four components and tracks changes in each share over time. The pension expenditure to GDP ratio can be expressed as follows:

$$\text{Pe/GDP} = \underset{(1)}{(\text{Pop55+/Pop15-54})} \ \underset{(2)}{(\text{Pen/Pop55+})} \ \underset{(3)}{[(\text{Pe/Pen})/(\text{GDP/Emp})]} \ \underset{(4)}{(\text{Pop15-54/Emp})}$$

The first component, the *old age ratio*, is the share of the old in the total population and is determined largely by long-run demographic factors (birth rates, age-specific mortality rates). The second ratio, the *eligibility ratio*, is the share of pensioners in the old age population and is determined largely by the coverage and maturity of pension programs (higher in mature programs with wider coverage). The third component, the *transfer ratio*, measures the transfer of resources from the employed to pensioners. The final component is an indicator of economic activity: the higher the number of employed, the lower the *pension expenditure* to GDP *ratio* (Holzmann 1990 "Reforming Public Pensions," Paris: OECD).

Pensioners' income levels deteriorated relative to those of the working labor force.[2] A small but favorable change in the demographic composition of the population—the share of old people in the total population fell—also kept expenditures lower than they would otherwise have been.

Table 5.4: Social Benefit Expenditures, 1989-92 (Sk million)				
Benefit	1989	1990	1991	1992
Pensions				
Old age pension				
Expenditures	10,827	11,610	14,886	17,498
Beneficiaries	480,128	498,463	523,934	539,493
Disability				
Expenditures	3,295	3,478	4,427	5,221
Beneficiaries	162,899	166,273	174,323	184,649
Survivors				
Expenditures	2,551	2,645	3,281	3,783
Beneficiaries	269,970	274,750	279,041	282,778
Sickness				
Expenditures	2,908	3,147	3,400	3,822
Average days per case	18.1	20.0	21.7	23.7
Claimants as share of total insured (%)	4.4	4.7	5.2	5.3
Health expenditures	--	--	--	15,900
Family benefits				
Birth grant				
Expenditures	170	153	198	210
Average cases per month	5,808	5,693	6,205	5,793
Maternity leave				
Expenditures	7	7	5	5
Beneficiaries	1,367	1,193	848	633
Child allowance expenditures	6,139	6,104	5,761	5,820
Maternity allowance				
Expenditures	765	764	756	778
Beneficiaries	na	na	37,604	36,480
Child care leave				
Expenditures	494	441	330	320
Beneficiaries	111,428	89,096	77,895	56,505
Parent benefit				
Expenditures	666	873	1,623	2,103
Beneficiaries	68,577	83,790	153,297	161,663
Social assistance	--	--	--	2,400
Source: na is not available; -- is not applicable				

2   The transfer ratio fell by more than 2 times the increase in pension expenditures; the eligibility ratio rose 1.2 times and the old age ratio 1.5 times; the old age ratio explained 15% of the increase in pension expenditures.

Pension expenditures increased sharply between 1991 and 1992, as the old age ratio rose 30% and the number of pensioners in the old age population rose by 15%. The transfer ratio rose as well, explaining more than half of the increase in the pension expenditure to GDP ratio. That suggests that pensioners improved their income position relative to that of the working-age population over the previous years.

Box 5.1: An Overview of the Pension System

Slovakia has a pay-as-you-go pension plan—today's contributors fund today's pensioners. An employee contributing to the social security fund may be eligible for three major pension benefits: old age security (60% of pension spending), disability (20%), and survivor pensions (15%). There are minor benefits as well, such as widow's benefits for women who have never worked, benefits for the severely handicapped, and burial and birth benefits. Pensioners are eligible to receive full retirement pensions after twenty-five years of employment if they have reached 53-57 years of age for women (depending on the number of children) and 60 years for men.

Pensions are calculated on the basis of the best five years of (unindexed) earnings in the last ten years before retirement. Earnings are converted to the pension base by a formula that adds 100% of the first Sk 2,500, 33% of earnings between Sk 2,500 and Sk 6,000, and 10% of earnings between Sk 6,000 and Sk 10,000. The maximum pension base is Sk 4,100. The benefit level is composed of a fixed portion that is 50% of the pension base plus a variable portion that increases 1% for each year worked after twenty-five years of employment. (For example, someone working forty-two years would have a wage replacement rate of 67% of the pension base.) Individuals can also qualify for partial pension benefits if they have worked for a specified period and are at least 60 (women) or 65 years old (men). A minimum pension of Sk 1,980 (Sk 3,360 for a two-person household) is allotted to those for whom the pension is the only source of income. Sk 550 is guaranteed to pensioners with other sources of income. Pensioners can receive full pensions if they continue to work after retirement; there is no retirement earnings test. However, for each year worked in which the pension is not claimed, individuals receive an additional 4% accrual rate.

Disability pensions are granted to individuals who suffer a work-related injury or disability and have worked at least one to five years prior to the disability. Claimants must be certified as full or partially disabled from working in their previous occupation. Moreover, earnings in the new job must have declined 33% over those in their previous occupation. The benefits for disability pensions are calculated in the same way as for old age pensions, except that an employment record is created for the years between the onset of disability and normal retirement age.

Survivor pensions (60% of the full pension) can be claimed by the widow of a deceased pensioner for the duration of her lifetime under certain qualifying conditions (age, number of children raised). If the widow receives a pension of her own, she must give up 50% of the lower pension. Approximately 60% of survivors receive two pensions.

The number of disability pensioners also increased. Pension authorities attribute this trend to collusion between employees and employers as they seek the most attractive retirement package for redundant workers. Employees more than two years away from retirement age are economically better off with disability pensions than with unemployment benefits. Recent measures to tighten eligibility criteria for unemployment benefits and to reduce the level and duration of these benefits have made them even less attractive. The shift in the age distribution of disability pensioners toward early claimants between 1990 and 1992 supports this hypothesis.[3]

As pension claims have risen, revenues have fallen. The increase in the number of unemployed and early retirees has reduced the contribution base, while collection rates fall far short of potential revenues. Actual pension system revenues were only 44% of potential revenues in the first quarter of 1993, implying that the pension fund will require major budgetary transfers to meet obligations if first quarter trends continue. A concerted effort to improve collection rates is needed.

Whether the social insurance system will require substantial government transfers over the medium term depends on the impact of demographic and macroeconomic developments on the level of social security expenditures and revenues over time. A simulation model using demographic projections and forecasts of unemployment, inflation, and growth rates under existing policy parameters (revenue collection and eligibility rates) was applied to simulate the path of social security revenues, expenditures, and transfers.

The model projections indicate that, with the aging of the postwar generation and its offspring, a smaller labor force will find it increasingly difficult to support a

Figure 5.1

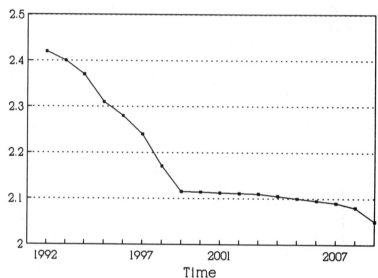

growing number of pensioners over the next ten to fifteen years (Figure 5.1). The ratio of contributors to beneficiaries is projected to decline from 2.42 in 1992 to 2.05 in 2010, a trend that will continue well into the next decade as the demographic impact of the post-war generation plays itself out.[4]

---

3   The age distribution of disability claimants should remain constant over time unless there are changes in work conditions in the economy or in the health of the population.

4   The projections assume that current mortality and fertility rates will continue over the medium term. Improvements in mortality rates will drive up the number of pensioners on social security, while increases in the birth rate will reduce the ratio of pensioners to contributors.

The model also forecasts the effect of alternate macroeconomic scenarios—median, optimistic, and pessimistic—[5] on the revenues, expenditures, and budgetary transfers[6] required to finance pensions, as well as the payroll taxes necessary to finance the social security system under the assumption of full revenue collection. The model indicates that transfers to the pension fund will increase sharply in 1993, from 4.5% of GDP in the optimistic case to 5% of GDP if the pessimistic forecast comes to pass (Figure 5.2). The level of transfers will be higher the more arduous the road to economic recovery: transfers remain approximately 2% of GDP higher for the pessimistic case than for the optimistic scenario throughout the simulation period. Transfers to the pension fund decline from these levels over time, and the funds begin to show a surplus by the end of the simulation period.

The drop in transfers over time reflects the increasing divergence between the growth in revenues, which increases with nominal wages, and the growth in expenditures, which increases with prices. Transfers also decline because the dampening effect of price indexation of benefits on expenditures more than offsets the positive effect on fund outlays of an increase in the number of pensioners (Figure 5.3).

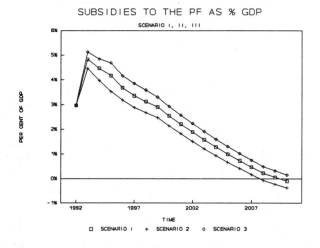

Figure 5.2

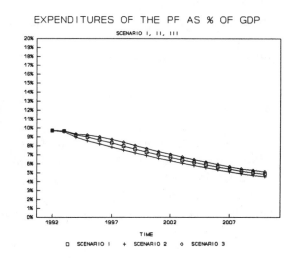

Figure 5.3

---

5 The scenarios are based on the following long-run equilibrium assumptions: inflation = 5%, GDP growth = 5%, and unemployment = 6%. These assumptions differ from the macroeconomic projections presented in chapter 1 and are only meant to be illustrative of possible long-run effects on the social funds. In the median scenario, convergence to this long run equilibrium is achieved in 1997, in the optimistic scenario in 1995, and in the pessimistic scenario in 1998. In the base case, the labor force participation rate for women will decline to 65% over the next seven years. Also taken as given are existing revenue collection rates (66% of hypothetical revenues for the pension fund), unemployment claimants, and average benefit levels prevalent in 1992. More important, benefits are indexed to prices. This assumption was made because the price compensation in 1993 of 11% closely approximates inflation rates in 1992. The model assumes that the employment fund will contribute social security contributions on behalf of the unemployed to the pension fund.

6 In this chapter, transfers refer to one-period deficits in fund finances. They do not take into account any implicit taxes across generations that may be inherent in the current system.

The payroll taxes required to match revenues and expenditures (under full revenue collection) will fall over the medium term. The decline in expenditures and increase in revenues could allow for a cut in payroll taxes from 25% in 1993 to 12% by 2010 (Figure 5.4). Again, the level of payroll taxes required to balance the fund will be higher the more arduous the path to stable economic growth.

Though transfers to the pension fund will decline over the medium term, the simulations show that large and positive transfers will be required to finance the social security system over this period. The surpluses achieved by the end of the study period require the economy to achieve a positive growth path without further shocks to output. A period of negative growth would cause inflation-indexed expenditures to rise faster than revenues, jeopardizing the financing of the social security system. Over the longer term, the aging of the population could increase pension expenditure, straining the financing of the pay-as-you-go social insurance system.

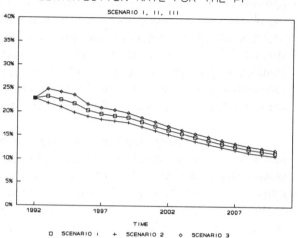

Figure 5.4

CONTRIBUTION RATE FOR THE PF

SCENARIO I, II, III

Short-Term Reform Options

There are two ways to reduce social insurance obligations in the short run: reducing benefit levels and tightening eligibility requirements. System solvency can also be improved through better revenue collection. Such short-term measures to contain costs and boost revenues could reduce the state transfers required to finance the fund and allow for a lower payroll tax, with positive effects on labor market efficiency. But for reforms to achieve such results, positive economic growth rates and stable employment rates are required since periods of high unemployment and negative growth cause program expenditures to soar. The long-run effect of the aging of the population may require continuous adjustments in benefit levels and eligibility criteria to avoid deficits.

Reducing benefit levels. Individual benefits are based on a relatively short assessment period, a very progressive calculation of the pension base, and uneven accrual rates. The assessment period of the five best years of the last ten creates incentives for employers and employees to claim that the employee retired at a higher wage than was actually the case. A short assessment period also weakens the link between contributions and benefits. Individuals with positive and steeply rising earning profiles gain relatively more than earners with a flatter lifetime earnings path. The uneven accrual rate—2% for the first twenty-five years, 1% thereafter—is an additional incentive to retire early. The caps on the pension base and pension amount are likely to create a transfer from high-income to low-income pensioners, particularly as there is no cap on payroll tax contributions. This phenomenon will tend to increase as the level and dispersion of wages increase throughout the economy.

If lifetime earnings follow a rising path for the average earner and the economy is growing, increasing the assessment period from five years to lifetime earnings would reduce the average monthly earnings used to calculate pension benefits. Smoothing out accrual rates for all categories of pensioners should reduce incentives to retire early. As the financial position of the pension fund improves, caps on taxable wages might be introduced to reduce transfers from high- to low-income workers.

The average monthly earnings used in the pension base calculation are not adjusted for inflation. Nor have pension benefits been fully adjusted for inflation, though the government increased pension benefits by 11% in 1993, closely following estimates of expected inflation for the year. Under current macroeconomic conditions, the government may not have adequate resources to fully protect all pension benefits against inflation. But minimum pensions should be protected, to keep pensioners from slipping into poverty during the transition. Failing to adjust benefits for the effects of inflation is not a recommended means of containing pension costs. It is likely to increase uncertainty, favor new entrants over old pensioners, and reduce confidence in the system. It may also promote labor market distortions if workers believe that the value of their contributions will be eroded by inflation.

Tightening eligibility criteria. Early retirement provisions for women and certain categories of workers may increase the number of pensioners in the economy. The earlier retirement age for women has been justified by their double burden of work. But at age fifty-five, women have ended their direct child-care responsibilities and do not have to withdraw from the labor force for that reason. In fact, 65% of working pensioners under age fifty-nine are women. Early retirement is also granted to "high risk" workers such as miners and ballet dancers. Early retirees neither pay higher contributions nor receive lower benefits, inducing higher expenditures for a given contribution stream for these individuals. Current incentives for delaying retirement—a 4% increase in pension levels for each year of delayed retirement—are inadequate. Benefit levels should be reduced or contributions increased on an actuarially fair basis for persons electing to retire early. Also, to control pension costs and improve labor-supply incentives, the retirement ages for men and women should be raised. The retirement age for women should be raised to reflect their longer life expectancy, and the retirement ages of both men and women should be increased gradually as mortality rates rise to OECD levels.

Retirements on disability pensions have also been increasing dramatically in many Eastern European economies since 1989. The jump in the number of individuals claiming disability between 1990 and 1992 indicates a weakness in the system's enforcement and monitoring capabilities. For workers who are being laid off, disability benefits are generally more generous than unemployment benefits. Employers find disability retirement attractive because government bears the cost of the higher rate of claims. Tightening eligibility criteria and monitoring disability pensioners regularly should reduce the number of claimants. Children receiving orphan pensions should lose them once they enter the work force. In 1992, half of the 40,809 orphan pensions were going to people twenty to twenty-nine years old.

Eliminating pensions for people who continue to work after retirement age may help reduce pension outlays in the short run, but the gains could be partially offset by higher outlays for social assistance.[7] Pension benefits paid to working pensioners might be recovered in part by taxing retirement benefits or reduced by applying an earnings test. In any case, the problem is shrinking along with the number of working pensioners, which dropped sharply from 230,000 in 1990 to 93,054 in 1992.

Improving revenue collection. Better enforcement and better compliance by enterprises should increase total pension fund revenues as growth in the economy picks up and the financial position of enterprises improves.

---

7   This occurred in Bulgaria, for example (see L. Fox and H. Ribe, 1991, "Social Security and Social Assistance Benefits in Bulgaria: Crisis and Transition to a Market Economy", World Bank).

Effect of short-term reforms on social insurance financing. Short-term reforms that reduce the number of pensioners on social insurance could allow the system to sustain current payment rates and become self-financing at lower contribution rates over the medium term. Gradually reducing eligibility would allow the pension fund to become self-financing at existing payment rates and at contribution rates of 7.7% over the medium term and would bring the fund into surplus three years earlier than in the base case (Figures 5.5 and 5.6). Specifically, with measures that reduce the number of retirees by 30% over the simulation period, the contribution rate needed for self-financing drops from 22.8% in 1992 to 9.2% by 2010. Gradually reducing the number of people on disability pensions by 20% lowers the contribution rate to 8.6% by 2010, while gradually reducing the number on survivor pensions by 60% brings the contribution rate down to 7.7%.

Figure 5.5   Figure 5.6

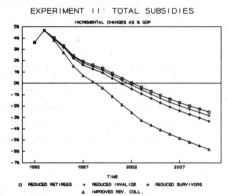

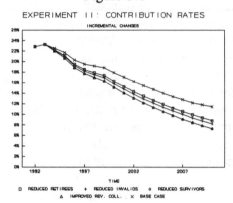

Improving revenue collection rates from 44% to 60% has an even more dramatic impact on fund deficits than reducing the number of retirees.[8] The pension fund will begin to show a surplus by 1998—five years earlier than otherwise—if collection procedures are improved along with a tightening of eligibility criteria.[9]

The model also shows the divergent impacts of indexation policies on social security financing. Wage indexation of benefits is more expensive than price indexation during periods of positive growth, but price indexation of minimum pensions reduces transfers by only about 1.5% of GDP over the simulation period. One result of the short-term reforms discussed above is that the fund realizes a

---

8   Marginal changes in revenue collection over time act through nominal wages, while changes in the number of pensioners act through changes in benefit levels. Since nominal wages are growing faster than average benefits are decreasing, improving revenue collection rates will have a greater marginal impact on reducing transfers to the pension fund.

9   Revenue collection rates reflect the percentage of the hypothetical payroll (total employment times the average wage) collected by the government. Improved enforcement procedures and better enterprise performance may increase the rates. But it is important to note that the rates may be low because part-time employment, and associated lower wages, drive down the ratio. Also, insurance contributions on behalf of women on maternity leave are supposed to be paid by the insurance fund, but may not be. The fund has not, for example, been paid insurance contributions on behalf of the unemployed.

surplus by 1998, five years before the non-intervention base case. Indexation of minimum pensions plus the other short-term reforms just described would allow a balanced pension fund before 1998.

Long-Term Reform: A Multitier Pension Scheme

Pension schemes in most market economies have evolved from a universal, single tier, pay-as-you-go public pension system to a multitiered mixed public-private system. There are several alternative models of such a system. A fully market-oriented approach would separate the insurance and redistribution functions of social security programs. A redistributive tier would provide a minimum guaranteed income for everyone or for low-income people on a means-tested basis. It might be administered by the government and financed from general budget revenues. The second, insurance-based tier might consist of a mandatory or voluntary fully funded, privately managed, defined-contribution scheme. If the state is involved in the second tier as well, the possibilities are a defined-benefit, pay-as-you-go second tier or a fully funded, defined-contribution, state-managed scheme. A third tier composed of supplementary, fully funded, defined contribution private insurance might be added as private capital markets develop.[10]

No system could fully insulate individuals against the effects of demographic changes and uncertainty in the macroeconomic climate. For example, one drawback of state-funded, defined benefit, pay-as-you-go schemes is that some intergenerational redistributive elements would remain. Moreover, any progressive benefit structure financed through payroll taxes would continue to combine redistribution and insurance. If payroll obligations are viewed as taxes to finance transfers rather than as contributions for old age insurance, there may be disincentives to participation.

A compelling argument for the move to a private, fully funded system is precisely because doing so would separate the earnings-related insurance objective from the redistributive objective, which should strengthen the link between contributions and benefits and improve labor market efficiency. It would also make intergenerational transfers more transparent. But there are likely to be important redistributive effects in switching from a pay-as-you-go to a fully funded system, and care must be taken during the transition to ensure that poor and older workers and pensioners are not left unprotected.[11]

The government would need to play a major role in financing the move from a pay-as-you-go to a fully funded system. This could entail meeting obligations to all retirees at the time the reform is implemented. The government could also finance fund contributions for individuals who are close to retirement. The transition could be financed through higher income taxes or by issuing

---

10   A version of this system was proposed by Topinski and Wisniewski (1992) for Poland. Another multitiered system along these lines has been put forth by D. Vittas, 1993 "Swiss Chilanpore: The Way forward for Pension Reform?" Policy Research Working Paper, Policy Research Department, World Bank, Washington, D.C.

11   See P. Arrau and K. Schmidt-Hebbel, 1992, "Macro-economic and Intergenerational Effect of a Transition from Pay-as-you Go to Fully Funded Systems," World Bank, December, for the implications for labor market efficiency and income distribution of changing from a pay-as-you-go to a funded system. Essentially, the old age pensioner would lose if the redistributive pillar of the existing system were removed without a targeted income support program.

government debt—with important welfare implications for each alternative.[12] An effective supervisory and regulatory system must also be put in place before private insurance schemes are introduced.[13] The move to a private pension system would also require well-functioning financial markets, though there is evidence from Chile and the United States that private pension schemes can contribute to the development and deepening of capital markets.[14]

Sickness Insurance

Sickness insurance in Slovakia covers employees who cannot work because of personal illness, childbirth, or the need to care for sick family members. Workers receive 70% of their wages for the first three days of illness and 90% thereafter. The maximum benefit is Sk 180 a day. Insurance indemnities are paid by the enterprises but are reimbursed by the state. The lower replacement rate for the first three days and the less than full replacement rate thereafter can be considered a deductible to prevent problems of moral hazard: consumption smoothing allowed by the insurance system is less than complete, forcing employees to bear some of the income risk themselves.

Because sickness benefits are provided for up to a year at relatively high replacement rates, the possibility of abuse is high—particularly in an economy with limited monitoring and enforcement capabilities. Data from early 1993 indicate that 113,000 workers were out sick each day, which is equivalent to 5.3% of the labor force. The rates were substantially higher for cooperative organizations and lower for private sector workers. At 23.7 days in 1992, the average number of sick days claimed is far higher than in most industrial countries, where the average number varies from 7.5 days (Netherlands 1987) to 18 days (Sweden 1981). With employees and employers bearing such a small share of the costs, collusion between them becomes appealing, particularly during the high-unemployment and low-productivity phase of the transition. Workers may find it in their interest to claim the more generous sickness benefits rather than unemployment benefits, which are also of shorter duration. The increase in the average number of personal sick days claimed and in the share of workers claiming sickness benefits supports this supposition. Both variables were relatively stable before the transition, at 18.4 days of sick leave and 4.4% of workers. In 1992, average sick leave days were up to 23.7 and the share of workers claiming sick leave was up to 5.3%. The average number of employees claiming child care sick leave and the number of women on maternity leave have declined meanwhile, perhaps reflecting declining fertility rates.

Government expenditure on sickness benefits increased by 8% in 1991 and 12.4% in 1992, but it was budgeted to increase by only 9.8% in 1993—probably an underestimate. Claiming sickness benefits will become even more attractive if unemployment benefit rates are lowered to 50% of average wages, as proposed. Without changes in the current incentive structure, low productivity growth

---

12   For the efficiency gains and losses from substituting income taxes for payroll taxes, see A. Auerbach, and L. Kotlikoff, 1987, "Dynamic Fiscal Policy," Cambridge University Press; A. Auerbach, L. Kotlikoff, and J. Skinner, 1983, "Efficiency Gains from Dynamic Tax Reform," *International Economic Review*.

13   The government might still be required to play the role of lender of last resort.

14   Although there is general agreement in the literature about the potential redistributive effects of the pay-as-you-go system, there is less consensus on the effects of a such system on aggregate savings (Thompson 1983). The move from a pay-as-you-go system to a fully funded system may have similar ambiguous impacts on savings. In addition, the accumulation and decumulation in the funds caused by the uneven size of the work force over time may increase the fluctuations in aggregate savings in the economy.

in 1993 and low labor demand may well lead to a continuation of the rising trend in sickness benefit claims.

Several measures could reduce the dependence on sickness benefits. Lowering the wage replacement rates, increasing the deductible, and shortening the duration of benefits are ways of overcoming the moral hazard problem associated with sickness benefits. One approach would be to shift the burden of sickness costs to employees for the first few days and to employers for the next 30-40 days. The U.S. model is another option. Employees are allowed to accumulate a fixed number of sick days that are paid for by the firm. After this quota is exhausted, employees pay for additional days off through a loss in annual leave or, for insurable illnesses, through health insurance schemes. As a first step, the government has proposed that benefits be reduced from 70% to 50% of wages for the first three days of illness, but Parliament rejected the proposal.

Health Insurance

Although the health sector consumes over 5.5% of GDP or 10.2% of general government revenues, it has been remarkably ineffective in promoting health and reducing preventable illness and disease. Cardiovascular disease, cancer, and accidents take a far higher toll than necessary, and health status and life expectancy have actually deteriorated during the past twenty years. About half of all adults smoke; many are overweight, hypertensive, and drink too much alcohol; 40% of calories consumed come from fat; work-related accidents and injury (often associated with alcohol) are frequent; and few people exercise regularly. Thanks to a massive buildup of acute-care delivery services in the 1970s, there are more physicians and hospital beds per thousand people in Slovakia than in Western Europe or North America. That buildup comes at the expense of effective public health interventions, primary health care, and community health services. The supply-dominated health sector provides virtually no incentives to motivate patients to maintain good health or to encourage health care workers and institutions to provide effective, efficient, and high-quality care. There have been few if any public education campaigns to discourage smoking or promote exercise, injury control, or occupational safety.

Strategy for Health Care Management

In January 1992, the Czechoslovak Ministry of Health presented its recommendations for a national health support program that included:

- An intersectoral approach to health protection to deal with environmental and occupational threats to health.

- A strategy to promote more healthful behavior with respect to smoking, alcohol and drug abuse, fat and cholesterol consumption, exercise, and occupational and highway safety.

- A prevention strategy of vaccination programs, screening, primary health care, social services, and self-help groups.

The government began to decentralize the ownership, management, and financing of health and social services to district- and community-level governments in 1984. Further steps are under way to strengthen performance-based incentives for health-care workers and to achieve an efficient balance between public and private service providers. Candidates for privatization include pharmaceutical and medical-equipment producers, ambulatory clinics, diagnostic centers, laboratories, general practitioners' offices, dentists, and some ancillary support services. Slovakia faces a major challenge in continuing with these management reforms given the limited availability of qualified public sector staff.

Proposals for Health Care Finance

The new health insurance fund will move health care financing from the state budget to enterprises and employees, but the system still lacks the regulatory, organizational, and electronic infrastructure needed to operate an efficient health financing administration. Simply shifting health care finance from the state budget to the health insurance fund will not in itself solve the problems of finance and efficiency. Without further reform, the system will be vulnerable to many of the same problems that afflict contributory health insurance schemes in other countries, particularly evasion, waste, fraud, and cost escalation. Such strategies complicate the task of setting appropriate payment rates, benefit schedules, and incentives for the various classes of affiliates of the system. In other countries, third-party payment systems have discouraged cost-containment measures and led to a dual health care system, as workers seek to avoid the formal sector and its high rates of social contributions and income taxes by moving into the informal sector of unregulated activities.

Managers of the National Insurance Corporation have expressed considerable skepticism about the financial viability of the health insurance fund and its ability to assume responsibility for health care financing during the current economic recession. Rising unemployment and bankruptcy are likely to shrink the contribution base, while the already-high total social insurance levy of 50% of net wages leaves no room for increasing the health insurance contribution rate should revenues fail or costs escalate. The high contribution rate encourages escape to the informal sector, further increasing the likelihood that fund revenues will fall short of projections that are based on full participation by the labor force. The government should continue to strengthen primary and community care, public health services, and health care management training and private sector development. In the short run, cost-effective health care measures and tight budget-capping mechanisms are needed to contain costs. Following a study to assess monitoring and cost control capacity throughout the national health care system, a fee-for-service compensation scheme will be implemented gradually as adequate monitoring mechanisms are put in place.

Family Allowances

Contributing to sickness insurance also make employees eligible for a number of additional state-funded benefits: childbirth benefits of Sk 3,000 per child, spa treatments, funeral benefits, child allowances, and extra child allowances for disabled children. Socialist economies, with their relatively flat wage structures, have generally used such allowances to direct additional income to larger families. But today the eligibility cutoff does not target only relatively poor households. Most Slovak households qualify for child and other family allowances. As the link between wages and marginal labor productivity strengthens, family allowances will no longer be needed to target income transfers. As economic growth resumes, these benefits can be allowed to decline over time, replaced by an efficient, well administered means-tested social assistance program for transfers to poor households.

Child allowances, at 3.3% of total government expenditures in 1992, are the largest single expenditure item among family allowances. Each employee (or eligible unemployed) contributing to the sickness insurance fund who can prove that monthly household income does not exceed Sk 16,800 is eligible for child benefits. Benefits are Sk 200 a month for the first child, Sk 450 for the second, Sk 610 for the third, Sk 510 for the fourth child, and Sk 350 per month for each additional child, a pronatalist benefit structure that has not had the desired effect on fertility. Nominal expenditures on child allowances have decreased from Sk 6,139 million in 1989 to Sk 5,820 million in 1992, largely because fewer families are claiming benefits. Supplementary family allowances of Sk 220 per child per month are provided as well, to compensate families for price increases associated with liberalization. An income ceiling for eligibility for child allowances was adopted recently, but the ceiling is set so high that it excludes fewer than 20 percent of households. It should become more discriminating in the future as incomes rise, however.

Other family allowances or state social benefits include income support to parents taking care of young children, rental support, and dependent benefits for individuals in military service. The largest of these are parent benefits, which provide SK 1,200 a month to parents whose annual income is less than Sk 12,000. This benefit is intended to compensate workers (or the eligible unemployed) for the income loss associated with withdrawing from the labor market to raise a child up to three years of age—or seven years for a disabled child. The average number of monthly claimants doubled between 1990 and 1992, and expenditures have increased nearly one and a half times. As in the case of other inadequately monitored benefits, it may be that employees and employers are colluding to allow workers to claim parent benefits from the state, instead of the less generous unemployment benefits.

Social Assistance

Slovakia has a means-tested social assistance program that is intended to keep individuals from becoming destitute during times when their income alone would not protect them. In practice, however, that is not quite the way this safety net functions. Budgetary allocations for the 1993 program were capped at 1992 levels precisely at a time when economic conditions can be expected to increase the number of people requiring assistance. Further, the budgeted amount covers a multitude of other benefits as well, in addition to means-tested social assistance, that are not separately budgeted, such as foster care for orphans and recreation benefits for pensioners. Not only is the total amount budgeted probably too small, but the income support level is set too high relative to the minimum wage, possibly distorting incentives to work.[15]

Maintaining the plethora of social benefit programs inherited from the socialist economy is inefficient and inequitable. There is a widespread perception—though difficult to document—that some groups benefit unfairly from public programs of social benefits. The diversity of programs is itself an invitation to abuse by making it possible to accumulate benefits from different programs in a total amount that greatly exceeds any intended level of benefits. Slovakia should switch to a streamlined system of social benefits, with a single means-tested program of social assistance to protect people from destitution. Legislation similar to the Law on a Living Minimum of October 1991, which defines minimum household incomes to meet basic consumption requirements, could serve as the basis of an effective, means-tested social assistance program—although the amounts would need to be scaled down to more realistic levels.

The government is considering a proposal for replacing child allowances and supplementary family allowances with a means-tested program that links eligibility for social assistance to the schedule of minimum household incomes. Under this proposal, families with incomes up to 150

---

15 To see this, consider that a two- (nonworking) adult and two-child family is eligible for Sk 6000 in basic income support. Subtracting other benefits for which the family is eligible—parent benefits, child allowances, and associated price compensations—brings the transfer amount to Sk 3,000, which is 36% above the minimum wage.

percent of the minimum household income would receive a transfer equal to half the minimum household income, and families with incomes between 150 percent and 200 percent of the minimum would receive a transfer equal to one-third the minimum. At current levels of household income, this plan would provide benefits to 88% of households, which is likely to make it very costly to implement. Some of the cost would presumably be offset by savings in social assistance outlays. Implementation also requires having a practical, objective means of establishing household incomes as a basis for eligibility. The Ministry of Labor, Social Affairs, and Family proposes to use income declarations from the personal income tax as a basis for determining eligibility. It is still too early to tell whether tax returns will be complete enough to be used for this purpose.

STATISTICAL APPENDIX

LIST OF STATISTICAL TABLES

Table 1.1. Slovakia: Social Indicators   1/

	1985	1986	1987	1988	1989	1990	1991	1992	1993 Prel.
Population and Vital Statistics									
Total population (in thousands)	5179.0	5208.7	5237.0	5264.2	5287.7	5310.7	5295.9	5307.9	5330.0
Total population growth (%)	0.67	0.57	0.54	0.52	0.45	0.43	-0.28	0.23	0.42
Life expectancy at birth (in years):									
Male	66.9	67.1	67.2	67.1	66.9	66.6	66.8	66.6	66.6
Female	74.7	74.6	75.1	75.5	75.4	75.4	75.2	75.4	75.4
Population age structure (in %):									
0-14	26.4	26.4	26.2	25.9	25.5	25.0	24.6	24.1	23.6
15-64	64.1	63.9	63.9	64.0	64.2	65.6	65.0	65.4	65.8
65 and above	9.5	9.7	9.9	10.1	10.3	10.4	10.4	10.5	10.6
Crude birth rate (per thousand)	17.6	16.9	16.2	15.9	15.3	15.2	14.9	14.1	13.8
Crude death rate (per thousand)	10.2	10.2	10.0	10.0	10.2	10.3	10.3	10.1	9.9
Infant mortality rate (per thousand)	16.3	15.0	14.2	13.3	13.5	12.0	13.2	12.6	10.6
Food, health, and nutrition									
Per capita supply of:									
Calories (per day)	2999.0	3030.0	3084.0	3185.0	3234.0	3333.0	..	..	..
Proteins (grams per day)	95.1	97.6	99.1	101.0	104.1	105.0	..	..	..
Population per physician	283.0	279.0	277.0	282.0	282.0	274.0	282.0	286.0	282.0
Population per hospital bed	7.4	7.4	7.4	7.4	7.4	7.4	7.6	7.6	..
Labor force 2/									
Total labor force (in thousands)	2501.0	2532.0	2554.0	2568.0	2555.0	2511.0	2548.0	2502.0	2350.0
Female (in percent)	48.3	48.4	48.5	48.5	48.6	49.0	47.6	46.9	46.1
Agriculture (in percent)	0.1	0.1	0.1	0.1	0.1	0.1	0.1	0.1	0.1
Industry (in percent)	0.4	0.4	0.4	0.4	0.4	0.4	0.4	0.4	0.4
Education									
Enrollment rates (% of school age children): 3/									
Primary: Total	99.2	99.0	98.3	97.9	97.7	98.1	99.6	99.6	99.5
Secondary: Total	96.8	95.9	95.6	95.6	95.8	96.3	96.6	96.6	95.9
Colleges, specialized schools and universities	24.5	24.0	23.8	24.3	24.8	26.1	26.9	29.5	29.1
Pupil-teacher ratio:									
Primary	26.4	26.5	26.1	25.7	25.0	23.9	23.2	22.1	22.4
Secondary	16.7	16.9	16.9	16.8	16.7	16.3	16.0	14.7	14.7
Other									
Telephones (per thousand)	194.0	201.0	209.0	217.0	227.0	236.0	247.0	257.0	..
Private cars (per thousand) 4/	136.0	141.0	147.0	151.0	158.0	165.0	173.0	180.0	..

Source: Slovak Statistical Office.

Notes:

1/ 1993: Preliminary data

2/ End of year. Excludes the armed forces and double employment, includes women on maternity leave.

3/ All children between the ages 6-15 have compulsory school attendance.

4/ Personal cars.

Table 1.2. Slovakia: Total Population   1/

	Total Population (In thousands)	Growth Rate (In percent)
1980	4996.3	
1981	5035.9	0.79
1982	5074.3	0.76
1983	5109.6	0.70
1984	5144.6	0.68
1985	5179.0	0.67
1986	5208.7	0.57
1987	5237.0	0.54
1988	5264.2	0.52
1989	5287.7	0.45
1990	5310.7	0.43
1991	5295.9	-0.28
1992	5307.9	0.23
1993 Prel.	5330.0	0.42

Source: Slovak Statistical Office.

Notes:
1/ end of year

Table 1.3. Slovakia: Employment by Sector 1/
(In thousands, yearly averages)

	1970	1975	1980	1981	1982	1983	1984	1985	1986	1987	1988	1989	1990	1991	1992	1993 Prel.
Total employment 2/	1958	2111	2277	2303	2318	2343	2377	2408	2452	2478	2503	2498	2478	2281	2163	2051
Material sphere	1556	1641	1740	1756	1762	1780	1801	1819	1845	1861	1864	1843	1812	1645	1560	1479
Agriculture	459	368	336	334	330	327	327	328	327	324	319	304	301	243	229	216
Industry	603	695	760	776	783	792	802	813	827	836	843	836	819	755	682	616
Construction	185	222	239	236	237	238	242	242	254	260	259	259	251	229	219	209
Other	309	356	405	410	412	423	430	436	437	441	443	446	441	418	430	438
Nonmaterial sphere	402	470	537	547	556	563	576	589	607	617	639	653	666	636	603	572
Education	109	126	139	142	145	148	152	155	160	162	169	172	173	160	181	185
Health	66	82	93	96	99	102	104	106	109	111	114	116	118	114	115	116
Transport	40	44	48	47	47	45	46	46	48	47	49	60	49	48	49	50
Science, research and development	30	39	48	49	50	51	53	55	56	58	60	60	52	39	34	30
Other	157	179	209	213	215	217	221	227	234	239	247	255	274	275	224	191
Memorandum items:																
Women in workforce (In %) 3/	42.8	43.8	44.6	44.7	45.0	45.0	45.3	45.4	45.4	45.5	46.5	45.5	44.5	43.3	42.8	-
Workers in the state and cooperative sector (%)	-	-	-	-	-	-	-	98.4	98.2	98.2	98.1	99.0	95.1	87.2	84.0	80.8

Source: Slovak Statistical Office.

Notes:

1/ Data for 1992 and 1993 are preliminary.

2/ Excludes women on maternity leave, trainees and the armed forces; includes double employment.

3/ Year end data.

Table 1.4. Slovakia: Structure of Employment and Employment by Training 1/ 2/
(in percent)

	1985	1986	1987	1988	1989	1990	1991	1992	1993 Prel.
Structure of Employment									
Total	100.0	100.0	100.0	100.0	100.0	100.0	100.0	100.0	100.0
State	81.6	81.5	81.5	81.5	81.1	78.9	72.5	69.6	66.8
'Cooperatives' of which:	16.8	16.7	16.7	16.6	16.5	15.0	13.1	12.0	11.0
Agricultural	-	-	-	-	-	-	-	-	-
Self-Employed of which:	0.4	0.5	0.5	0.5	1.0	5.0	12.8	18.4	22.2
Farmers	0.2	0.2	0.2	0.1	0.1	0.1	0.3	0.4	0.4

	1983	1989	1991
Employment by Training 3/ 4/			
University	8.3	10.0	10.8
Secondary school	24.7	27.8	30.7
School for apprentices	31.7	34.3	37.5
Primary school	35.3	27.9	20.3

Source: Slovak Statistical Office.

Notes:
1/ As of end year.
2/ Preliminary for 1992 and 1993.
3/ Civil employment excluding the private sector.
4/ 1983 data are as of end October; 1989 data are as of end September; 1991 data are as of Census 3.3.1991.

Table 1.5. Slovakia: Total Employment by Industry   1/
(Annual averages, in thousands)

	1990	1991	1992 Prel.	1993 Prel.
Total employment	2514.0	2377.8	2244.8	2120.0
As a percent of total	100.0	100.0	100.0	100.0
1. Agriculture, hunting, forestry and fishing	346.0	292.0	274.9	218.3
As a percent of total	13.7	12.5	12.3	10.3
2. Mining and quarrying, manufacturing, electricity, gas and water	865.0	824.0	732.8	667.8
As a percent of total	34.4	34.6	32.7	31.5
3. Construction	235.0	254.2	219.8	188.7
As a percent of total	9.4	10.7	9.8	8.9
4. Wholesale and retail trade, restaurants and hotels	287.0	257.3	244.7	256.5
As a percent of total	11.4	10.8	10.9	12.1
5. Transport, storage and communication	171.0	177.8	169.0	165.4
As a percent of total	6.8	7.5	7.5	7.8
6. Financing, insurance real estate, business services	86.0	72.7	97.3	101.8
As a percent of total	3.4	3.1	4.3	4.8
7. Community, social and personal services	514.0	485.3	498.6	515.1
As a percent of total	20.5	20.4	22.2	24.3
8. Activities not adequately defined	10.0	8.8	7.1	6.4
As a percent of total	0.4	0.4	0.3	0.3

Source: Slovak Statistical Office.

Notes:
1/ ISIC-68 major divisions
2/ Data are preliminary and include women on maternity leave, exclude
    armed forces and double employment.

Table 1.6. Slovakia: Employment by Ownership Forms
(In thousands)

	1990	1991	1992	1993 Prel.
Total	2477.6	2044.2	2007.5	1924.9
State organizations	1829.4	1424.3	1256.9	892.8
Economic organizations	1265.0	727.2	578.1	508.2
Budgetary organizations	343.0	273.2	278.3	256.3
Organizations based on contributions	43.8	114.6	122.6	128.3
Other	177.4	309.3	278.0	..
Local organizations	..	12.7	14.6	20.6
Cooperatives of which:	390.1	272.4	242.0	187.2
Agriculture	256.6	199.1	160.6	131.6
Private enterprises & organizations 1/	121.5	279.9	365.0	410.9
Social organizations	22.5	16.8	17.0	11.8
International organizations	..	5.6	10.2	..
Other	114.1	32.5	101.8	401.6

Source: Slovak Statistical Office.

Note:
1/ Including international and foreign organizations.

Table 2.1. Slovakia: Gross Domestic Product 1/ 2/
(In billions of koruny)

(In current prices)

	1980	1981	1982	1983	1984	1985	1986	1987	1988	1989	1990	1991	1992 6/	1992 7/	1993
Gross domestic product	171.5	165.4	173.8	182.1	193.1	203.3	211.7	216.9	225.0	234.2	243.6	280.1	285.9	301.8	336.7
By sector: 3/															
Agriculture	11.6	10.1	12.2	13.0	13.8	13.1	15.2	15.0	15.1	21.9	18.0	15.9	12.9	18.1	22.4
Industry	108.7	98.5	103.4	110.2	115.4	125.1	129.5	131.7	135.3	136.9	144.0	168.3	143.0	162.4	160.2
Services	51.2	56.8	58.2	58.9	63.9	65.1	67.0	70.2	74.6	75.4	81.6	95.9	130.0	121.3	154.1
By expenditure:															
Total consumption	118.5	120.1	125.4	130.0	136.8	141.2	148.3	154.3	158.7	167.4	184.7	200.9	226.0	244.0	270.4
Gross investment	64.0	56.9	58.2	59.1	61.7	64.3	66.7	63.2	67.0	69.6	81.5	98.4	87.8	74.6	84.4
Fixed investment	54.3	53.1	52.5	53.8	58.6	59.7	61.3	59.4	61.1	64.5	76.2	79.2	95.8	86.1	95.5
Changes in stocks	9.7	3.8	5.7	5.3	3.1	4.6	5.4	3.8	5.9	5.1	5.3	19.2	-8.0	-11.5	-11.1
Resource balance	-11.0	-11.6	-9.8	-7.0	-5.4	-2.2	-3.3	-8.1	-4.1	-7.8	-22.0	-2.3	-27.9	-12.3	-17.8
Exports of goods and nonfactor services								70.2	72.4	67.5	64.6	129.8		225.7	223.8
Imports of goods and nonfactor services								78.3	76.5	75.3	86.6	138.1		238.1	241.6
Net factor income 5/	-2.2	-2.7	-1.8	-1.1	-1.3	-1.0	-0.7	-0.7	-2.0	-0.4	-1.6	0.2	-2.9	-2.9	-1.3
Gross national product	169.3	162.7	172.0	181.0	191.8	202.3	211.0	216.2	223.0	233.8	242.0	280.3	283.0	298.9	335.4

(In 1984 prices)

	1980	1981	1982	1983	1984	1985	1986	1987	1988	1989	1990	1991	1992 6/	1992 7/	1993
Gross domestic product					193.1	201.1	209.2	214.6	218.6	220.9	215.4	184.1	171.2	179.6	172.2
By sector:															
Agriculture					13.8	12.3	13.4	13.2	13.9	14.5	13.0	12.5	9.0	15.0	15.7
Industry					115.4	118.9	123.9	128.2	131.8	133.3	129.7	98.7	88.9	89.4	75.4
Services					63.9	69.9	71.9	73.2	72.9	73.1	72.7	72.9	73.3	75.1	81.1
By expenditure:															
Total consumption					136.8	138.6	144.6	151.2	156.1	164.0	169.4	126.9	133.2	140.9	130.2
Gross investment					61.7	64.1	66.5	65.2	69.0	70.7	78.7	66.5	40.5	40.3	40.0
Fixed investment					58.6	59.5	61.2	61.5	63.3	65.8	73.5	55.0	46.6	46.6	45.5
Changes in stocks					3.1	4.6	5.3	3.7	5.7	4.9	5.2	11.5	-6.1	-6.3	-5.5
Resource balance 4/						-1.6	-1.9	-1.8	-6.5	-13.8	-32.7	-9.3	-1.2	-1.2	-5.5
Exports of goods and nonfactor services 4/								76.8	74.0	69.4	55.0	65.6	121.0	121.0	118.7
Imports of goods and nonfactor services 4/								78.6	80.5	83.2	87.7	74.9	122.2	122.2	124.2
Net factor income					-1.3	-1.0	-0.7	-0.7	-1.9	-0.4	-1.4	0.1	-1.6	-1.6	-0.6
Gross national product					191.8	200.1	208.5	213.9	216.7	220.5	214.0	184.2	169.6	178.0	171.6

Source: Staff estimates and Slovak Statistical Office.

Notes:
1/ The transformation methodology was used to calculate the national accounts data until 1987. During the period 1988-91 a conversion factor was used to make the data consistent with the earlier period. SNA methodology has been used for the years 1992-93. However for this presentation the transformation methodology has been used for years 1980-92. The SNA methodology has been used for 1992-93.
2/ Includes foreign trade organizations.
3/ Estimate for 1992 and 1993 since sectoral data are not available.
4/ Estimate for 1992 and 1993 include trade with Czech Republic.
5/ Data for 1980-91 exclude the Czech Republic.
6/ Transformation methodology.
7/ SNA methodology.

Table 2.2. Slovakia: Percentage Distribution of Gross Domestic Product by Industrial Origin
and by Final Use
(In current prices)

	1980	1981	1982	1983	1984	1985	1986	1987	1988	1989	1990	1991 1/	1992 2/	1993 2/ 3/
Gross domestic product	100.0%	100.0%	100.0%	100.0%	100.0%	100.0%	100.0%	100.0%	100.0%	100.0%	100.0%	100.0%	100.0%	100.0%
By sector:														
Agriculture	6.8%	6.1%	7.0%	7.1%	7.1%	6.4%	7.2%	6.9%	6.7%	9.4%	7.4%	5.7%	6.3%	6.7%
Industry	63.4%	59.6%	59.5%	60.5%	59.8%	61.5%	61.2%	60.7%	60.1%	58.5%	59.1%	60.1%	45.9%	43.9%
Services	29.9%	34.3%	33.5%	32.3%	33.1%	32.0%	31.6%	32.4%	33.2%	32.2%	33.5%	34.2%	47.9%	49.4%
By expenditure:														
Total consumption	69.1%	72.6%	72.2%	71.4%	70.8%	69.5%	70.1%	71.1%	70.5%	71.5%	75.8%	71.7%	78.7%	77.5%
Gross investment	37.3%	34.4%	33.5%	32.5%	32.0%	31.6%	31.5%	29.1%	29.8%	29.7%	33.5%	35.1%	24.7%	24.8%
Fixed investment	31.7%	32.1%	30.2%	29.5%	30.3%	29.4%	29.0%	27.4%	27.2%	27.5%	31.3%	28.3%	28.5%	28.0%
Changes in stocks	5.7%	2.3%	3.3%	2.9%	1.6%	2.3%	2.6%	1.8%	2.6%	2.2%	2.2%	6.9%	-3.8%	-3.3%
Resource balance	-6.4%	-7.0%	-5.6%	-3.8%	-2.8%	-1.1%	-1.6%	-3.7%	-0.3%	-1.2%	-9.3%	-6.9%	..	-2.4%
Exports of goods and nonfactor services								32.4%	33.7%	31.0%	26.3%	42.4%	..	..
Imports of goods and nonfactor services								36.1%	34.0%	32.2%	35.6%	49.3%	..	..

Source: Staff estimates and Slovak Statistical Office.

Note:

1/ Estimate of the transformation method.

2/ Quarterly national accounts ESA method.

3/ Preliminary.

Table 2.3. Slovakia: Derivation of Gross Domestic Product
(In billions of current koruny)

	1980	1981	1982	1983	1984	1985	1986	1987	1988	1989	1990	1991	1992	1993 Prel.
Domestic demand	149.3	144.1	148.8	152.1	160.3	166.3	173.5	174.2	183.7	190.9	214.4	250.4	219.0	..
Personal consumption	78.7	81.0	83.6	86.6	89.7	93.3	96.8	99.9	104.6	109.1	121.3	130.4	167.0	..
Social consumption	27.5	29.0	30.4	31.8	35.7	37.1	40.1	42.6	45.3	47.0	48.2	62.8		..
Total accumulation	43.1	34.0	34.8	33.6	34.9	35.9	36.6	31.7	33.7	34.8	44.9	57.2		..
Foreign balance	-10.8	-11.1	-9.6	-6.5	-4.4	-1.4	-2.6	0.3	-1.5	-3.3	-19.0	-21.6	-2.1	..
Losses on fixed capital and works	1.6	1.7	2.2	1.8	2.3	1.7	1.8	2.2	2.6	2.5	3.1	3.7	..	..
Net material product	140.1	134.6	141.4	147.3	158.2	166.6	172.7	176.7	184.8	190.1	198.4	232.5	222.0	..
Value added on non-material services	21.5	21.3	22.7	23.5	23.3	23.6	24.7	25.7	25.9	28.5	29.7	42.4	..	..
Less nonmaterial costs of material sphere	9.3	11.6	11.5	12.4	12.9	13.6	14.0	14.8	16.3	16.7	18.1	32.2	..	..
Depreciation 1/	19.2	21.1	21.2	23.6	24.5	26.7	28.3	29.3	30.7	32.3	33.5	37.4	..	..
GDP at market prices	171.5	165.4	173.8	182.1	193.1	203.3	211.7	216.9	237.5	247.2	257.1	295.7	301.8	336.7

Source: Staff estimates and Slovak Statistical Office.

1/ Less losses on stocks.
2/ Data for 1992 are estimated.

Table 2.4. Slovakia: Net Material Product by Industrial Origin and by Final Use
(In millions of current koruny)

	1980	1981	1982	1983	1984	1985	1986	1987	1988	1989	1990	1991	1992
Net material product 1/ 2/	140082	134565	141421	147347	158186	166559	172665	176674	184754	190124	198431	232548	:
By origin													
Agriculture	11253	9386	11502	12297	12794	10192	12117	12186	12405	18116	15371	13187	:
Industry	87420	78514	83164	89414	92547	98350	101799	104855	107993	108952	115578	144322	:
Construction	16503	16540	17259	16779	19014	20288	19921	21013	21529	22095	22298	22298	:
Trade and catering	14046	19160	18771	18362	22985	23588	24401	24890	28737	26777	30564	29726	:
Other	10860	10965	10725	10495	10846	14141	14427	13730	14090	14184	14620	23015	:
By final use	149287	144052	148789	152050	160325	166273	173513	174209	183673	190905	214364	250440	:
Personal consumption	78700	81020	83609	86647	89674	93299	96798	99925	104598	109106	121272	130382	:
Social consumption	27499	29013	30422	31777	35746	37096	40109	42613	45333	46997	48189	62809	:
Total accumulation	43088	34019	34758	33626	34905	35878	36606	31671	33742	34802	44903	57249	:
Net fixed investment	28212	27476	24369	27013	32976	32426	29326	25378	25504	22947	21184	23048	:
Change in stocks	9661	3848	5710	5200	3098	4581	5453	3799	5911	5079	5326	19203	:
Unfinished construction	5215	2695	4679	1413	-1169	-1129	1827	2494	2327	6776	18393	14998	:
Residual	-9205	-9487	-7368	-4703	-2139	286	-848	2465	1081	-781	-15933	-17892	:
Trade balance 3/	-10846	-11216	-9609	-6457	-4427	-1430	-2685	264	-1498	-3346	-19030	-21577	:
Exports of goods and services								74004	70461	66701	60961	101701	:
Imports of goods and services								73740	71959	70047	79991	123869	:
Losses on fixed capital and stocks	1641	1729	2241	1754	2288	1716	1837	2201	2579	2565	3097	3685	:

Source: Slovak Statistical Office.

Notes:
1/ Includes foreign trade organizations. For 1980-86, estimates of net material product for foreign trade organizations
   was done separately for the republics.
2/ 1991 figures are estimates.
3/ Calculated as a residual and not done separately by republics.

Table 2.5. Slovakia: Net Material Product by Industrial Origin and by Final Use
(In constant prices, millions of koruny)

	1980	1981	1982	1983	1984	1985	1986	1987	1988	1989	1990	1991	1992
Net material product 1/2/3/	128395	130044	130372	134928	142295	149981	165099	169259	173473	172373	166420	133193	..
By origin	128395	130044	130372	134928	142295	149981	165099	169259	173473	172373	166420	133193	..
Agriculture	11816	9769	11066	11517	12949	10949	10945	10910	11684	12307	11547	11270	..
Industry	73607	74692	73442	76266	81613	86613	96376	100996	104597	106680	103695	82420	..
Construction	17332	17234	16746	17097	16320	17729	20269	21519	21662	21051	20532	15547	..
Trade and catering	16609	18957	19695	20869	22363	23290	24089	22568	22291	19860	19263	14409	..
Other	9031	9392	9423	9179	9050	11400	13420	13266	13239	12475	11383	9547	..
By final use	128395	130044	130372	134928	142295	149981	165099	169259	173473	172373	166420	133193	..
Personal consumption	71281	73129	71039	73542	75363	77029	93482	96134	101243	103377	105999	75585	..
Social consumption	27275	28588	29152	30307	31351	33515	41392	43811	46416	49726	49155	46714	..
Accumulation	40050	31568	31033	28643	25745	25887	30879	28278	30278	30545	36749	19868	..
Net fixed investment	26696	25759	21707	22834	26872	24719	24617	19931	20017	18374	15622	7050	..
Change in stocks	8005	3087	6664	5541	3127	3981	5355	3740	5704	4900	5153	11517	..
Unfinished construction	5349	2722	2662	268	-4254	-2813	907	4607	4557	7271	15974	1301	..
Residual	-10211	-3241	-852	2436	9836	13550	-654	1036	-4464	-11275	-25483	-8974	..
Trade balance 4/	-11762	-4862	-2761	889	7836	12057	-2550	-991	-6868	-13546	-28429	-11808	..
Exports of goods and services								73100	68780	63840	52585	55357	..
Imports of goods and services								74091	75648	77386	81014	67165	..
Losses on fixed capital and stocks	1551	1621	1909	1547	2000	1493	1896	2027	2404	2271	2946	2834	..

Source: Staff estimates and Slovak Statistical Office.

Notes:
1/ Includes foreign trade organizations. For 1980-86, estimates of net material product for foreign trade organizations
  was done separately for the republics.
2/ Data for 1980-85 are in constant January 1, 1977 prices, for 1986-90 in constant January 1, 1984 prices.
3/ 1991 figures are estimates.
4/ Calculated as a residual and not done separately by republics.

Table 2.6. Slovakia: Annual Growth of Net Material Product by Industrial Origin and by Final Use
(In Constant Prices)

	1981	1982	1983	1984	1985	1986	1987	1988	1989	1990	1991	1992
Net material product 1/ 2/	1.3	0.3	3.5	5.5	5.4	3.8	2.5	2.5	-0.6	-3.5	-20.0	..
By origin												
Agriculture	-17.3	13.3	4.1	12.4	-15.4	12.7	-0.3	7.1	5.3	-6.2	-2.4	..
Industry	1.5	-1.7	3.8	7.0	6.1	4.4	4.8	3.6	2.0	-2.8	-20.5	..
Construction	-0.6	-2.8	2.1	-4.5	8.6	-1.7	6.2	0.7	-2.8	-2.5	-24.3	..
Trade and catering	14.1	3.9	6.0	7.2	4.1	3.3	-6.3	-1.2	-10.9	-3.0	-25.2	..
Other	4.0	0.3	-2.6	-1.4	26.0	1.6	-1.1	-0.2	-5.8	-8.8	-16.1	..
By final use												
Personal consumption	2.6	-2.9	3.5	2.5	2.2	3.1	2.8	5.3	2.1	2.5	-28.7	..
Social consumption	4.8	2.0	4.0	3.4	6.9	7.5	5.8	5.9	7.1	-1.1	-5.0	..
Accumulation	-21.2	-1.7	-7.7	-10.1	0.6	2.7	-8.4	7.1	0.9	20.3	-45.9	..
Net fixed investment	-3.5	-15.7	5.2	17.7	-8.0	-17.7	-19.0	0.4	-8.2	-15.0	-54.9	..
Change in stocks	-61.4	115.9	-16.9	-43.6	27.3	15.9	-30.2	52.5	-14.1	5.2	123.5	..
Unfinished construction	-49.1	-2.2	-89.9	-1687.3	33.9	-20.3	407.9	-1.1	59.6	119.7	-91.9	..
Trade balance 3/	58.7	43.2	132.2	781.4	53.9	34.9	61.1	-593.0	-97.2	-109.9	58.5	..
Exports of goods and services								-5.9	-7.2	-17.6	5.3	..
Imports of goods and services								2.1	2.3	4.7	-17.1	..
Losses on fixed capital and stocks	4.5	17.8	-19.0	29.3	-25.4	4.6	6.9	18.6	-5.5	29.7	-3.8	..

Source: Slovak Statistical Office.

Notes:
1/ Includes foreign trade organizations. For 1980-86, estimates of net material product for foreign trade organizations
   was done separately for the republics.
2/ Data for 1980-85 are in constant January 1, 1977 prices, for 1986-90 in constant January 1, 1984 prices.
3/ 1991 figures are estimates.
4/ Calculated as a residual and not done separately by republics.

Table 2.7. Slovakia: Gross Output, Input, and Net Material Product by Sector
(In billions of current koruny)

	1980	1981	1982	1983	1984	1985	1986	1987	1988	1989	1990	1991	1992
Industry													
Gross output	246.2	252.4	267.6	276.1	304.4	317.3	329.9	340.7	344.5	334.1	346.9	430.5	..
Material input	158.8	173.8	184.4	186.7	211.9	218.9	228.1	235.8	236.5	225.2	231.3	286.1	..
Net product	87.4	78.5	83.2	89.4	92.5	98.4	101.8	104.9	108.0	109.0	115.6	144.3	..
Agriculture													
Gross output	38.7	38.5	43.8	45.2	48.6	46.0	48.2	51.3	52.7	62.5	59.5	57.3	..
Material input	27.4	29.1	32.3	32.9	35.9	35.8	36.1	39.1	40.3	44.4	44.1	44.1	..
Net product	11.3	9.4	11.5	12.3	12.8	10.2	12.1	12.2	12.4	18.1	15.4	13.2	..
Construction													
Gross output	41.3	41.2	43.4	43.8	48.0	49.5	48.5	50.2	51.4	52.7	52.8	53.6	..
Material input	24.8	24.7	26.2	27.0	29.0	29.2	28.6	29.2	29.9	30.6	30.5	31.3	..
Net product	16.5	16.5	17.3	16.8	19.0	20.3	19.9	21.0	21.5	22.1	22.3	22.3	..
Trade and Catering													
Gross output	21.0	25.2	25.4	25.2	29.4	31.6	32.2	32.2	36.5	34.9	39.8	48.7	..
Material input	6.9	6.0	6.5	6.8	6.4	8.0	7.8	7.3	7.8	8.1	9.2	18.2	..
Net product	14.0	19.2	18.8	18.4	23.0	23.6	24.4	24.9	28.7	26.8	30.6	29.7	..
Other sectors													
Gross output	18.1	18.6	18.9	18.8	20.1	25.7	26.1	26.4	26.9	27.8	31.0	48.7	..
Material input	7.3	7.6	8.3	8.4	9.3	11.6	11.7	12.7	12.8	13.6	16.4	25.7	..
Net product	10.9	11.0	10.7	10.5	10.8	14.1	14.4	13.7	14.1	14.2	14.6	23.0	..
Total economy													
Gross material output	365.3	375.9	399.1	409.1	450.5	470.1	484.9	500.8	512.0	512.0	530.0	638.0	..
Material input	225.2	241.2	257.7	261.8	292.4	303.5	312.3	324.1	327.3	321.9	331.6	405.4	..
Net material product	140.1	134.6	141.4	147.3	158.2	166.6	172.7	176.7	184.8	190.1	198.4	232.5	..

Source: Slovak Statistical Office.

Table 2.8. Slovakia: Gross Fixed Investment 1/
(In billions of current koruny)

	1989	1990	1991	1992	1993 Prel.
Material sphere	42.0	47.9	48.1	64.3	..
Agriculture	8.0	7.8	5.5	4.4	..
Forestry	0.6	0.5	0.5	0.5	..
Water economy	3.9	3.9	3.4	4.6	..
Industry	23.0	27.8	29.1	39.3	..
Construction	2.0	2.0	2.8	3.0	..
Mining and development	0.2	0.3	0.1	2.5	..
Freight transport	1.6	2.3	2.6	3.0	..
Trade	2.7	3.3	4.1	5.8	..
Nonmaterial sphere	21.3	21.8	21.7	26.3	..
Housing	7.3	6.9	7.1	6.1	..
Passenger transport	3.3	3.0	3.4	3.2	..
Other	10.7	11.9	11.2	17.0	..
Total	63.3	69.7	69.8	90.6	101.8
Gross fixed investment (In constant 1989 prices)	63.3	66.7	47.9	58.4	56.2
Index of gross fixed investment	100.0	105.4	75.7	92.3	88.8

Source: Slovak Statistical Office.

1/ Preliminary data for 1993.

Table 2.9. Slovakia: Percentage Distribution of Gross Fixed Investment

	1989	1990	1991	1992
Material sphere	66.4%	68.7%	68.9%	71.0%
Agriculture	12.6%	11.2%	7.9%	4.9%
Forestry	0.9%	0.7%	0.7%	0.6%
Water economy	6.2%	5.6%	4.9%	5.1%
Industry	36.3%	39.9%	41.7%	43.4%
Construction	3.2%	2.9%	4.0%	3.3%
Mining and development	0.3%	0.4%	0.1%	2.8%
Freight transport	2.5%	3.3%	3.7%	3.3%
Trade	4.3%	4.7%	5.9%	6.4%
Nonmaterial sphere	33.6%	31.3%	31.1%	29.0%
Housing	11.5%	9.9%	10.2%	6.7%
Passenger transport	5.2%	4.3%	4.9%	3.5%
Other	16.9%	17.1%	16.0%	18.8%
Total	100.0%	100.0%	100.0%	100.0%

Source: Slovak Statistical Office.

Table 2.10. Slovakia: Personal and Social Consumption

	1980	1981	1982	1983	1984	1985	1986	1987	1988	1989	1990	1991	1992 3/	1993 3/
Personal Consumption (In billions of current koruny)														
Total	78.7	81.0	83.6	86.6	89.7	93.3	96.8	99.9	104.6	109.1	121.3	130.4	167.0	199.1
Purchases - retail stores	70.9	73.1	75.0	77.4	80.1	83.4	85.9	88.8	93.7	97.0	108.5	114.2	..	
Purchases - agricultural markets	0.9	0.9	1.0	0.9	0.9	0.9	1.1	1.1	0.8	1.1	1.1	1.7	..	
Own consumption:	3.1	3.0	3.4	4.0	4.1	4.0	4.5	4.6	4.6	5.5	5.2	6.3	..	
Agricultural goods	2.9	2.8	3.1	3.6	3.7	3.6	4.0	4.1	4.1	5.0	4.6	5.5	..	
Other	0.2	0.2	0.3	0.4	0.4	0.4	0.5	0.5	0.5	0.5	0.6	0.8	..	
Other 1/	3.8	4.0	4.2	4.3	4.6	5.0	5.3	5.4	5.5	5.5	6.5	8.2	..	
Social Consumption (In billions of current koruny)														
Social consumption 2/	27.5	29.0	30.4	31.8	35.7	37.1	40.1	42.6	45.3	47.0	48.2	62.8	..	
Institutions providing services	19.4	20.6	21.6	22.1	24.5	25.9	28.0	29.8	31.4	33.2	34.9	44.8	..	
Other social consumption	8.1	8.4	8.8	9.7	11.2	11.2	12.1	12.8	13.9	13.8	13.3	18.0	..	

Source: Slovak Statistical Office.

Notes:
1/ Including sales by the small private sector.
2/ Figures from Material Product System.
3/ ESA method used from 1992 onwards.

Table 2.11. Slovakia: Capital Stocks
(In billions of current koruny)

	1980	1981	1982	1983	1984	1985	1986	1987	1988	1989	1990	1991
Material sphere	261.3	279.9	294.0	310.0	329.2	351.7	367.2	382.9	396.4	406.7	419.2	433.2
Agriculture	47.3	51.0	54.3	58.1	62.3	67.6	71.8	76.2	79.9	82.7	84.7	85.3
Forestry	4.8	5.2	5.6	5.8	6.1	6.4	6.8	7.3	7.7	7.9	8.1	8.3
Water economy	23.1	24.6	25.7	27.1	28.9	31.0	34.1	36.0	38.1	39.2	41.4	42.2
Industry	130.6	139.4	145.4	153.4	163.7	175.8	178.4	183.7	188.4	192.5	198.6	205.3
Construction	10.4	10.8	11.2	11.5	11.6	12.0	12.8	13.6	14.2	14.6	14.1	13.9
Mining and development	1.1	1.1	1.2	1.2	1.2	1.3	1.5	1.6	1.7	1.7	1.8	1.7
Freight transport	20.2	22.6	23.7	24.3	24.8	25.5	27.8	29.0	29.9	29.6	29.8	31.0
Trade 2/	23.8	25.2	26.9	28.6	30.6	32.1	34.0	35.5	36.5	38.5	40.6	44.1
Nonmaterial sphere	192.4	201.7	212.7	224.3	238.6	249.6	264.1	274.2	287.3	300.7	312.1	320.1
Housing	97.0	101.2	107.1	113.2	119.7	125.5	130.9	135.7	141.1	146.2	150.6	151.0
Passenger transport	33.0	34.3	35.4	37.1	39.1	39.6	43.4	43.8	45.2	47.8	48.3	47.9
Other	62.4	66.2	70.2	74.0	79.8	84.5	89.8	94.7	101.0	106.7	113.2	121.2
Total	453.7	481.6	506.7	534.3	567.8	601.3	631.3	657.1	683.7	707.4	731.2	753.5

Source: Slovak Statistical Office.

Notes:
1/ At depreciated value.
2/ Trade and other.

Table 2.12. Slovakia: Changes in Stocks by Type and by Economic Sector
(In millions of current koruny)

	1980	1981	1982	1983	1984	1985	1986	1987	1988	1989	1990	1991
Increase in stocks	9661	3848	5710	5200	3098	4581	5453	3799	5911	5079	5326	19203
By type												
Raw materials	4484	2880	-5642	1401	-4254	839	4010	1695	3853	3540	2882	
Intermediate goods	7008	1614	19859	-117	10348	3837	-6409	-13662	23572	-8746	5686	
Finished goods	-3162	-561	-8443	2108	-2485	3454	1428	13377	-9933	7123	707	
Work-in-progress	1331	-90	-64	1808	-511	-3549	6424	2389	-11521	3162	-3949	
By sector												
Agriculture 1/	1621	959	1243	1224	1156	265	580	163	835	839	-822	-637
Mining and industry	5831	1788	1103	2137	-628	2042	2032	2533	2864	2021	-1070	18273
Construction	539	445	194	-208	60	21	813	143	17	-302	-1944	3516
Freight transport	32	44	-22	30	26	20	20	10	-4	78	150	167
Trade and catering	1554	685	2483	1227	1250	1977	1059	138	1729	1405	4350	-848
Other material sphere	99	-285	594	509	1222	111	722	632	318	844	3029	-1270
Nonmaterial sphere	-15	207	115	281	12	145	227	180	152	194	1633	2

Source: Slovak Statistical Office.

Notes:
1/ Includes forestry and fishing.

Table 2.13. Slovakia: Indices of Agricultural Production 1/
(In constant 1989 prices)

	1980	1981	1982	1983	1984	1985	1986	1987	1988	1989	1990	1991	1992	1993
Crop production	85.9	80.1	92.1	93.4	100.0	89.7	96.7	101.7	101.9	100.0	88.4	93.5	79.9	75.1
of which:														
Grains 2/	87.4	75.2	84.1	88.0	99.1	92.4	87.2	101.5	102.7	100.0	83.5	93.7	82.6	74.4
Fodder and root crops	84.9	84.2	87.9	86.5	96.8	99.9	94.9	99.7	100.7	100.0	86.6	86.8	66.2	60.4
Potatoes	103.7	136.0	147.3	126.4	137.5	105.3	133.3	119.5	119.7	100.0	104.5	89.8	88.2	114.9
Vegetables	71.5	75.9	85.4	82.0	92.9	81.9	89.4	102.8	98.2	100.0	87.0	96.7	85.3	93.8
Animal production	86.3	86.7	85.1	89.7	93.0	93.0	94.8	97.4	97.4	100.0	96.2	79.9	69.4	62.5
of which:														
Livestock for slaughter 3/	88.1	89.3	81.6	86.3	91.1	93.8	92.8	97.8	96.8	100.0	98.9	91.0	82.4	78.8
of which:														
Cattle	88.2	87.2	86.9	86.1	93.5	98.6	100.9	97.3	97.6	100.0	101.0	99.3	82.4	81.5
Pigs	88.2	91.2	77.9	86.0	88.2	89.0	85.9	98.2	96.1	100.0	98.3	86.0	82.0	77.0
Milk	85.0	85.9	85.3	91.1	95.8	98.4	100.0	99.3	99.8	100.0	96.2	76.5	66.7	60.9
Eggs	79.4	81.6	85.3	89.5	92.8	94.0	96.9	97.0	98.5	100.0	99.8	91.8	81.8	76.9
Total agricultural gross production	86.1	83.8	88.2	91.3	96.1	91.5	93.9	99.4	99.4	100.0	92.8	85.9	74.0	68.1

Source: Slovak Statistical Office.

Notes:
1/ 1993: Preliminary data.
2/ Cereals.
3/ Excludes poultry.

Table 2.14. Slovakia: Annual Growth Rates of Agricultural Production
(1989=100)

	1981	1982	1983	1984	1985	1986	1987	1988	1989	1990	1991	1992	1993 Prel.
Crop production of which:	-6.8	15.0	1.4	7.1	-10.3	7.8	5.2	0.2	-1.9	-11.6	5.8	-14.5	-6.0
Grains 1/	-14.0	11.8	4.6	12.6	-6.8	-5.6	16.4	1.2	-2.6	-16.5	12.2	-11.8	-9.9
Fodder and root crops	-0.8	4.4	-1.6	11.9	3.2	-5.0	5.1	1.0	-0.7	-13.4	0.2	-23.7	-8.8
Potatoes	31.1	8.3	-14.2	8.8	-23.4	26.6	-10.4	0.2	-16.5	4.5	-14.1	-1.8	30.3
Vegetables	6.2	12.5	-4.0	13.3	-11.8	9.2	15.0	-4.5	1.8	-13.0	11.1	-11.8	10.0
Animal production of which:	0.5	-1.8	5.4	3.7	0.0	1.9	2.7	0.0	2.7	-3.8	-16.9	-13.1	-9.9
Livestock for slaughter 2/	1.4	-8.6	5.8	5.6	3.0	-1.1	5.4	-1.0	3.3	-1.1	-8.0	-9.5	-4.4
of which:													
Cattle	-1.1	-0.3	-0.9	8.6	5.5	2.3	-3.6	0.3	2.5	1.0	-1.7	-17.0	-1.1
Pigs	3.4	-14.6	10.4	2.6	0.9	-3.5	14.3	-2.1	4.1	-1.7	-12.5	-4.7	-6.1
Milk	1.1	-0.7	6.8	5.2	2.7	1.6	-0.7	0.5	0.2	-3.8	-20.5	-12.8	-8.7
Eggs	2.8	4.5	4.9	3.7	1.3	3.1	0.1	1.5	1.5	-0.2	-8.0	-10.9	-6.0
Total agricultural gross production	-2.7	5.3	3.5	5.3	-4.8	2.6	5.9	0.0	0.6	-7.2	-7.4	-13.9	-8.0

Source: Slovak Statistical Office.

Notes:
1/ Cereals
2/ Excludes poultry

Table 2.15 Slovakia: Production and Yields of Selected Agricultural Crops and Livestock Products
(In thousands of tonnes)

	1980	1981	1982	1983	1984	1985	1986	1987	1988	1989	1990	1991	1992	1993 1/
					Selected Agricultural Crops									
Production					(In thousands of tons)									
Grain overall	3727.0	3172.0	3525.0	3746.0	4195.0	3884.0	3669.0	4239.0	4370.0	4249.0	3617.0	4004.0	3710.0	3151.9
Barley	985.0	1009.0	867.0	883.0	1013.0	859.0	897.0	930.0	883.0	937.0	913.0	960.0	1038.4	822.7
Corn	657.0	629.0	838.0	649.0	826.0	905.0	793.0	913.0	824.0	825.0	370.0	711.0	675.8	673.7
Wheat	1920.0	1373.0	1650.0	2001.0	2135.0	1940.0	1774.0	2180.0	2442.0	2266.0	2083.0	2124.0	1697.4	1528.5
Potatoes	773.0	1014.0	1098.0	942.0	1025.0	785.0	994.0	800.0	892.0	745.0	779.0	669.0	657.8	856.7
Rye	125.0	111.0	126.0	165.0	171.0	135.0	153.0	168.0	167.0	151.0	178.0	131.0	76.2	69.3
Sugar beets	2150.0	1945.0	2273.0	1716.0	2103.0	1922.0	1697.0	1611.0	1752.0	1877.0	1582.0	1501.0	1338.2	1128.0
Yields					(In tons per hectare)									
Grain overall	4.5	3.8	4.1	4.4	5.0	4.7	4.4	5.1	5.3	5.2	4.7	5.0	4.4	3.8
Barley	4.2	3.5	3.7	3.9	4.9	4.1	4.2	4.5	4.6	4.7	4.8	4.6	4.1	3.3
Corn	4.8	4.3	5.4	4.6	5.0	5.6	4.9	5.8	5.6	5.6	3.6	5.4	4.5	4.6
Wheat	4.8	4.0	4.1	4.8	5.3	4.9	4.4	5.4	5.8	5.5	5.0	5.2	4.8	3.9
Potatoes	11.5	15.6	16.4	14.9	16.6	13.3	17.1	14.2	15.6	13.6	14.1	12.3	12.9	18.2
Rye	3.2	2.9	2.9	3.4	3.4	2.9	3.3	3.8	3.7	3.8	3.9	3.4	3.2	3.0
Sugar beets	36.9	31.3	37.8	29.0	37.1	32.8	30.6	30.9	33.1	34.3	30.8	31.1	29.4	34.2
					Selected Livestock Products									
Production					(In thousands of tons)									
Meat (tons, live yield)														
Beef (thousand tons)	184.0	182.0	181.0	180.0	195.0	206.0	211.0	207.0	204.0	209.0	211.0	207.0	172.0	170.4
Veal (thousand tons)	4.0	4.0	3.0	4.0	6.0	6.0	4.0	4.0	3.0	3.0	2.0	1.0	0.7	6.2
Pork (thousand tons)	337.0	348.0	297.0	328.0	337.0	340.0	328.0	344.0	367.0	382.0	376.0	328.0	313.2	294.2
Eggs (million pcs.)	1531.0	1577.0	1654.0	1743.0	1804.0	1824.0	1886.0	1927.0	1953.0	1985.0	1983.0	1824.0	1720.8	1526.8
Milk (liters) (mill.1)	1696.0	1714.0	1702.0	1818.0	1912.0	1963.0	1996.0	1972.0	1991.0	1995.0	1920.0	1526.0	1330.6	1214.4
Yields					(In tons per hectare)									
Average live weight (kg)														
Slaughtered cattle	465.0	458.0	439.0	439.0	444.0	448.0	455.0	456.0	462.0	475.0	483.0	479.0	471.5	426.0
Slaughtered pigs 2/	116.1	111.0	110.9	116.2	120.1	123.3	123.3	124.0	122.7	125.3	129.0	133.3	136.1	119.0
Average annual milk yield/cow (liters)	3012.0	3051.0	3015.0	3183.0	3345.0	3479.0	3577.0	3573.0	3616.0	3654.0	3573.0	2887.0	2887.1	2952.8
Average annual egg production/chicken	215.0	215.0	218.0	226.0	233.0	239.0	241.0	244.0	244.0	249.0	249.0	241.0	240.0	226.5
Number of calves born per 100 cows	99.3	98.0	99.6	101.7	104.1	104.5	104.2	104.4	105.0	103.7	101.8	92.0	90.6	93.5
Number of piglets born per sow	17.4	17.5	17.2	17.8	18.4	18.5	18.4	18.4	18.4	18.2	17.5	16.7	15.7	15.2

Source: Slovak Statistical Office.

Note:
1/ Prelimiary data.
2/ Estimate for 1993.

Table 2.16. Slovakia: Indices of Industrial Production
(1989=100)

	1980	1981	1982	1983	1984	1985	1986	1987	1988	1989	1990	1991	1992	1993 Prel.
Fuels	76.5	81.0	86.3	83.5	90.2	93.2	97.8	102.5	102.5	100.0	98.0	59.3	53.2	51.8
Energy	80.9	85.6	87.7	85.8	83.8	91.6	97.5	97.1	96.5	100.0	100.4	80.4	76.4	73.3
Ferrous metallurgy	82.2	85.3	84.4	84.4	89.1	93.0	93.5	96.5	98.6	100.0	102.6	91.1	87.5	86.1
Nonferrous metallurgy	91.3	91.7	89.1	89.3	89.5	91.4	94.1	96.0	98.6	100.0	95.2	64.0	61.4	60.5
Chemicals and rubber	85.8	82.6	80.4	83.8	87.7	91.4	95.0	98.7	100.1	100.0	89.3	71.2	66.4	51.8
Machinery	66.9	71.1	74.5	81.2	90.1	97.1	103.2	107.9	110.7	100.0	94.5	63.3	43.4	35.4
Electrical engineering	43.8	46.9	48.5	53.7	63.2	68.7	76.1	86.7	97.2	100.0	94.7	59.1	46.5	43.1
Construction materials	92.4	94.2	92.6	93.3	93.9	94.5	96.2	97.3	100.0	100.0	92.1	59.8	55.0	50.1
Wood Processing	85.5	83.1	86.8	89.6	93.3	94.5	96.3	97.4	99.2	100.0	97.6	73.5	66.0	57.4
Paper and cellulose	70.6	71.7	78.1	81.0	86.7	89.7	93.2	93.2	96.6	100.0	100.2	86.2	88.0	75.1
Glass, ceramics, porcelain	68.6	69.8	72.3	75.3	79.7	82.1	85.1	87.1	90.0	100.0	105.2	87.9	88.2	87.3
Textiles	74.1	76.6	76.6	79.0	78.9	80.9	83.9	85.4	98.7	100.0	100.7	66.4	56.9	48.6
Clothing	73.5	77.7	79.9	81.7	84.1	89.0	92.2	93.1	94.8	100.0	97.8	61.5	63.2	54.5
Leather processing	87.5	88.6	89.9	87.8	89.8	91.5	94.6	95.2	98.4	100.0	97.9	59.8	49.4	37.7
Printing	71.1	71.1	73.6	75.6	79.4	83.2	87.7	91.1	97.0	100.0	108.5	109.6	84.3	90.6
Food and beverages	84.7	87.1	85.0	88.1	90.4	93.8	95.4	96.9	98.5	100.0	98.9	85.4	69.7	56.7
Frozen foods, spring water and tobacco	76.5	79.3	77.3	78.3	82.5	85.2	88.6	93.5	93.5	100.0	100.6	71.3	58.1	29.1
Other	54.6	42.8	43.7	45.9	59.9	72.9	75.0	78.3	91.1	100.0	92.2	60.8	50.7	45.8
Total gross output	76.6	78.3	78.9	82.0	86.6	91.0	94.7	97.9	100.9	100.0	96.3	73.0	62.7	54.3

Source: Slovak Statistical Office

Table 2.17. Slovakia: Annual Growth Rates of Industrial Production
(In constant prices of January 1, 1989)

	1981	1982	1983	1984	1985	1986	1987	1988	1989	1990	1991	1992	1993 Prel.
Fuels	5.9	6.5	-3.2	8.0	3.3	4.9	4.8	0.0	-2.4	-2.0	-39.5	-10.3	-2.6
Energy	5.8	2.5	-2.2	-2.3	9.3	6.4	-0.4	-0.6	3.6	0.4	-19.9	-5.0	-4.1
Ferrous metallurgy	3.8	-1.1	0.0	5.6	4.4	0.5	3.2	2.2	1.4	2.6	-11.2	-4.0	-1.6
Nonferrous metallurgy	0.4	-2.8	0.2	0.2	2.1	3.0	2.0	2.7	1.4	-4.8	-32.8	-4.1	-1.5
Chemicals and rubber	-3.7	-2.7	4.2	4.7	4.2	3.9	3.9	1.4	-0.1	-10.7	-20.3	-6.7	-22.0
Machinery	6.3	4.8	9.0	11.0	7.8	6.3	4.6	2.6	-9.7	-5.5	-33.0	-31.4	-18.4
Electrical engineering	7.1	3.4	10.7	17.7	8.7	10.8	13.9	12.1	2.9	-5.3	-37.6	-21.3	-7.3
Construction materials	1.9	-1.7	0.8	0.6	0.6	1.8	1.1	2.8	0.0	-7.9	-35.1	-8.0	-8.9
Woodworking	-2.8	4.5	3.2	4.1	1.3	1.9	1.1	1.8	0.8	-2.4	-24.7	-10.2	-13.0
Metal working	5.0	2.8	3.6	3.3	5.3	2.9	1.7	-1.5	-0.7	-2.0	-31.6	-16.3	1.4
Paper & pulp	1.6	8.9	3.7	7.0	3.5	3.9	0.0	3.6	3.5	0.2	-14.0	2.1	-14.7
Glass, ceramics, porcelain	1.7	3.6	4.1	5.8	3.0	3.7	2.4	3.3	11.1	5.2	-16.4	0.3	-1.0
Textiles	3.4	0.0	3.1	-0.1	2.5	3.7	1.8	15.6	1.3	0.7	-34.1	-14.3	-14.6
Clothing	5.7	2.8	2.3	2.9	5.8	3.6	1.0	1.8	5.5	-2.2	-37.1	2.8	-13.8
Leather processing	1.3	1.5	-2.3	2.3	1.9	3.4	0.6	3.4	1.6	-2.1	-38.9	-17.4	-23.7
Printing	0.0	3.5	2.7	5.0	4.8	5.4	3.9	6.5	3.1	8.5	1.0	-23.1	7.5
Food and beverages	2.8	-2.4	3.6	2.6	3.8	1.7	1.6	1.7	1.5	-1.1	-13.7	-18.4	-18.7
Frozen foods, spring water and tobacco	3.7	-2.5	1.3	5.4	3.3	4.0	5.5	0.0	7.0	0.6	-29.1	-18.5	-49.9
Other	-21.6	2.1	5.0	30.5	21.7	2.9	4.4	16.3	9.8	-7.8	-34.1	-16.6	-9.7
Total gross output	2.2	0.8	3.9	5.6	5.1	4.1	3.4	3.1	-0.9	-3.7	-24.2	-14.1	-10.6

Source: Slovak Statistical Office.

Table 2.18. Slovakia: Construction 1/

	1988	1989	1990	1991	1992	1993 3/
In millions of current koruny:						
Construction production						
carried out by delivery contracts 2/		73328	66807	42741	56560	42716
Shares in total construction output:						
Private housing		0.1	0.5	0.4		
Other residential construction		30.9	29.7	38.4		4.5 4/
Industrial and commercial construction		22.8	25.3	26.0		28.7
Roads and infrastructure		31.5	29.0	30.3		14.8
Index of construction						
(In constant 1992 prices)	99.4	100.0	91.1	58.3	77.1	58.3

Source: Slovak Statistical Office.

Notes:
/1 NACE classification used for the estimation of the table.
/2 The data is based on 1992 annual data conversions.
/3 The data is based on monthly statement.
/4 Aggregate for private housing and other residential construction.

Table 2.19. Slovakia: Money Incomes and Expenditures
(In billions of current koruny)

	1980	1981	1982	1983	1984	1985	1986	1987	1988	1989	1990	1991	1992	1993 Prel.
Total money incomes	108.0	111.4	116.4	120.6	124.8	129.3	134.4	139.2	146.2	151.0	161.5	186.1	214.3	256.3
Wages	65.7	67.7	69.4	71.8	73.9	76.5	79.0	81.6	84.7	86.9	89.7	93.0	102.8	119.7
Social money benefits 1/	20.3	20.7	22.6	23.7	24.4	26.0	26.6	27.2	28.2	29.8	31.4	40.3	45.2	50.9
Nonwage incomes from economic activity 2/	8.9	9.3	9.8	10.6	11.1	11.2	11.7	11.9	12.8	13.2	13.1	9.5	8.0	7.6
Interest income	1.3	1.4	1.5	1.6	1.8	1.9	2.1	2.3	2.5	2.7	2.9	7.5	7.3	7.8
Other 3/	11.8	12.3	13.1	12.9	13.6	13.7	15.0	16.2	18.0	18.4	24.4	35.8	50.9	70.3
Total money expenditures	104.5	107.9	111.6	115.4	119.5	124.2	128.2	132.7	139.7	144.5	163.1	174.1	207.2	247.3
Retail purchases	70.8	73.0	75.4	78.0	80.6	83.8	86.3	89.3	94.2	97.7	109.5	109.7	131.9	159.6
Services	14.3	14.6	15.2	15.5	16.2	16.8	17.2	17.6	18.5	18.5	21.2	23.8	25.8	31.4
Taxes and levies to government	11.7	12.2	12.5	13.1	13.6	14.2	14.8	15.3	16.0	16.9	17.1	19.2	24.6	29.2
Interest payments	0.3	0.3	0.4	0.4	0.4	0.5	0.5	0.5	0.6	0.6	0.6	0.8	1.0	1.0
Other	7.4	7.8	8.1	8.4	8.7	8.9	9.4	10.0	10.4	10.8	14.7	20.6	23.9	26.1
Financial savings	3.5	3.5	4.8	5.2	5.3	5.1	6.2	6.5	6.5	6.5	-1.6	12.0	7.0	8.9
Cash	0.7	0.5	0.9	0.9	0.8	0.3	0.7	0.8	1.1	1.6	1.9	3.7	1.7	-5.1
Savings	2.8	3.0	3.9	4.3	4.5	4.8	5.5	5.7	5.4	4.9	-3.5	8.3	5.3	14.0
Savings ratio in percent	3.2	3.1	4.1	4.3	4.2	3.9	4.6	4.7	4.4	4.3	-1.0	6.4	3.3	3.5

Source: Slovak Statistical Office.

Notes:
1/ Social benefits comprise mainly pensions, sickness benefits and social aid for families with children.
2/ Includes income of cooperative farms.
3/ Includes interest payments on savings accounts, payments from insurance claims, gambling wins, business travel allowances, subsidies paid by enterprises in connection with work mobility and borrowing by the household sector from the banking system.

Table 3.1. Slovakia: Balance of Payments with the Rest of the World in Covertible Currencies
(Im millions of Current US$)

	1980	1981	1982	1983	1984	1985	1986	1987	1988	1989	1990	1991	1992	1993 Prel.
Trade balance	-324.3	-197.1	-104.2	-68.8	-22.8	192.0	28.1	-35.2	-90.7	-34.9	-533.0	-787.1	-229.0	-1095.1
Exports, f.o.b.	909.4	819.4	733.6	698.0	750.8	967.5	1078.7	1138.6	1202.1	1251.5	1326.1	2525.2	3321.0	2998.6
Imports, f.o.b.	1233.7	1016.5	837.8	766.8	773.6	775.5	1050.6	1173.8	1292.8	1286.4	1859.1	3312.3	3550.0	4093.7
Nonfactor services balance	-42.9	-33.3	-7.0	-3.7	20.2	77.6	92.1	53.7	43.1	-2.7	-115.3	23.3	199.0	337.6
Receipts NFS	263.3	250.4	214.0	202.6	248.4	296.1	355.1	351.4	346.2	321.7	353.9	665.3	612.0	1181.0
Shipment and other	185.4	176.0	146.9	138.2	150.2	191.9	221.4	216.2	212.2	203.6	212.2	256.7	275.0	378.1
Travel	14.1	13.7	13.3	12.4	11.8	12.6	15.8	20.2	22.8	24.3	52.0	126.5	200.0	309.4
Other	63.8	60.7	53.8	52.0	86.4	91.6	117.9	115.0	111.2	93.8	89.7	282.1	137.0	493.5
Expenditures NFS	306.2	283.7	221.0	206.3	228.2	218.5	263.0	297.7	303.1	324.4	469.2	642.0	413.0	843.4
Shipment and other	210.8	158.4	130.4	112.5	110.5	108.0	137.4	143.6	148.3	151.7	191.9	147.7	200.0	126.3
Travel	17.9	21.2	16.4	17.9	20.3	18.3	21.1	24.1	34.5	54.3	124.4	115.3	165.0	154.6
Other	77.5	104.1	74.2	75.9	97.4	92.2	104.5	130.0	120.3	118.4	152.9	379.0	48.0	562.5
Net factor income	-174.6	-219.2	-155.8	-96.1	-84.9	-67.5	-55.0	-57.8	-152.5	-54.4	-105.3	-21.8	30.0	-24.5
Factor receipts	104.1	113.9	83.4	79.5	81.7	81.8	90.2	103.6	112.2	130.0	147.5	176.1	160.0	169.0
Factor payments	278.7	333.1	239.2	175.6	166.6	149.3	145.2	161.4	264.7	184.4	252.8	197.9	130.0	193.5
Unrequited transfers	-14.1	-11.2	-54.6	-12.0	-9.8	-13.3	-11.9	-15.4	-16.2	-11.5	-13.1	-0.6	68.0	73.9
Private	-0.5	-0.6	-0.6	-0.6	-0.6	-0.7	-1.2	-1.2	-2.1	-1.2	-1.4	5.5	60.0	3.9
Official	-13.6	-10.6	-54.0	-11.4	-9.2	-12.6	-10.7	-14.2	-14.1	-10.3	-11.7	-6.1	8.0	70.0
Current account after official transfers	-555.9	-460.8	-321.6	-180.6	-97.3	188.8	53.3	-54.7	-216.3	-103.5	-766.7	-786.2	68.0	-708.1
Net medium- and long-term capital	136.8	87.5	-10.0	-97.4	-179.9	-231.7	-119.8	69.5	-12.9	-3.9	230.4	165.0	447.0	725.0
Direct foreign investment											10.5	17.9	81.6	100.0	144.2
Portfolio investment														7.8
MLT Credits received	176.6	125.3	34.8	-10.7	-83.8	-111.9	-39.5	103.1	101.5	36.1	238.7	81.3	55.0	314.2
MLT Credits extended	-39.8	-37.8	-44.8	-86.7	-96.1	-119.8	-80.3	-33.6	-114.4	-50.5	-26.2	2.1	292.0	258.8
Net short-term capital 3/	268.0	-237.2	-99.9	-99.3	15.5	-23.9	121.9	28.7	126.7	41.0	-190.9	-759.0	-481.0	-22.7
Clearing account balance (-,surplus)														
Total capital account	404.8	-149.7	-109.9	-196.7	-164.4	-255.6	2.1	98.2	113.8	37.1	39.5	-594.0	-34.0	702.3
Errors and omissions, nei	176.1	576.0	396.2	454.3	275.9	88.4	-15.9	-25.5	38.0	92.3	514.6	1240.2	-168.0	292.4
Overall Balance	25.0	-34.5	-35.3	77.0	14.2	21.6	39.5	18.0	-64.5	25.9	-212.6	-140.0	-134.0	286.6
Change in reserves	-25.0	34.5	35.3	-77.0	-14.2	-21.6	-39.5	-18.0	64.5	-25.9	212.6	140.0	-0.7	-286.6
Use of IMF Credit	0.0	0.0	0.0	0.0	0.0	0.0	0.0	0.0	0.0	0.0	0.0	437.5	94.3	90.1
Change in gross reserves	-25.0	34.5	35.3	-77.0	-14.2	-21.6	-39.5	-18.0	64.5	-25.9	212.6	-297.5	-95.0	-376.7

Source: Slovak National Bank

Note:
1/ Excluding the Czech Republic.
2/ For 1980-91, net short term capital figures were revised by the National Bank of Slovakia; hence, errors and omissions
   were changed.
3/ Net Short-term capital includes short-term bank liabilities.

Table 3.2. Slovakia: Balance of Payments with the Rest of the World in Nonconvertible Currencies 1/ 2/
(In millions of current US dollars)

	1980	1981	1982	1983	1984	1985	1986	1987	1988	1989	1990	1991	1993 Prel.
Trade balance	182.9	102.8	148.0	198.6	267.5	244.4	452.8	660.9	700.7	328.8	-105.4	-28.8	13.4
Exports, f.o.b.	1852.3	1566.2	1737.6	1809.6	1774.9	2175.4	2580.3	3042.4	2781.9	2263.8	1420.2	692.9	27.3
Imports, f.o.b.	1669.4	1463.4	1589.6	1611.0	1507.4	1931.0	2127.5	2381.5	2081.2	1935.0	1525.6	721.7	13.9
Nonfactor services balance	53.9	50.0	87.3	89.3	78.7	107.5	128.9	192.4	220.7	156.3	62.0	21.2	6.8
Receipts NFS	247.2	233.0	262.3	259.5	268.2	321.5	366.2	435.1	444.0	364.0	266.5	98.7	29.5
Shipment and other	145.3	139.7	162.2	161.7	162.4	200.7	219.4	243.1	217.3	191.5	160.3	17.8	0.0
Travel	74.0	70.8	70.7	74.3	79.2	88.2	107.9	139.1	177.0	109.2	59.8	6.8	28.2
Other	27.9	22.5	29.4	23.5	26.6	32.6	38.9	52.9	49.7	63.3	46.4	74.1	1.3
Expenditures NFS	193.3	183.0	175.0	170.2	189.5	214.0	237.3	242.7	223.3	207.7	204.5	77.5	22.7
Shipment and other	95.0	89.0	88.0	77.7	69.1	83.8	94.2	96.8	87.8	82.5	79.2	3.6	0.0
Travel	64.0	64.7	62.4	68.6	69.2	85.4	87.6	103.4	89.7	78.7	76.0	4.0	22.3
Other	34.3	29.3	24.6	23.9	51.2	44.8	55.5	42.5	45.8	46.5	49.3	69.9	0.4
Net factor income	20.2	12.7	23.5	15.4	8.0	10.1	10.4	8.5	15.7	25.0	18.8	29.0	0.2
Factor receipts	28.6	22.0	31.7	22.8	15.8	19.1	19.0	20.3	24.5	37.2	28.4	42.4	0.2
Factor payments	8.4	9.3	8.2	7.4	7.8	9.0	8.6	11.8	8.8	12.2	9.6	13.4	0.0
Unrequited transfers	8.8	9.2	8.8	4.5	7.3	8.4	6.2	21.0	24.8	24.0	35.1	3.7	-0.1
Private	5.5	5.2	6.2	3.6	5.1	6.0	9.3	15.9	16.4	21.2	41.5	2.5	0.0
Official	3.3	4.0	2.6	0.9	2.2	2.4	-3.1	5.1	8.4	2.8	-6.4	1.2	-0.1
Current account after official transfers	265.8	174.7	267.6	307.8	361.5	370.4	598.3	882.8	961.9	534.1	10.5	25.1	20.3
Net medium- and long-term capital	-4.1	4.0	-11.7	-18.8	5.6	-12.8	-2.5	-30.5	-99.2	-165.6	-49.3	-3.5	1.7
Direct foreign investment										-0.2	6.2	0.4	0.0
Portfolio investment													0.0
MLT Credits received	-9.9	-5.3	-2.2	-5.6	-3.6	-3.5	-5.7	-2.1	2.3	76.2	6.3	-1.3	1.7
MLT Credits extended	5.8	9.3	-9.5	-13.2	9.2	-9.3	3.2	-28.4	-101.5	-241.6	-61.8	-2.6	0.0
Net short-term capital	-30.5	-38.5	-15.4	38.8	44.7	-28.5	32.3	-136.5	-324.0	32.9	150.2	-276.1	37.0
Total capital account	-34.6	-34.5	-27.1	20.0	50.3	-41.3	29.8	-167.0	-423.2	-132.7	100.9	-279.6	38.7
Errors and omissions, nei	-231.2	-140.2	-240.5	-327.8	-411.8	-329.1	-628.1	-715.8	-538.7	-401.4	-111.4	254.5	-59.0
Overall Balance	0.0	0.0	0.0	0.0	0.0	0.0	0.0	0.0	0.0	0.0	0.0	0.0	0.0
Change in reserves	0.0	0.0	0.0	0.0	0.0	0.0	0.0	0.0	0.0	0.0	0.0	0.0	0.0

Source: National Bank of Slovakia.

Note:
1/ Excluding the Czech Republic.

Table 3.3. Slovakia: Consolidated Balance of Payments with the Rest of the World 1/
(In millions of current US$)

	1980	1981	1982	1983	1984	1985	1986	1987	1988	1989	1990	1991	1992	1993 Prel.
Trade balance	-141.4	-94.3	43.8	129.8	244.7	436.4	480.9	625.7	610.0	293.9	-638.4	-815.9	-74.0	-1081.7
Exports, f.o.b.	2761.7	2385.6	2471.2	2507.6	2525.7	3142.9	3659.0	4181.0	3984.0	3515.3	2746.6	3218.1	3489.0	3025.9
Imports, f.o.b.	2903.1	2479.9	2427.4	2377.8	2281.0	2706.5	3178.1	3555.3	3374.0	3221.4	3385.0	4034.0	3563.0	4107.6
Nonfactor services balance	11.0	16.7	80.3	85.6	98.9	185.1	221.0	246.1	263.8	153.6	-53.3	44.4	587.0	344.4
Receipts NFS	510.5	483.4	476.3	462.1	516.6	617.7	721.3	786.5	790.2	685.7	620.4	764.0	1142.0	1210.5
Shipment and other	330.7	315.7	309.1	299.9	312.6	392.6	440.8	459.3	429.5	395.1	372.5	274.5	405.0	378.1
Travel	88.1	84.5	84.0	86.7	91.0	100.9	123.7	159.3	199.8	133.5	111.8	133.3	200.0	337.6
Other	91.7	83.2	83.2	75.5	113.0	124.2	156.8	167.9	160.9	157.1	136.1	356.2	537.0	494.8
Expenditures NFS	499.5	466.7	396.0	376.5	417.7	432.6	500.3	540.4	526.4	532.1	673.7	719.6	555.0	866.1
Shipment and other	305.8	247.4	218.4	190.2	179.6	191.8	231.6	240.4	236.1	234.2	271.1	151.4	76.0	126.3
Travel	81.9	85.9	78.8	86.5	89.5	103.7	108.7	127.5	124.2	133.0	200.4	119.3	165.0	176.9
Other	111.8	133.4	98.8	99.8	148.6	137.1	160.0	172.5	166.1	164.9	202.2	448.9	314.0	562.9
Net factor income	-154.4	-206.5	-132.3	-80.7	-76.9	-57.4	-44.6	-49.3	-136.8	-29.4	-86.5	7.2	-101.0	-24.3
Factor receipts	132.7	135.9	115.1	102.3	97.5	100.9	109.2	123.9	136.7	167.2	175.9	218.5	82.0	169.2
Factor payments	287.1	342.4	247.4	183.0	174.4	158.3	153.8	173.2	273.5	196.6	262.4	211.3	183.0	193.5
Unrequited transfers	-5.3	-1.9	-45.8	-7.5	-2.5	-4.9	-5.7	5.7	8.6	12.5	22.0	3.2	68.0	73.8
Private	5.0	4.6	5.6	3.0	4.6	5.3	8.1	14.9	14.3	20.0	40.1	8.1	60.0	69.9
Official	-10.3	-6.5	-51.4	-10.5	-7.1	-10.2	-13.8	-9.2	-5.7	-7.5	-18.1	-4.9	8.0	3.9
Current account after official transfers	-290.1	-286.0	-54.0	127.2	264.2	559.2	651.6	828.2	745.6	430.6	-756.2	-761.1	480.0	-687.8
Net medium- and long-term capital	132.7	91.5	-21.8	-116.2	-174.3	-244.5	-122.3	39.0	-112.1	-169.5	181.1	161.5	335.0	726.7
Direct foreign investment	0.0	0.0	0.0	0.0	0.0	0.0	0.0	0.0	0.0	10.3	24.1	82.0	100.0	144.2
Portfolio investment	0.0	0.0	0.0	0.0	0.0	0.0	0.0	0.0	0.0	0.0	0.0	0.0	0.0	7.8
MLT Credits received	166.7	120.0	32.6	-16.3	-87.4	-115.4	-45.2	101.0	103.8	112.3	245.0	80.0	180.0	315.9
MLT Credits extended	-34.0	-28.5	-54.4	-99.9	-86.9	-129.1	-77.1	-62.0	-215.9	-292.1	-88.0	-0.5	55.0	258.8
Net short-term capital 2/ 3/	237.5	-275.7	-115.3	-60.5	60.2	-52.4	154.2	-107.8	-197.3	73.9	-40.7	-1035.1	-100.0	14.3
Total capital account	370.2	-184.2	-137.1	-176.7	-114.1	-296.9	31.9	-68.8	-309.4	-95.6	140.4	-873.6	235.0	741.0
Errors and omissions, nei 2/	-55.1	435.7	155.7	126.5	-135.9	-240.7	-644.0	-741.4	-500.7	-309.1	403.2	1494.7	-714.3	233.4
Overall Balance	25.0	-34.5	-35.4	77.0	14.2	21.6	39.5	18.0	-64.5	25.9	-212.6	-140.0	0.7	286.6
Change in reserves	-25.0	34.5	35.3	-77.0	-14.2	-21.6	-39.5	-18.0	64.5	-25.9	212.6	140.0	-0.7	-286.6
Use of IMF Credit	0.0	0.0	0.0	0.0	0.0	0.0	0.0	0.0	0.0	0.0	0.0	437.5	94.3	90.1
Change in gross reserves	-25.0	34.5	35.3	-77.0	-14.2	-21.6	-39.5	-18.0	64.5	-25.9	212.6	-297.5	-95.0	-376.7

Source: National Bank of Slovakia.

Note:
1/ Excluding the Czech Republic.
2/ For 1980-91, net short term capital data were revised by the National Bank of Slovakia; hence, errors and omissions
   were changed.
3/ Net Short-term capital includes short-term bank liabilities.

Table 3.4. Slovakia: Balance of Payments with the Czech Republic
(In millions of current US$)

	1991	1992	1993 Prel.
Trade balance	-366.0	-640.0	43.6
Exports, f.o.b.	3491.0	3026.0	2275.7
Imports, f.o.b.	3857.0	3666.0	2232.1
Nonfactor services balance		-310.0	63.1
Receipts NFS		330.0	733.7
Shipment and other		0.0	80.2
Travel		0.0	47.6
Other		330.0	605.9
Expenditures NFS		640.0	670.6
Shipment and other		0.0	16.3
Travel		0.0	44.1
Other		640.0	610.2
Net factor income		0.0	-14.6
Factor receipts		0.0	19.4
Factor payments		0.0	34.0
Unrequited transfers		746.0	26.2
Private		10.0	0.0
Official Transfers		736.0	26.2
Current account after official transfers	..	-204.0	118.3
Capital Transfers			529.4
Net medium- and long-term capital		0.0	-596.3
Direct foreign investment		0.0	-10.3
Portfolio investment		0.0	-510.8
MLT Credits received		0.0	-65.2
MLT Credits extended		0.0	-10.0
Net short-term capital		204.0	26.3
Total capital account		204.0	148.8
Clearing account balance (-,surplus)			189.4
Errors and omissions, nei		0.0	-267.1
Overall Balance	..	0.0	0.0

Source: National Bank of Slovakia.

Table 3.5. Slovakia: Consolidated Balance of Payments with the Rest of the World
and with the Czech Republic
(In millions of current US$)

	1991	1992	1993 Prel.
Trade balance	-690.0	-714.0	-1038.1
Exports, f.o.b.	6775.0	6515.0	5301.6
Imports, f.o.b.	7465.0	7229.0	6339.7
Nonfactor services balance		277.0	407.5
Receipts		1472.0	1944.2
Expenditures		1195.0	1536.7
Net factor income		-101.0	-38.9
Factor receipts		82.0	188.6
Factor payments		183.0	227.5
Unrequited transfers		814.0	100.0
Private		70.0	3.9
Official		744.0	96.1
Current account after official transfers	..	276.0	-569.5
Capital Transfers			529.4
Net medium- and long- term capital		335.0	130.4
Direct foreign investment		100.0	133.9
Portfolio investment		0.0	-503.0
MLT Credits received		180.0	250.7
MLT Credits extended		55.0	248.8
Net short-term capital 2/		104.0	40.6
Clearing account balance (-,surplus)			189.4
Total capital account		439.0	889.8
Errors and omissions, nei		-714.3	-33.7
Overall Balance	..	0.7	286.6
Change in reserves	437.5	-0.7	-286.6
Use of IMF Credit	437.5	94.3	90.1
Purchases	437.5	110.7	90.1
Repurchases	0.0	16.4	0.0
Change in gross reserves		-95.0	-376.7

Source: National Bank of Slovakia.

Note:
1/ 1993 figures have been provided by the IMF.
2/ Net Short-term capital includes short-term bank liabilities.

Table 3.6. Slovakia: External Reserves 1/
(In millions of current US$)

	1980	1981	1982	1983	1984	1985	1986	1987	1988	1989	1990	1991	1992	1993 Prel.
Total Assets 2/	780.6	793.5	770.9	945.2	1039.0	1241.8	1512.5	1697.4	1810.2	1884.9	1651.6	2294.6	..	..
Total external reserves	227.1	192.5	157.1	234.1	248.3	269.9	309.4	327.2	345.3	369.7	151.2	772.6	899.9	1402.2
External reserves: IMF definition	227.1	192.5	157.1	234.1	248.3	269.9	309.4	327.2	345.3	369.7	151.2	772.6	409.2	449.5
Official reserves 3/	227.1	192.5	157.1	234.1	248.3	269.9	309.4	327.2	345.3	369.7	151.2	535.1	409.2	449.5
Gold 4/	43.0	42.9	49.5	52.6	53.4	53.6	53.1	50.8	52.5	51.0	33.3	30.7	53.1	54.5
Foreign exchange held by State Bank	184.1	149.6	107.6	181.5	194.9	216.3	256.3	276.4	292.8	318.7	117.9	504.4	343.3	415.3
Of which: foreign currency from gold swaps														20.6
SDR Holding	0.0	0.0	0.0	0.0	0.0	0.0	0.0	0.0	0.0	0.0	0.0		12.8	0.3
Foreign exchange held by other banks	0.0	0.0	0.0	0.0	0.0	0.0	0.0	0.0	0.0	0.0	0.0	237.5	490.7	952.7
Other foreign assets in convertible currencies	553.5	601.0	613.8	711.1	790.7	971.9	1203.1	1370.2	1464.9	1515.2	1500.4	1522.0	..	..
Held by enterprises	331.5	362.4	371.2	388.7	416.2	479.8	600.1	641.6	643.3	673.0	627.4	655.0		
Held by government institutions	216.3	227.9	240.4	294.8	349.5	461.4	573.4	700.8	787.9	811.9	843.3	831.8		
Long term assets of other banks	5.7	10.7	2.2	27.6	25.0	30.7	29.6	27.8	33.7	30.3	29.7	35.2	-10.1	..
Direct investment abroad														
Foreign assets in nonconvertible currencies	567.4	509.1	497.3	178.5	459.7	515.9	582.7	717.4	756.4	958.5	494.2	755.0	927.3	..
Held by State Bank	22.7	19.5	24.0	30.7	31.2	41.2	58.8	56.7	60.6	70.1	7.2	0.0	0.1	..
Held by other banks	0.0	0.0	0.0	6.2	1.0	3.6	1.4	2.6	1.9	2.4	4.1	15.4	2.3	..
Held by enterprises	178.6	167.3	158.2	-133.4	203.7	235.1	267.8	343.4	310.5	262.6	163.4	2.0	38.4	..
Held by government institutions	366.1	322.3	315.1	275.0	223.8	236.0	254.7	314.7	383.4	623.4	319.5	737.6	885.0	..
Direct investment abroad													1.5	..
Total reserves & other assets	1348.0	1302.6	1268.2	1123.7	1498.7	1757.7	2095.2	2414.8	2566.6	2843.4	2145.8	3049.6	1326.4	..

Source: Staff estimates and National Bank of Slovakia.

1/ For 1980-91, data were derived by applying 2:1 ratio to Czechoslovakia's assets.
2/ Valuation by the National Bank of Slovakia.
3/ Changes in method of calculation of "Official reserves of NBS". Foreign currency from gold swaps is excluded
   from the Official reserves.
4/ Gold in accounting value = USD 42.22 per ounce.

Table 3.7. Slovakia: Trade by SITC with the Rest of the World 5/
(In millions of current koruny)

	1991	1992	1993
By SITC Classification			
Exports to Nonsocialist Ctrys 1/			
0 Food & live animals	4092.1	3671.5	
1 Beverages & tobacco	22.7	62.5	
2 Inedible crude matls., nonfuel	3148.1	4025.3	
3 Minerals, fuels	806.1	401.8	
4 Animal & vegetable oils & fats	89.7	54.9	
5 Chemicals	6535.4	7419.7	
6 Manufactures by material	19111.4	30999.5	
7 Machinery & equipment	7764.4	10535.4	
8 Manufactures: Miscellaneous	9167.9	11851.2	
9 Others	36.4		
Total	50774.2	69021.7	

	1991	1992	1993
Exports to Socialist Ctrys 1/			
0 Food & live animals	2579.2	4141.9	
1 Beverages & tobacco	690.4	468.1	
2 Inedible crude matls., nonfuel	1203.9	1710.9	
3 Minerals, fuels	308.6	435.9	
4 Animal & vegetable oils & fats	4.7	48.7	
5 Chemicals	5254.7	4307.2	
6 Manufactures by material	15953.5	12935.7	
7 Machinery & equipment	14018.5	7652.9	
8 Manufactures: Miscellaneous	6012.8	4084.8	
9 Others		11.5	
Total	46026.3	35797.5	

	1991 1/	1991 2/	1992 1/	1992 2/	1993 3/	1993 2/
Total Exports						
0 Food & live animals	6671.3	6954.0	7813.4	7971.0	9225.0	5272.0
1 Beverages & tobacco	713.1	721.0	530.6	540.0	1471.0	550.0
2 Inedible crude matls., nonfuel	4352.0	4665.0	5736.2	5994.0	8296.0	5212.0
3 Minerals, fuels	1114.7	1122.0	837.7	850.0	8255.0	3256.0
4 Animal & vegetable oils & fats	94.4	96.0	103.6	107.0	172.0	75.0
5 Chemicals	11790.1	12199.0	11726.9	12275.0	20187.0	10269.0
6 Manufactures by material	35064.9	37095.0	43935.2	45916.0	65464.0	41016.0
7 Machinery & equipment	21782.9	22739.0	18188.3	18834.0	32578.0	16263.0
8 Manufactures: Miscellaneous	15180.7	16042.0	15936.0	16866.0	22485.0	15242.0
9 Others 4/	36.4	37.0	11.5	12.0	146.0	102.0
Total	96800.5	101670.0	104819.2	109365.0	168279.0	97257.0

Table 3.7. Slovakia: Trade by SITC with the Rest of the World -- cont.

	1991	1992	1993
Imports from Nonsocialist Ctrys 2/			
0 Food & live animals	3785.7	4018.6	
1 Beverages & tobacco	623.1	559.1	
2 Inedible crude matls., nonfuel	5116.2	3365.3	
3 Minerals, fuels	4341.5	674.0	
4 Animal & vegetable oils & fats	90.6	40.7	
5 Chemicals	6683.4	7462.5	
6 Manufactures by material	4078.9	6219.8	
7 Machinery & equipment	21526.1	32647.2	
8 Manufactures: Miscellaneous	4436.7	7623.9	
9 Others	3.8	1.8	
Total	50686.0	62612.9	

	1991	1992	1993
Imports from Socialist Ctrys 2/			
0 Food & live animals	1233.7	1046.6	
1 Beverages & tobacco	278.6	264.9	
2 Inedible crude matls., nonfuel	8943.5	4926.1	
3 Minerals, fuels	34738.9	29880.0	
4 Animal & vegetable oils & fats	9.5	11.7	
5 Chemicals	3038.5	3263.4	
6 Manufactures by material	4747.0	3189.4	
7 Machinery & equipment	4922.6	3364.8	
8 Manufactures: Miscellaneous	2230.0	1472.8	
9 Others	0.1	0.0	
Total	60142.4	47419.7	

	1991 2/	1991 1/	1992 2/	1992 1/	1993 3/	1993 1/
Total Imports						
0 Food & live animals	5019.4	4550.0	5065.2	4860.0	14197.0	8238.0
1 Beverages & tobacco	901.7	861.0	824.0	814.0	2832.0	846.0
2 Inedible crude matls., nonfuel	14059.7	12564.0	8291.4	7628.0	10003.0	8181.0
3 Minerals, fuels	39080.4	38370.0	30554.0	30325.0	40735.0	32078.0
4 Animal & vegetable oils & fats	100.1	99.0	52.4	52.0	478.0	152.0
5 Chemicals	9721.9	9318.0	10725.9	10608.0	22005.0	13353.0
6 Manufactures by material	8825.9	8649.0	9409.2	9359.0	29208.0	11026.0
7 Machinery & equipment	26448.7	25920.0	36012.0	35789.0	56767.0	40104.0
8 Manufactures: Miscellaneous	6666.7	6123.0	9096.7	8992.0	17430.0	10388.0
9 Others 4/	3.9	4.0	1.8	2.0	337.0	141.0
Total	110828.4	106458.0	110032.6	108429.0	193992.0	124507.0

Source: Slovak Statistical Office.
Notes:
1/ F.O.B. methodology.
2/ C.I.F. methodology
3/ Including the Czech Republic.
4/ Includes Gold, Coinage and Non specific.
5/ Excluding the Czech Republic.

Table 3.8. Slovakia: Geographical Composition of Trade with the Rest of the World 1/
(In millions of current koruny)

	1980	1981	1982	1983	1984	1985	1986	1987	1988	1989	1990	1991	1992
Exports, f.o.b /FCO/	40554	32447	35226	36890	43553	56063	57007	59185	59502	54790	52032	96800	104915
of which: hard currency	14221							17365	19344	20518	26336	90402	104093
Nonconvertible area	26143	21603	24642	26042	29904	37699	39504	42580	40437	34327	26084	46026	35798
of which: hard currency	901							1203	875	844	1454	39768	35186
of which:													
China	335							1135	1139	766	439	775	804
of which: hard currency	0							-	6	0	9	112	803
Yugoslavia	2583							2489	2606	2470	3038	3910	3706
of which: hard currency	406							2	10	75	297	3675	3662
CMEA	23188	19047	21961	23101	25976	34132	36163	38906	36577		22500	40564	31181
of which: hard currency	496							1201	859	769	1147	35851	30625
of which:													
Bulgaria	717							1880	1880	964	497	676	626
of which: hard currency	45							69	16	8	27	591	621
G.D.R.	2733							4493	3637	3541	1514		
of which: hard currency	89							675	207	167	112		
Hungary	2327							3550	3409	2977	2801	6582	7255
of which: hard currency	80							26	25	93	127	5676	7233
Poland	3650							6286	6209	5608	3401	7729	4303
of which: hard currency	95							24	74	95	180	6967	4287
U.S.S.R.	12723	10487	12795	13545	15726	19224	20494	20961	19689	16560	13066	24139	17584
of which: hard currency	21								61	234	363	21573	17086
Convertible area and	14410	10844	10584	10848	13649	18364	17503	16605	19065	20464	25948	50774	69022
bilateral trade													
of which: hard currency	13319							16162	18468	19674	24882	50634	68813
Industrial countries	9407	8077	8394	8632	11088	11529	10811	11238	14360	16124	22217	42511	56756
of which: hard currency	9199							11238	14360	16124	22217	42393	56581
of which:													
Austria	1876							2202	3180	3357	3769	5702	7771
of which: hard currency	1876							2202	3180	3357	3769	5682	7732
France	482							775	1029	1241	2107	2364	3978
of which: hard currency	482							775	1029	12405	2107	2359	3977
Italy	590							692	913	1165	1895	4947	5746
of which: hard currency	590							692	913	1165	1895	4945	5738
Germany	3339							3850	4270	4785	7180	19154	25618
of which: hard currency	3339							3850	4270	4785	7180	19104	25583
United Kingdom	507							520	760	760	1233	1064	1937
of which: hard currency	507							520	777	760	1233	1064	1936
Netherlands	481							586	681	881	1313	2614	2466
of which: hard currency	481							586	681	881	1313	2607	2408
U.S.A.	175							198	256	264	339	819	1371
of which: hard currency	175							198	256	264	339	803	1360
Developing countries	5003	2767	2190	2216	2562	6836	6692	5367	4705	4340	3731	8263	12266
of which: hard currency	4120							4924	4108	3551	2665	8241	12232
of which:													
India	370							200	420	563	750	538	1374
of which: hard currency	0							0	0	3	1	533	1374
Syria	950							188	96	48	68	2511	2096
of which: hard currency	950							188	96	48	68	2511	2096
Brazil	36							83	155	229	107	177	256
of which: hard currency	36							83	155	229	107	176	256

1/ Excl. the Czech Republic. Data converted at average commercial exchange rate for each year. Data are on customs basis.

Table 3.8. Slovakia: Geographical Composition of Trade with the Rest of the World 1/
(In millions of current koruny)

Cont...	1980	1981	1982	1983	1984	1985	1986	1987	1988	1989	1990	1991	1992
Imports, f.o.b /FCO/	44866	36558	37010	36004	39871	46346	49569	50563	53540	51642	61258	110864	110051
of which: hard currency	20515							18138	21371	21795	33587	105410	108682
Nonconvertible area	24955	20326	23251	23510	25252	30233	31537	32247	32349	29831	28951	60142	47428
of which: hard currency	1045							190	626	501	1497	55028	46140
of which:													
China	549							1155	1709	1898	2697	839	382
of which: hard currency								-	13	3	0	285	380
Yugoslavia	2153							1852	2019	1784	2201	2518	1558
of which: hard currency	288							18	60	18	174	2241	1557
CMEA	22102	17992	20451	20631	22513	26733	27961	29098	28479		23926	56735	45451
of which: hard currency	758							172	553	479	1323	52493	44166
of which:													
Bulgaria	689							1816	1745	1362	707	538	239
of which: hard currency	19							43	14	11	4	351	237
G.D.R.	3257							4127	3985	3315	3470		
of which: hard currency	56							63	88	59	23		
Hungary	3067							3331	3245	3230	2742	3284	2833
of which: hard currency	463							6	24	25	70	2521	2827
Poland	2275							5349	5544	5210	5458	3990	3484
of which: hard currency	70							37	68	127	658	3669	3483
U.S.S.R.	11219	9323	10436	10485	10838	12043	12276	12316	11516	10764	9674	47489	38187
of which: hard currency	51							5	111	59	341	45571	36965
Convertible area and bilateral trade	19911	16232	13759	12494	14620	16113	18032	18316	21191		32307	50686	62613
of which: hard currency	19470							17948	20745	21294	32090	50346	62531
Industrial countries	16332	12860	11217	10132	11544	12960	14628	15298	17653		28843	41278	56904
of which: hard currency	16216							15298	17653	18002	28843	40953	56825
of which:													
Austria	1938							2857	3409	3426	3769	9215	11130
of which: hard currency	1938							2857	3409	3426	3769	9180	11118
France	517							880	901	563	1007	2104	2552
of which: hard currency	517							880	901	563	1007	2101	2541
Italy	743							682	1150	1292	1631	3113	6205
of which: hard currency	743							682	1150	1292	1631	3104	6204
Germany	3159							4818	5402	5391	8835	15553	22850
of which: hard currency	3159							4818	5402	5391	8835	15325	22816
United Kingdom	1943							1105	1189	1156	1674	1043	1249
of which: hard currency	1943							1105	1189	281	1674	1043	1248
Netherlands	775							586	775	797	855	1463	1895
of which: hard currency	775							586	775	797	855	1458	1892
U.S.A.	1506							163	229	281	243	1250	1820
of which: hard currency	1506							163	229	281	243	1237	1820
Developing countries	3579	3371	2542	2363	3076	3154	3404	3018	3538	3810	3464	9408	5709
of which: hard currency	3254							2650	3538	3293	3247	9393	5707
of which:													
India	259							311	378	501	209	375	261
of which: hard currency	0								2	11	27	375	261
Syria	88							18	21	53	8	25	12
of which: hard currency	88							18	21	53	8	25	12
Brazil	887							472	651	808	1063	1465	862
of which: hard currency	887							472	651	808	1063	1465	862

1/ Excl. the Czech Republic. Data converted at average commercial exchange rate for each year. Data are on customs basis.

Table 3.8. Slovakia: Geographical Composition of Trade with the Rest of the World 1/
(In millions of current koruny)

Cont...	1980	1981	1982	1983	1984	1985	1986	1987	1988	1989	1990	1991	1992
Exports to the European Community:													
Belgium								265	342	370	482	1594	1575
Denmark								168	194	199	295	331	334
France	482							775	1029	1241	2107	2364	3978
Germany	3339							3850	4270	4785	7180	19154	25618
Greece								172	303	282	240	343	677
Ireland								32	62	74	90	73	103
Italy	590							692	913	1165	1895	4947	5746
Luxemburg								6	9	9	22	68	73
Netherland	481							586	681	881	1313	2614	2466
Portugal								17	44	69	51	60	148
Spain								119	176	180	224	626	1083
United Kingdom	507							520	760	760	1233	1064	1937
Imports from the European Community:													
Belgium								426	525	499	495	1061	1070
Denmark								163	211	207	287	331	1014
France	517							880	901	563	1007	2104	2552
Germany	3159							4818	5402	5391	8835	15553	22850
Greece								127	150	159	99	378	306
Ireland								129	165	140	361	170	115
Italy	743							682	1150	1292	1631	3113	6205
Luxemburg								11	19	16	19	24	93
Netherland	775							586	775	797	855	1463	1895
Portugal								10	10	7	15	17	42
Spain								151	216	327	160	393	482
United Kingdom	1943							1105	1189	1156	1674	1043	1249

Source: Slovak Statistical Office.

Table 3.9. Slovakia: Exchange Rates
(Koruny per US$)

	1980	1981	1982	1983	1984	1985	1986	1987	1988	1989	1990	1991	1992	1993 Prel.
Period average														
Official rate 1/	5.4	5.9	6.1	6.3	6.6	6.9	6.0	5.5	5.3					
Commercial rate 2/ 5/	14.3	13.3	13.7	14.2	16.6	17.2	15.0	13.7	14.4	15.1	18.0	29.5	28.3	33.0
Noncommercial rate 3/ 5/	9.4	10.3	10.7	11.0	11.6	12.0	10.5	9.6	9.3	9.8	18.0	29.5		
Auction rate 4/										121.2	50.6			
Tourist rate 6/											31.4			
End of period														
Official rate	5.6	5.9	6.3	6.5	6.9	6.4	5.8	5.2	5.3					
Commercial rate 2/ 5/	14.8	13.2	14.1	14.6	17.1	16.0	14.4	13.0	14.3	14.3	28.0	27.8	28.9	33.2
Noncommercial rate 3/ 5/	9.8	10.2	10.9	11.4	12.0	11.2	10.1	9.1	9.3	9.3	28.0	27.8		
Auction rate 4/										114.4	39.4			
Tourist rate 6/											28.0			

Source: State Bank of Czechoslovakia and National Bank of Slovakia.

Notes:
1/ The official rate was discontinued on January 1, 1989.
2/ Until December 31, 1988, the commercial rate equaled the official rate multiplied by a coefficient for commercial payments.
3/ Until December 31, 1988, the noncommercial rate equaled the official rate multiplied by a coefficient for commercial payments.
4/ First auction took place on August 30, 1989; last auction took place on December 12, 1990.
5/ The commercial and noncommercial rates were unified on January 8, 1990.
6/ Separate tourist rates were in effect during 1990, then unified with the commercial rate on December 28, 1990.

Table 4.1. Slovakia: External Debt
(In millions of current US$)

	1980	1981	1982	1983	1984	1985	1986	1987	1988	1989	1990	1991	1992	1993
Debt with the Rest of the World 1/ 2/ 4/														
Convertible debt	1124.0	1275.0	1362.0	1288.0	1235.0	1234.0	1395.0	1515.3	1717.9	1816.1	2007.1	2676.4	2783.7	3316.0
Medium and long-term	925.0	1010.0	985.0	940.0	912.0	854.0	910.0	998.5	1146.9	1222.1	1504.1	2184.4	2216.6	2601.1
Multilateral	0.0	0.0	0.0	0.0	0.0	0.0	0.0	87.8	89.3	89.3	89.2	238.9	333.6	361.2
IBRD	0.0	0.0	0.0	0.0	0.0	0.0	0.0	0.0	0.0	0.0	0.0	66.0	110.0	150.0
EEC								0.0	0.0	0.0	0.0	76.0	151.4	151.4
Other								87.8	89.3	89.3	89.2	96.9	72.2	59.8
Bilateral								56.2	46.5	38.2	36.4	45.1	123.6	140.9
Suppliers credits								211.3	321.8	341.1	399.4	390.5	319.3	293.0
Banks								643.2	662.9	707.0	760.9	797.0	668.9	698.6
Bonds								0.0	26.5	46.5	218.2	313.8	277.8	523.8
IMF	0.0	0.0	0.0	0.0	0.0	0.0	0.0	0.0	0.0	0.0	0.0	399.1	493.5	583.6
Short-term	199.0	265.0	377.0	348.0	323.0	380.0	485.0	516.8	571.0	594.0	503.0	492.0	567.1	714.9
Nonconvertible debt	132.0	131.0	135.0	140.0	134.0	162.0	166.0	180.0	131.0	157.0	58.0	32.0	0.0	0.0
Medium and long-term	54.0	46.0	41.0	32.0	25.0	25.0	19.0	19.0	19.0	21.0	14.0	12.0	0.0	0.0
Short-term	78.0	85.0	94.0	108.0	109.0	137.0	147.0	161.0	112.0	136.0	44.0	20.0	0.0	0.0
Total	1256.0	1406.0	1497.0	1428.0	1369.0	1396.0	1561.0	1695.3	1848.9	1973.1	2065.1	2708.4	2783.7	3316.0
Medium and long-term	979.0	1056.0	1026.0	972.0	937.0	879.0	929.0	1017.5	1165.9	1243.1	1518.1	2196.4	2216.6	2601.1
Short-term	277.0	350.0	471.0	456.0	432.0	517.0	632.0	677.8	683.0	730.0	547.0	512.0	567.1	714.9
Memorandum items:														
Convertible debt to Czech Republic 1/ 3/													854.7	854.7
Convertible debt including debt to Czech Republic 1/ 3/													3638.4	4170.7

Source: Staff estimates and National Bank of Slovakia.

Notes:
1/ Preliminary estimates for debt contracted as of end-1992.
2/ Data for 1980-91 were derived by territorial principal and by applying 2:1 ratio to Czechoslovakia's debt.
3/ Debt related to the splitting of the balance sheet of the State Bank of Czechoslovakia.
4/ The number of enterprises reporting principal and interest payments increased in 1993.

Table 4.2. Slovakia: Debt Service in Covertible Currencies   1/
(In millions of current US$)

	1992	1993 2/
Principal Repayments		
Convertible debt with the rest of the world		
Medium and long-term	380.0	423.8
Multilateral	31.0	12.4
IBRD	0.0	0.0
Bilateral	11.9	0.0
Suppliers credits	111.2	243.0
Banks	173.4	168.4
Bonds	36.0	0.0
IMF	16.4	0.0
Interest Payments		
Convertible debt with the rest of the world		
Medium and long-term	152.0	175.5
Multilateral	22.5	32.0
IBRD	5.0	8.4
Bilateral	4.2	19.3
Suppliers credits	26.1	15.7
Banks	41.4	75.3
Bonds	25.8	11.7
IMF	32.0	21.6
Short-term 3/	31.0	21.0
Total interest payments	183.0	196.5
Total debt service	563.0	620.4

Source: Staff estimates and National Bank of Slovakia.

Notes:
1/ Data for 1993-2002 are based on debt contracted as of end 1992.
2/ The number of enterprises reporting principal and interest payments
   increased in 1993.
3/ Preliminary.

Table 5.1. Slovakia: Government Budget
(In billions of current koruny)

	1992	1993 Actual
State Budget 1/		
Total revenue	153.1	163.5
Current revenue	153.1	163.5
Tax revenue	100.8	91.7
Indirect tax	40.3	47.0
VAT/Turnover	15.8	27.5
Excises 3/	24.5	19.5
Customs duties	5.3	4.5
Direct tax	54.4	36.5
Profits taxes	31.2	22.0
Income tax	23.2	14.5
On Wages	21.8	10.7
On Entrep. activity	1.4	3.2
On Dividends/interest		0.6
Other tax revenue	0.8	3.7
Property tax 4/	0.8	2.1
Road tax	0.0	1.6
Social security contributions	30.1	42.9
From employer	27.9	
From employee	0.0	
From self-employed	2.2	
Nontax revenue	22.2	29.0
Fees	3.3	3.8
Revenue from ROPOs 2/	6.3	6.3
Other nontax revenue	12.7	18.9
Payments on federal loans/deposits	5.9	4.2
Interest	1.7	
Repayments	4.3	
Sales of local property		
Other 5/	6.8	14.7
Total expenditure	192.6	189.0
Subsidies to enterprises	16.2	16.2
Agriculture		
Economy	1.2	
Transport		
Heating	2.0	
"For stabilization"	0.9	
Financial institutions	2.0	
Investment transfers to enterprises	3.0	3.1
Other current expenditure of ROPOs 2/	151.9	154.7
Wages and salaries ROs 2/	15.4	15.9
Other	136.5	138.8
Labor and Social Affairs	54.3	56.8
Unemployment benefits	2.0	1.8
Active empl. pol. & admin	3.8	1.1
General income support 6/	7.2	8.3
Other	41.3	45.5
Pensions		32.7
Other transfers		8.5
Other		4.3
Interior	8.8	
of which: Social assistance	2.4	3.1

Table 5.1. Slovakia: Government Budget -- cont.

	1992	1993 Actual
Education	8.0	7.9
Health	15.3	15.8
Debt service	0.0	12.5
Own interest	0.0	11.4
Interest on federal debt	0.0	
Guarantees	0.0	1.1
Lending abroad	0.0	
Other 7/	1.1	42.7
Investment expenditure ROPOs 2/	12.5	18.1
Surplus/deficit	-39.5	-25.4
Extrabudgetary spending		
Total	9.1	
Gabcikovo	7.7	
Health sector investment		
Other	1.4	
OVERALL surplus/deficit	-48.6	-25.4
Financing	39.5	25.4
Foreign		0.0
Domestic	39.5	25.4
Memorandum items on revenue:		
Fiscal transfers in revenue	13.6	..
Slovak state budget revenue	112.6	..
Slovak local budget revenue	9.1	..
Federal state budget revenue	127.1	..
Taxes on wage bill		..
Paid by employers	28.1	..
Paid by employees	21.8	..
Taxes paid by self-employed	4.1	..
On "wage bill"	2.2	..
On "profit"	1.9	..

Source: Slovak authorities.

Note:
1/ State Budget includes central government, local government and social funds.
2/ RO: Budgetary organizations; PO: Subsidized organizations.
3/ Includes taxes from previous year.
4/ Includes other current taxes.
5/ Includes NBS profits transfered and other current revenue.
6/ Includes sickness benefits and social assistance.
7/ Since break-up for some categories was not available, the other is a residual item for 1993.

Table 6.1. Slovakia: Monetary Survey 1/
(In billions of current koruny)

	1991	1992	1993 Prel. 4/
Net foreign assets 1/	-0.1	-25.5	-33.4
Foreign assets 1/	20.7	26.9	
Foreign liabilities	20.8	52.4	
Net domestic assets			
Domestic credit	233.0	298.8	357.8
Net credit to government 2/	20.1	61.2	89.4
Net credit to Property Funds	6.6	0.4	6.8
Credit to enterprises and households	206.3	237.2	261.6
Credit to households	19.2	19.8	..
Credit to enterprises	185.4	215.3	..
Credit in foreign currency	1.7	2.1	8.3
Liquid liabilities	204.8	214.4	253.8
Money	111.6	108.2	153.9
Currency	28.8	30.9	25.1
Demand deposits	82.8	77.3	128.8
Enterprises	52.9	50.0	..
Households	28.5	26.5	..
Insurance companies	1.4	0.8	..
Quasi-money	93.2	106.2	99.9
Local currency time & savgs dep	86.9	92.8	99.9
Enterprises	4.8	5.0	
Households	65.7	72.9	..
Insurance companies	16.4	14.9	..
Foreign currency deposits	6.3	13.4	..
Other items (net) 3/	28.1	58.9	70.6

Source: National Bank of Slovakia.

Notes:
1/ Includes impact of gold swaps in 1992.
2/ Increased by Slovak share (Sk 4 billion) of Kcs 12 billion transfer to Obchodni Banka.
3/ Includes nonconvertible foreign assets and liabilities. Also includes net claims on Slovak system by the Czech Rep. arising from the split of the former State Bank.
4/ These are projected end-1993 magnitudes valued at the end-October SK/$US exchange rate of 32.68.

Table 7.1. Slovakia: Developments in Wholesale and Consumer Prices
(In constant 1980 prices)

	1980	1981	1982	1983	1984	1985	1986	1987	1988	1989	1990	1991	1992	1993 Prel.
Wholesale Prices														
Industry	100.0	104.3	112.1	113.1	122.4	124.6	124.6	124.7	124.4	121.1	126.9	214.4	225.7	264.6
Agriculture	100.0	101.2	108.7	108.9	112.5	113.2	115.2	115.3	114.3	148.0	148.6	155.1	165.2	189.3
Agricultural inputs	100.0	101.3	116.1	116.4	123.0	123.6	125.3	126.1	126.0	131.3	140.4			
Consumer Prices														
Goods and Services	100.0	100.8	106.1	107.1	108.1	110.4	111.0	111.2	111.4	112.8	124.5	200.7	220.8	272.0
Food	100.0	100.0	109.7	110.2	110.7	113.5	114.0	114.2	114.0	114.1	126.7	186.6	199.7	242.2
Nonfood	100.0	101.5	102.6	103.8	105.0	105.9	106.6	106.9	107.1	109.8	122.3	217.7	239.0	287.8
Catering	100.0	100.0	114.8	115.5	116.5	125.8	126.4	126.5	127.0	128.1	138.5	214.7	229.1	310.4
Services	100.0	100.8	101.1	102.2	103.4	103.4	103.4	103.5	104.2	104.8	113.7	160.8	193.8	248.1

Source: Slovak Statistical Office.

Table 7.2. Slovakia: Indices of Energy Wholesale Prices
(In constant 1980 prices)

	1980	1981	1982	1983	1984	1985	1986	1987	1988	1989	1990	1991	1992	1993 Prel.
Coking coal														
Steam coal	100.0	123.5	125.3	127.2	155.8	158.4	161.6	161.3	161.3	186.9	240.5	931.9	984.1	1157.3
Coke	100.0	109.8	111.4	112.9	131.4	133.6	133.6	133.6	134.7	180.9	220.7	495.9	457.7	
Natural gas	100.0	145.0	146.0	147.3	232.4	234.5	234.5	234.5	234.5	170.2	223.8			
Electricity	100.0	109.3	111.0	112.7	121.5	123.3	125.4	127.8	127.8	134.8	150.3	373.0	436.8	457.8
Heat	100.0	121.8	124.1	126.3	142.7	145.3	148.2	151.2	151.2	150.3	178.7	319.9	340.1	468.3

Source: Slovak Statistical Office.

Table 7.3. Slovakia: Average Monthly Wages and Earnings of Persons Employed in the State and Cooperative Sector
(In current koruny)

	1980	1981	1982	1983	1984	1985	1986	1987	1988	1989	1990	1991	1992	1993 Prel.
Total 2/	2594	2638	2692	2756	2809	2864	2914	2970	3064	3142	3281	3766	4538	5372
Cooperatives	2513	2608	2669	2834	2949	3018	3107	3187	3404	3550	3819	3934	4181	4471
Small private sector 3/												4000	4950	5850
Material sphere	2630	2669	2730	2791	2842	2893	2945	3000	3083	3158	3277	3765	4510	
of which:														
Agriculture 4/	2515	2557	2596	2716	2812	2860	2906	2980	3105	3212	3365	3629	3929	4556
Industry	2641	2688	2763	2836	2897	2955	3007	3053	3128	3199	3299	3852	4522	5496
Building and Construction	2865	2886	2945	2993	3036	3122	3176	3249	3335	3431	3530	3920	4656	5533
Nonmaterial sphere	2540	2569	2599	2618	2650	2708	2736	2787	2858	2920	3073	3711	4480	
of which:														
Education	2610	2661	2663	2666	2688	2769	2783	2852	2903	2941	3075	3555	4448	4701
Health	2516	2574	2582	2564	2601	2694	2712	2754	2800	2851	3087	3909	4605	4823

Source: Slovak Statistical Office.

Notes:
1/ Includes wages, bonuses and other payments.
2/ Includes estimates for employees working at private entrepreneurs.
3/ Estimate.
4/ Less cooperatives; 1993 data includes all cooperatives in agro-activities.

Table 7.4. Slovakia: Indices of Average Monthly Wages and Earnings

	1980	1981	1982	1983	1984	1985	1986	1987	1988	1989	1990	1991	1992	1993 Prel.
NOMINAL WAGES														
Total state	100.0	101.7	103.8	106.2	108.3	110.4	112.3	114.5	118.1	121.1	126.5	145.2	174.9	207.1
1. Material sphere	100.0	101.5	103.8	106.1	108.1	110.0	112.0	114.1	117.2	120.1	124.6	143.2	171.5	
Agriculture	100.0	101.7	103.2	108.0	111.8	113.7	115.5	118.5	123.5	127.7	133.8	144.3	156.2	181.2
Industry	100.0	101.8	104.6	107.4	109.7	111.9	113.9	115.6	118.4	121.1	124.9	145.9	171.2	208.1
Construction	100.0	100.7	102.8	104.5	106.0	109.0	110.9	113.4	116.4	119.8	123.2	136.8	162.5	193.1
2. Nonmaterial sphere	100.0	101.1	102.3	103.1	104.3	106.6	107.7	109.7	112.5	115.0	121.0	146.1	176.4	
Consumer price index	100.0	100.8	106.1	107.1	108.1	110.4	111.0	111.2	111.4	112.8	124.5	200.7	220.8	272.1
REAL WAGES														
Total wage	100.0	100.9	97.8	99.2	100.2	100.0	101.2	103.0	106.0	107.4	101.6	72.3	79.2	76.1
1. Material sphere	100.0	100.6	97.8	99.1	100.0	99.6	100.9	102.6	105.2	106.5	100.1	71.4	77.7	
Agriculture 1/	100.0	100.9	97.3	100.8	103.4	103.0	104.1	106.6	110.9	113.2	107.5	71.9	70.7	66.6
Industry	100.0	101.0	98.6	100.3	101.5	101.4	102.6	104.0	106.3	107.4	100.3	72.7	77.5	76.5
Construction	100.0	99.9	96.9	97.6	98.1	98.7	99.9	102.0	104.5	106.2	99.0	68.2	73.6	71.0
2. Nonmaterial sphere	100.0	100.3	96.4	96.3	96.5	96.6	97.0	98.7	101.0	102.0	97.2	72.8	79.9	

Source: Slovak Statistical Office.

Note:
1/ Less cooperatives; 1993 data includes all cooperatives in agro-activities.

Table 8.1. Slovakia: Regional Unemployment by Districts.

Area/Districts	As of 12/31/92 number of persons	rate in %	As of 3/31/93 number of persons	rate in %	As of 6/30/93 number of person	rate in %	As of 12/31/93 number of person	rate in %
Total	260,274	10.4	306,090	12.0	318,082	12.5	368,095	14.4
of which:								
Banska Bystrica	7,191	7.6	8,709	9.1	9,305	9.8	10,539	11.1
Bardejov	5,345	15.7	6,384	17.7	6,200	17.2	7,480	20.8
Bratislava,hl.m.SR	10,883	3.8	13,152	4.4	12,833	4.3	13,510	4.5
Bratislava-vidiek	5,104	9.6	6,149	12.3	5,730	11.5	6,620	13.3
Cadca	7,042	16.2	8,310	17.6	8,571	18.2	9,931	21.0
Dolny Kubin	6,932	12.9	8,635	16.0	8,374	15.5	9,635	17.9
Dunajska Streda	7,231	16.3	8,386	17.1	8,895	18.1	10,025	20.4
Galanta	8,292	14.9	10,109	17.0	10,334	17.4	11,824	19.9
Humenne	5,464	10.5	6,413	12.4	7,033	13.6	7,623	14.8
Komarno	6,028	12.7	7,961	19.7	8,771	18.4	10,361	21.7
Kosice-mesto	9,661	6.8	11,179	7.8	11,948	8.4	14,278	10.0
Kosice-vidiek	4,883	16.5	5,645	18.2	5,449	17.6	7,007	22.6
Levice	7,175	11.8	8,129	12.9	8,611	13.7	10,439	16.6
Liptovsky Mikulas	4,147	6.5	4,701	7.4	5,123	8.1	7,065	11.1
Lucenec	6,558	14.3	7,532	16.7	7,532	16.7	9,143	20.3
Martin	4,348	7.6	4,937	8.8	4,917	8.8	5,999	10.7
Michalovce	8,600	16.4	10,223	19.5	10,684	20.4	11,796	22.5
Nitra	11,763	12.6	13,709	14.0	13,093	13.4	14,405	14.7
Nove Zamky	7,405	11.3	9,289	13.5	10,196	14.8	12,276	17.8
Porad	7,845	10.6	9,867	13.0	9,926	13.0	11,957	15.7
Povazska Bystrica	7,213	9.3	8,973	11.2	9,683	12.1	10,884	13.6
Presov	9,406	10.4	12,312	13.5	13,414	14.7	15,031	16.4
Prievidza	5,847	8.9	6,752	10.3	7,612	11.6	8,929	13.6
Rimavska Sobota	7,348	16.6	8,701	19.6	9,565	21.6	11,703	26.4
Roznava	6,969	17.0	7,653	18.4	8,291	19.9	9,285	22.3
Senica	5,661	8.9	6,913	10.8	7,165	11.2	8,570	13.4
Spisska Nova Ves	9,226	14.8	10,964	17.7	11,878	19.2	14,407	23.3
Stara Lubovna	1,848	9.9	2,383	12.8	2,156	11.6	2,660	14.3
Svidnik	3,051	13.7	3,542	16.1	3,614	16.4	4,275	19.4
Topolcany	8,517	11.8	9,695	13.7	10,504	14.9	11,215	15.9
Trebisov	9,459	19.3	9,025	17.2	9,532	18.2	10,249	19.6
Trencin	6,903	8.2	6,856	8.1	6,514	7.7	6,844	8.1
Trnava	11,697	10.2	13,645	12.0	14,647	12.8	15,485	13.6
Velky Krtis	3,012	13.8	3,723	18.5	3,943	19.6	4,349	21.7
Vranov nad Toplou	4,599	16.0	5,206	18.1	5,405	18.7	6,524	22.6
Zvolen	5,740	9.0	6,398	10.4	6,144	10.0	7,770	12.7
Ziar nad Hronom	3,573	7.9	3,845	8.8	3,840	8.8	5,319	12.2
Zilina	8,308	9.0	10,085	10.5	10,650	11.0	12,683	13.2

Source: Slovak Statistical Office

Table 8.2. Slovakia: Vacancies by Districts and by Regions

Area/districts	As of 12/31/92	As of 3/31/93	As of 7/31/93	As of 12/31/93
Total	16204	12383	9625	7676
of which:				
Bratislava	3667	2838	1607	961
West Slovakia	4444	3173	3070	2276
of which:				
Bratislava-vicinity	545	299	306	191
Dunajska Streda	48	88	137	112
Galanta	231	94	85	60
Komarno	198	148	123	111
Levice	121	217	198	126
Nitra	568	461	485	496
Nove Zamky	143	177	121	83
Senica	465	151	166	147
Topolcany	366	353	321	213
Trencin	743	526	492	324
Trnava	896	659	636	413
Central Slovakia	3743	3084	2260	1865
of which:				
Banska Bystrice	751	438	363	292
Cadca	376	357	188	55
Dolny Kubin	335	598	272	263
Liptovsky Mikulas	510	249	187	160
Lucenec	41	47	94	29
Martin	459	323	158	160
Povazska Bystrica	338	121	241	268
Prievidza	172	175	218	80
Rimavska Sobota	26	78	76	77
Velky Krtis	21	34	14	22
Zvolen	178	171	94	142
Ziar nad Hronom	115	179	50	84
Zilina	421	314	305	233
East Slovakia	4340	3288	2688	2574
of which:				
Bardejov	718	703	318	433
Humenne	618	176	368	302
Kosice-city	813	817	455	497
Kosice-vicinity	389	274	236	105
Michalovce	130	179	294	370
Poprad	279	145	164	147
Presov	476	377	403	229
Roznaka	167	74	47	38
Spisska Nova Ves	320	257	107	121
Stara Lubovna	140	108	45	90
Svidnik	26	41	62	55
Trebisov	155	89	49	121
Vranov	109	48	140	66

Vacancies by Regions

	As of 12/31/92	As of 3/31/93	As of 7/31/93	As of 12/31/93
Total	16,204	12,383	9625	7676
of which:				
Bratislava	3,677	2,838	1607	961
West Slovakia	4,444	3,173	3070	2276
Central Slovakia	3,743	3,084	2260	1865
East Slovakia	4,340	3,288	2688	2574

Source: Slovak Statistical Office

Table 9.1. Slovakia: Industrial Production by Ownership

	1991		1992		1993	
	In mill. of 1992 Kcs	In %	In mill. of 1992 Kcs	In %	In mill. of 1992 Kcs	In %
Total	403,051	100.0	347,834	100.0	344,797	100.0
of which						
public 1/	353,941	87.8	293,062	84.3	256,404	74.4
cooperative	6,310	1.6	5,452	1.6	5,104	1.5
private 2/	28,459	7.1	32,899	9.5	66,968	19.4
other 3/	14,341	3.5	16,421	4.6	21,424	6.2

Source: Slovak Statistical Office.

Notes:
1/ State and municipal ownership
2/ Including international and foreign enterprises
3/ Ownership associations, political parties and parishes etc.

Table 9.2. Slovakia: Share of Private Sector in Production 1/ 2/
(Excludes Cooperatives)

	1990	1991	1992	1993
Share of private sector in:				
- Output	6.0	15.0	21.9	27.0
- Production of:				
industry		2.1	9.5	17.9
construction		8.0	32.0	49.5
commerce and repair services		22.2	59.3	75.7
other trade services		.	45.1	62.9
transport and communications		25.4	36.6	49.8
milk eggs 3/		4.8	8.6	10.3
eggs 3/		38.9	43.1	48.7

Source: Slovak Statistical Office.

Notes:
1/ Excludes cooperatives.
2/ Increase in 1991 reflects the conversion of state enterprises into
   joint stock companies.
3/ In terms of production of physical units.

Table 9.2.1. Slovakia: Share of Private Sector in Production 1/ 2/
(Includes Cooperatives)

	1991	1992	1993
Share of private sector in:			
-Output	26.6	32.4	39.0
-Production of			
industry	8.6	11.0	19.4
construction	24.0	35.0	51.7
retail sales	48.9	73.2	85.2
selected market services	..	55.5	66.7
road freight transport	..	..	..
milk 3/	77.5	78.5	77.7
eggs 3/	78.1	82.4	85.8

Source: Slovak Statistical Office.

Notes:
1/ Includes cooperatives, international and foreign organizations.
2/ Increase in 1991 reflects the conversion of state enterprises into
   joint stock companies.
3/ In production of physical units.

Table 9.3. Slovakia: Organizations According to Economic Sector and Type of Ownership (as of Dec. 31, 1992)

	Total Number	Index 1992/ 1991	Private Number	%	Cooperative Number	%	Public Number	%	International Number	%	Enterprises not included in commercial registation Number	Index 1992/ 1991
Total	34,534	144.0	13,939	40.4	1,879	5.4	10,135	29.3	2,822	8.2	300,637	148.8
of which economy of which:	21,498	177.0	13,819	64.3	1,863	8.7	2,540	11.8	2,803	13.0	300,637	148.8
Agric., forestry and fisheries	1,368	111.4	147	10.7	945	69.1	217	15.9	11	0.8	19,511	294.8
Mining mineral resources	53	115.2	9	17.0	5	9.4	29	54.7	8	15.1	445	50.3
Processed average	3,720	174.7	2,265	60.9	209	5.6	832	22.4	327	8.8	57,016	131.7
Production and transmission of power, gas, water	73	143.1	18	24.7	1	1.4	51	69.9	2	2.7	901	311.8
Construction	1,936	163.2	1,264	65.3	183	9.5	335	17.3	114	5.9	62,857	127.9
Commerce and service	8,122	243.4	6,093	75.0	131	1.6	275	3.4	1,535	18.9	71,607	203.7
Catering, housing	517	178.3	366	70.8	15	2.9	71	13.7	41	7.9	11,931	158.6
Transport activity	1,040	266.6	852	81.9	18	1.7	98	9.4	60	5.8	10,960	168.9
Communications	36	163.6	10	27.8	1	2.8	16	44.4	7	19.4	209	101.0
Financing and insurance	284	249.1	146	51.4	6	2.1	80	28.2	18	6.3	125	130.2
Realestate, service for enterprises, research, develop.	1,040	161.0	493	47.4	166	16.0	257	24.7	104	10.0	8,041	132.5
Other commercial service	2,752	119.5	1,830	66.5	148	5.4	187	6.8	514	18.7	41,276	130.6
Public admin., defense, social insurance	13	185.7	8	61.5	1	7.7	3	23.1	0	?	1,126	134.9
Education	56	112.0	27	48.2	4	7.1	9	16.1	7	12.5	2,485	142.0
Health, veterinary and social activity	29	93.5	10	34.5	3	10.3	12	41.4	3	10.3	539	151.0
Other public social and personal service	459	183.6	281	61.2	27	5.9	68	14.8	52	11.3	11,577	144.5
Private domestic and ex-territorial organizations	0	.	0	.	0	.	0	.	0	.	0	.

Source: Slovak Statistical Office.

Table 9.3.1. Slovakia: Organizations According to Economic Sector and Type of Ownership (as of Dec. 31, 1993)

	Total	Index 1993/ 1992	Private		Cooperative		Public		International		Enterprises not included in commercial registation	Index 1993/ 1992
	Number		Number	%	Number	%	Number	%	Number	%	Number	
Total	45,265	131.1	18,716	41.3	1,956	4.3	10,128	22.4	5,179	11.4	282,894	94.1
of which economy of which:	28,978	134.8	18,617	64.2	1,940	6.7	2,388	8.2	5,157	17.8	282,894	94.1
Agric., forestry and fisheries	1,527	111.6	189	12.4	1,026	67.2	230	15.1	26	1.7	21,543	110.4
Mining mineral resources	67	126.4	15	22.4	5	7.5	32	47.8	10	14.9	212	47.6
Processed average	4,960	133.3	3,226	65.0	226	4.6	755	15.2	576	11.6	50,462	88.5
Production and transmission of power, gas, water	85	116.4	28	32.9	2	2.4	49	57.6	3	3.5	1,341	148.8
Construction	2,592	133.9	1,845	71.2	161	6.2	298	11.5	204	7.9	50,841	80.9
Commerce and service	12,518	154.1	8,693	69.4	152	1.2	291	2.3	3,177	25.4	76,984	107.5
Catering, housing	745	144.1	549	73.7	16	2.1	68	9.1	71	9.5	13,650	114.4
Transport activity	1,220	117.3	961	78.8	14	1.1	103	8.4	123	10.1	11,580	105.7
Communications	46	127.8	15	32.6	1	2.2	16	34.8	10	21.7	152	72.7
Financing and insurance	380	133.8	188	49.5	6	1.6	78	20.5	53	13.9	167	133.6
Realestate, service for enterprises, research, develop.	1,433	137.8	748	52.2	185	12.9	238	16.6	193	13.5	7,740	96.3
Other commercial service	2,713	98.6	1,741	119.0	119	4.4	138	5.1	617	22.7	34,024	82.4
Public admin., defense, social insurance	17	130.8	7	41.2	0	0.0	8	47.1	0	0.0	852	75.7
Education	92	164.3	49	53.3	3	3.3	7	7.6	17	18.5	2,191	88.2
Health, veterinary and social activity	30	103.4	15	50.0	2	6.7	11	36.7	1	3.3	572	106.1
Other public social and personal service	553	120.5	348	62.9	22	4.0	66	11.9	76	13.7	10,555	91.2
Private domestic and ex-territorial organizations	.	.	.	.	.	.	.	.	.	.	28	90.3

Source: Slovak Statistical Office.

Table 9.4. Slovakia: Organizational Structure of the Economy According to Selected Legal Forms in 1993 1/

Legal Forms	As of 12/31/1992	Surpluses(+), decrease(-) for individual quarters according to registration as of end of quarters				As of 12/31/1993	Surpluses(+), decrease(-) for individual quarters according to registration as of end of quarters	
		1.Q	2.Q	3.Q	4.Q		1.Q 93	2.Q 93
Number of Units in the Register of Organizations total of which:	335,179	-3,777	-8,682	4,749	870	328,159	3,450	-8682
state enterprises	1,173	-65	-76	-146	33	1,049	65	-76
commerical companies total	12,779	1,690	2,321	1,992	1,923	20,705	1,690	2,321
of which joint stock cos.	1,450	66	45	48	82	1,691	66	45
agricultural cooperatives	1,513	-145	79	60	20	1,527	7	-26
non-agricultural cooperative	366	125	-41	-25	-30	395	12	64
budgetary organizations	1,771	-35	-1	146	135	2,016	35	-1
organizations based on contributions	1,966	-116	41	642	141	2,674	116	41
private entrepreneurs total of which	305,287	-5,935	-12,111	1,436	-1,782	286,895	5,935	-12111
natural persons total of	291,504	-7,405	-13,158	505	-2,200	269,246	7,445	-13427
which filed in business register	4,638	-169	-244	-93	-148	3,984	171	-257
private farmers total of	13,783	1,470	1,047	931	418	17,649	-1510	1,316
which filed in business register	12	3	2	0	0	17	-5	15

Source: Slovak Statistical Office.

1/ Data from the "Register of Organizations"
Note: Classification of data is not completely comparable to regulations in force.

Table 9.5. Slovakia: Financial Position of Enterprises 1/
(In millions of koruny)

	1990	1991	1992
1. Output	487502	579775	500286
of which:			
Price subsidies 2/	18495	6779	4179
2. Costs	463825	562818	505460
of which:			
Material costs	314116	403064	349100
of which:			
Depreciation	26870	34858	37373
Non-material costs	10519	22534	27877
Wage costs	65584	67026	62520
Wage tax	33800	32966	30423
Interest payments	9774	21699	20808
Other	30032	15529	14732
3. 1-2 = Gross profit	23677	16957	-5174
4. Price differences on foreign trade	-5477	109	-69
5. Extraordinary receipts	9045	5006	7377
6. 3+4+5 = Total gross profit	38199	21774	2270
7. Subsidies other than price			
subsidies	4791	8207	7436
8. Profit taxes	25786	23494	18245
9. 6+7+8 = Net profit after taxation	17204	6487	-8539
10. Other resources	-113	7714	9484
11. 9+10 = Profit for distribution	17091	14201	964
12. Distributed profit	15986	2333	-6132
of which:			
Wage fund			
Fund for cultural & social needs	1605	1275	1030
13. 11-12 = Retained earnings	1105	11902	7075
14. Depreciation after taxation	26870	32338	37164
15. Borrowing from banks	87320	155962	156984
16. 13+14+15 = Total financial resources	115295	200202	201223
17. Use of financial resources	88000	168000	164000
18. Investment	41000	18000	9000
19. Stocks	15000	8000	-24000
20. Financial assets	33000	84000	167000

Source: Slovak Statistical Office.

Notes:
1. Enterprises include those with more than 25 employees for 1991
   and 1992 and all employees for 1990.
2. Subsidies to selected agricultural products, heat and energy
   usage and transport.

Distributors of World Bank Publications

ARGENTINA
Carlos Hirsch, SRL
Galeria Guemes
Florida 165, 4th Floor-Ofc. 453/465
1333 Buenos Aires

AUSTRALIA, PAPUA NEW GUINEA,
FIJI, SOLOMON ISLANDS,
VANUATU, AND WESTERN SAMOA
D.A. Information Services
648 Whitehorse Road
Mitcham 3132
Victoria

AUSTRIA
Gerold and Co.
Graben 31
A-1011 Wien

BANGLADESH
Micro Industries Development
   Assistance Society (MIDAS)
House 5, Road 16
Dhanmondi R/Area
Dhaka 1209

   Branch offices:
   Pine View, 1st Floor
   100 Agrabad Commercial Area
   Chittagong 4100

BELGIUM
Jean De Lannoy
Av. du Roi 202
1060 Brussels

CANADA
Le Diffuseur
151A Boul. de Mortagne
Boucherville, Québec
J4B 5E6

Renouf Publishing Co.
1294 Algoma Road
Ottawa, Ontario
K1B 3W8

CHILE
Invertec IGT S.A.
Av. Santa Maria 6400
Edificio INTEC, Of. 201
Santiago

CHINA
China Financial & Economic
   Publishing House
8, Da Fo Si Dong Jie
Beijing

COLOMBIA
Infoenlace Ltda.
Apartado Aereo 34270
Bogota D.E.

COTE D'IVOIRE
Centre d'Edition et de Diffusion
   Africaines (CEDA)
04 B.P. 541
Abidjan 04 Plateau

CYPRUS
Center of Applied Research
Cyprus College
6, Diogenes Street, Engomi
P.O. Box 2006
Nicosia

DENMARK
SamfundsLitteratur
Rosenoerns Allé 11
DK-1970 Frederiksberg C

DOMINICAN REPUBLIC
Editora Taller, C. por A.
Restauración e Isabel la Católica 309
Apartado de Correos 2190 Z-1
Santo Domingo

EGYPT, ARAB REPUBLIC OF
Al Ahram
Al Galaa Street
Cairo

The Middle East Observer
41, Sherif Street
Cairo

FINLAND
Akateeminen Kirjakauppa
P.O. Box 128
SF-00101 Helsinki 10

FRANCE
World Bank Publications
66, avenue d'Iéna
75116 Paris

GERMANY
UNO-Verlag
Poppelsdorfer Allee 55
D-5300 Bonn 1

HONG KONG, MACAO
Asia 2000 Ltd.
46-48 Wyndham Street
Winning Centre
2nd Floor
Central Hong Kong

HUNGARY
Foundation for Market Economy
Dombovari Ut 17-19
H-1117 Budapest

INDIA
Allied Publishers Private Ltd.
751 Mount Road
Madras - 600 002

   Branch offices:
   15 J.N. Heredia Marg
   Ballard Estate
   Bombay - 400 038

   13/14 Asaf Ali Road
   New Delhi - 110 002

   17 Chittaranjan Avenue
   Calcutta - 700 072

   Jayadeva Hostel Building
   5th Main Road, Gandhinagar
   Bangalore - 560 009

   3-5-1129 Kachiguda
      Cross Road
   Hyderabad - 500 027

   Prarthana Flats, 2nd Floor
   Near Thakore Baug, Navrangpura
   Ahmedabad - 380 009

   Patiala House
   16-A Ashok Marg
   Lucknow - 226 001

   Central Bazaar Road
   60 Bajaj Nagar
   Nagpur 440 010

INDONESIA
Pt. Indira Limited
Jalan Borobudur 20
P.O. Box 181
Jakarta 10320

IRAN
Kowkab Publishers
P.O. Box 19575-511
Tehran

IRELAND
Government Supplies Agency
4-5 Harcourt Road
Dublin 2

ISRAEL
Yozmot Literature Ltd.
P.O. Box 56055
Tel Aviv 61560

ITALY
Licosa Commissionaria Sansoni SPA
Via Duca Di Calabria, 1/1
Casella Postale 552
50125 Firenze

JAPAN
Eastern Book Service
Hongo 3-Chome, Bunkyo-ku 113
Tokyo

KENYA
Africa Book Service (E.A.) Ltd.
Quaran House, Mfangano Street
P.O. Box 45245
Nairobi

KOREA, REPUBLIC OF
Pan Korea Book Corporation
P.O. Box 101, Kwangwhamun
Seoul

Korean Stock Book Centre
P.O. Box 34
Yeoeido
Seoul

MALAYSIA
University of Malaya Cooperative
   Bookshop, Limited
P.O. Box 1127, Jalan Pantai Baru
59700 Kuala Lumpur

MEXICO
INFOTEC
Apartado Postal 22-860
14060 Tlalpan, Mexico D.F.

NETHERLANDS
De Lindeboom/InOr-Publikaties
P.O. Box 202
7480 AE Haaksbergen

NEW ZEALAND
EBSCO NZ Ltd.
Private Mail Bag 99914
New Market
Auckland

NIGERIA
University Press Limited
Three Crowns Building Jericho
Private Mail Bag 5095
Ibadan

NORWAY
Narvesen Information Center
Book Department
P.O. Box 6125 Etterstad
N-0602 Oslo 6

PAKISTAN
Mirza Book Agency
65, Shahrah-e-Quaid-e-Azam
P.O. Box No. 729
Lahore 54000

PERU
Editorial Desarrollo SA
Apartado 3824
Lima 1

PHILIPPINES
International Book Center
Suite 1703, Cityland 10
Condominium Tower 1
Ayala Avenue, H.V. dela
   Costa Extension
Makati, Metro Manila

POLAND
International Publishing Service
Ul. Piekna 31/37
00-677 Warzawa

For subscription orders:
IPS Journals
Ul. Okrezna 3
02-916 Warszawa

PORTUGAL
Livraria Portugal
Rua Do Carmo 70-74
1200 Lisbon

SAUDI ARABIA, QATAR
Jarir Book Store
P.O. Box 3196
Riyadh 11471

SINGAPORE, TAIWAN,
MYANMAR,BRUNEI
Gower Asia Pacific Pte Ltd.
Golden Wheel Building
41, Kallang Pudding, #04-03
Singapore 1334

SOUTH AFRICA, BOTSWANA
For single titles:
Oxford University Press
   Southern Africa
P.O. Box 1141
Cape Town 8000

For subscription orders:
International Subscription Service
P.O. Box 41095
Craighall
Johannesburg 2024

SPAIN
Mundi-Prensa Libros, S.A.
Castello 37
28001 Madrid

Librería Internacional AEDOS
Consell de Cent, 391
08009 Barcelona

SRI LANKA AND THE MALDIVES
Lake House Bookshop
P.O. Box 244
100, Sir Chittampalam A.
   Gardiner Mawatha
Colombo 2

SWEDEN
For single titles:
Fritzes Fackboksforetaget
Regeringsgatan 12, Box 16356
S-103 27 Stockholm

For subscription orders:
Wennergren-Williams AB
P. O. Box 1305
S-171 25 Solna

SWITZERLAND
For single titles:
Librairie Payot
Case postale 3212
CH 1002 Lausanne

For subscription orders:
Librairie Payot
Service des Abonnements
Case postale 3312
CH 1002 Lausanne

THAILAND
Central Department Store
306 Silom Road
Bangkok

TRINIDAD & TOBAGO, ANTIGUA
BARBUDA, BARBADOS,
DOMINICA, GRENADA, GUYANA,
JAMAICA, MONTSERRAT, ST.
KITTS & NEVIS, ST. LUCIA,
ST. VINCENT & GRENADINES
Systematics Studies Unit
#9 Watts Street
Curepe
Trinidad, West Indies

UNITED KINGDOM
Microinfo Ltd.
P.O. Box 3
Alton, Hampshire GU34 2PG
England